Learner Contributions to Language Learning
New Directions in Research

APPLIED LINGUISTICS AND LANGUAGE STUDY

GENERAL EDITOR

CHRISTOPHER N. CANDLIN

Chair Professor of Applied Linguistics
Department of English
Centre for English Language Education &
Communication Research
City University of Hong Kong, Hong Kong

For a complete list of books in this series see pages v–vi

Learner Contributions to Language Learning

New Directions in Research

Edited by

MICHAEL P BREEN

Longman

An imprint of **Pearson Education**

Harlow, England · London · New York · Reading, Massachusetts · San Francisco
Toronto · Don Mills, Ontario · Sydney · Tokyo · Singapore · Hong Kong · Seoul
Taipei · Cape Town · Madrid · Mexico City · Amsterdam · Munich · Paris · Milan

Pearson Education Limited
Edinburgh Gate
Harlow
Essex CM20 2JE
England

and Associated Companies throughout the world

Visit us on the World Wide Web at:
www.pearsoned.co.uk

First published 2001

ISBN 0–582–40475–4 PPR

British Library Cataloguing-in-Publication Data

A catalogue record for this book is available from the British Library

Library of Congress Cataloging-in-Publication Data

Breen, Michael P.
  Learner contributions to language learning: new directions in research/Michael P. Breen.
    p.   cm. — (Applied linguistics and language study)
  Includes bibliographical references and index.
  ISBN 0–582–40475–4
  1. Second language acquisition.   2. Language and languages—Study and teaching.   I. Title.   II. Series.

P118.2 .B73   2001
418′.0071—dc21
                                                                  00–061390

 6 5 4 3 2
 08 07 06 05

Set in 10/12pt Baskerville by 35
Printed in Malaysia, VVP

APPLIED LINGUISTICS AND LANGUAGE STUDY

GENERAL EDITOR

CHRISTOPHER N. CANDLIN

Chair Professor of Applied Linguistics
Department of English
Centre for English Language Education &
Communication Research
City University of Hong Kong, Hong Kong

Error Analysis:
Perspective on Second Language
Acquisition
JACK C RICHARDS (ED.)

Contrastive Analysis
CARL JAMES

Language and Communication
JACK C RICHARDS *and*
RICHARD W SCHMIDT (EDS)

Reading in a Foreign Language
J CHARLES ALDERSON *and*
A H URQUHART (EDS)

An Introduction to Discourse Analysis
Second Edition
MALCOLM COULTHARD

Bilingualism in Education:
Aspects of Theory, Research and Practice
JIM CUMMINS *and* MERRILL SWAIN

Second Language Grammar:
Learning and Teaching
WILLIAM E RUTHERFORD

Vocabulary and Language Teaching
RONALD CARTER *and*
MICHAEL McCARTHY

The Classroom and the
Language Learner:
Ethnography and Second-Language
Classroom Research
LEO VAN LIER

Listening in Language Learning
MICHAEL ROST

An Introduction to Second Language
Acquisition Research
DIANE LARSEN-FREEMAN
and MICHAEL H LONG

Process and Experience in the Language
Classroom
MICHAEL LEGUTKE *and*
HOWARD THOMAS

Translation and Translating:
Theory and Practice
ROGER T BELL

Language Awareness in the Classroom
CARL JAMES *and* PETER GARRETT (EDS)

Rediscovering Interlanguage
LARRY SELINKER

Language and Discrimination:
A Study of Communication in
Multi-ethnic Workplaces
CELIA ROBERTS, EVELYN DAVIES *and*
TOM JUPP

Analysing Genre:
Language Use in Professional Settings
VIJAY K BHATIA

Language as Discourse:
Perspective for Language Teaching
MICHAEL McCARTHY *and*
RONALD CARTER

Second Language Learning:
Theoretical Foundations
MICHAEL SHARWOOD SMITH

Interaction in the Language
Curriculum:
Awareness, Autonomy and Authenticity
LEO VAN LIER

Contents

Author's Acknowledgements

My particular gratitude is due to two valued colleagues and long-time friends. First to Merrill Swain, who invited me to organize the colloquium at the conference of the American Association for Applied Linguistics that initially brought together most of the contributors to this volume to discuss the significance of learner contributions within second language acquisition research. Second to Chris Candlin, who encouraged the present publication of our various perspectives on the learner that have been developed and refined since the colloquium. Helen Maitland is due my particular thanks for her patience and care in her work on the manuscript. Requiring busy academics to conform to an agreed format in their writing has, for her, been a new venture and pretty much like herding cats. Jackie Sorley grappled with the indexing and I thank her for her care and enthusiasm. Finally, special thanks to Casey Mein, Verina Pettigrew and Sarah Bury who, on behalf of Pearson Education, enabled the whole project to reach fruition.

Publisher's Acknowledgements

We are grateful to Pearson Education – ELT & ISD for permission to re-produce an extract from *THE LEARNING STRATEGIES HANDBOOK* by Milada Broukal.

List of Contributors

Michael P. Breen is currently Professor of Language Education and Director of the Centre for English Language Teaching at the University of Stirling, Scotland. Previously he worked at Edith Cowan University, Western Australia and Lancaster University, England. He has published on communicative and task-based approaches to language teaching, language teachers' beliefs, and the social context of language learning. More recently his research has focused upon the educational provision and assessment of young bilingual learners and on the relationship between language teachers' thinking and their classroom practices. His recent publications include, with research colleagues in Australia, *Profiling ESL Children: Teachers' Interpretations and Use of State and National Assessment Frameworks* (Canberra: Department of Employment, Education, Training and Youth Affairs, 1997) and *Principles and Practices of ESL Teachers* (Perth: Centre for Applied Languages & Literacy Research, 1998) and, with Andrew Littlejohn, *Classroom Decision Making: Negotiation and Process Syllabuses in Practice* (Cambridge: Cambridge University Press, 2000).

Anna Uhl Chamot is Associate Professor of Secondary Education at the George Washington University in Washington, DC. Her research interests include language learning strategies, content-based ESL and foreign language instruction, elementary school foreign language immersion, and literacy development of adolescent immigrant students. She is co-director of the National Capital Language Resource Center, a partnership between Georgetown University, the George Washington University, and the Center for Applied Linguistics. Dr Chamot received her PhD in ESL and Applied Linguistics from the University of Texas at Austin, her MA in Foreign Language Education from Teachers College, Columbia University, and her BA in Spanish Literature from the George Washington University.

Rod Ellis is currently Professor in, and Director of, the Institute of Language Teaching and Learning, University of Auckland. His published work includes articles and books in second language acquisition, the most recent of which is *Learning a Second Language through Interaction* (Amsterdam: John Benjamins), and also several English language textbooks, including *Impact Grammar*

(London: Addison Wesley Longman). In addition to his current position in New Zealand, he has worked in teacher education in Zambia, England, Japan and the United States.

James P. Lantolf is currently Professor of Applied Linguistics and Spanish and Director of the Center for Language Acquisition at The Pennsylvania State University. He was on the faculty of Cornell University from 1991 to 1999 and from 1980 to 1991 he was on the faculty of the University of Delaware. He has held visiting appointments at the University of Auckland, Nottingham University, the University of Melbourne, the University of Rome (*La Sapienza*) and Kassel University. He is past co-editor of *Applied Linguistics* and continues to serve on its editorial panel as well on the editorial boards of *The Modern Language Journal* and *Spanish Applied Linguistics*. His research focus is on sociocultural and activity theory and second language acquisition.

Diane Larsen-Freeman is a Professor of Applied Linguistics in the Department of Language Teacher Education at the School for International Training in Brattleboro, Vermont, USA. She has published a number of articles in the areas of second language acquisition research, English grammar, language teaching methods and teacher education. Her books include: *Discourse Analysis in Second Language Research* (Rowley, MA: Newbury House, 1980), *The Grammar Book: An ESL/EFL Teacher's Course* (with Marianne Celce-Murcia, Rowley, MA: Newbury House, 1983, 1999), *Techniques and Principles in Language Teaching* (Oxford: Oxford University Press, 1986) and *An Introduction to Second Language Acquisition Research* (with Michael Long, London: Longman, 1991). Dr Larsen-Freeman is also series director for *Grammar Dimensions*, a four-level grammar series for ESL university students (Boston, MA: Heinle and Heinle Publishers, 1993, 1997, forthcoming). From 1980 to 1985, Dr Larsen-Freeman was Editor of the journal *Language Learning*. In 1997, she was inducted as a Fellow into the Vermont Academy of Arts and Sciences.

Bonny Norton is Associate Professor in the Department of Language and Literacy Education of the University of British Columbia, Canada. She has published widely on the relationship between language learning, sociocultural identity and educational change. In Autumn 1997 she edited the *TESOL Quarterly* special issue on 'Language and Identity' and has published *Identity and Language Learning: Gender, Ethnicity and Educational Change* (London: Addison Wesley Longman, 2000).

Rebecca Oxford is Professor at Teachers College, Columbia University and the author of a number of books on language learning strategies, motivation, and instructional methodology, and has co-edited the *Tapestry* ESL Program for Heinle and Heinle Publishers. She has over 100 refereed articles and chapters to her credit on topics such as language teaching, second language acquisition, learning styles and strategies, language learning motivation, learner-generated metaphors, gender and technology. She has presented keynote speeches at conferences for teachers and researchers on most continents of the world. She holds a PhD in educational psychology from the University of North Carolina, Master's degrees from Yale University (Russian Language) and Boston University (Educational Psychology), and a Bachelor's degree (Russian Language and History) from Vanderbilt University.

Aneta Pavlenko is currently Assistant Professor of TESOL at Temple University, Philadelphia. She received her PhD in 1997 from Cornell University. Her research focuses on the relationship between bilingualism and cognition, and on the interaction between second language learning in adulthood and identity. Her work has appeared in *Bilingualism: Language and Cognition, The International Journal of Bilingualism, Annual Review of Applied Linguistics* and *Issues in Applied Linguistics*.

Anita Wenden is Professor of ESL at York College, City University of New York. She has also recently taught as Visiting Professor in the Program in Applied Linguistics at the Regional English Language Centre (Singapore). Her professional interests are in metacognitive knowledge in language learning and the development of learner autonomy. Her publications in this area include *Learner Strategies in Language Learning* (co-edited with Joan Rubin) (London: Prentice-Hall, 1987), *Learner Strategies for Learner Autonomy*, a special issue on metacognitive knowledge and beliefs guest edited for *System*, and articles in *Applied Linguistics, Language Learning, Canadian Modern Language Journal, Language Classrooms of Tomorrow* (Anthology Series – RELC), *Language Learners of Tomorrow* (Northeast Conference Reports) and *New Developments in Language Learning: Self-Management and Autonomy* (Goethe Institute).

General Editor's Preface

Michael Breen's major contribution to the study of language learning and language teaching has always been characterised by an intense engagement with the reflexivity of theory and practice. In re-reading now his earliest work, one senses a scholar-practitioner who discerns from the richness of educational theory and research ways forward for the teacher, ways which are always couched in terms of principle, not just of emulatable models of practice. This focus on principle is important since in invests his work with a challengeable quality; it urges reaction not some blind adoption. From his early contributions to the basic philosophy of what has now become a somewhat tarnished product, though at that time communicative language teaching shone with some brilliance, to his most recent characterisations of the social context and culture of the classroom, the learner as a cognitive, human and social being has always been at the centre of his inquiry.

So it is in this finely edited and remarkably coherent collection of original chapters for which, quite typically, he chooses as a title *Learner Contributions to Language Learning*. Even from a cursory glance at the titles of the individual chapters, contributed by some of the most distinguished writers in the field, one senses the bones of the argument, the outline of the map, landmarks for the reader: learner contributions and differential success; the importance of metacognitive knowledge and learner beliefs; how learners construct themselves and their teachers; whether to participate or not to participate in classroom activity as merely a learner's social decision or one implicative for relative success or failure at learning; whether learners are *people* and in what ways; how the worlds and discourses learners inhabit outside the classroom impinge upon their construction of, and participation in, the worlds and discourses within the classroom. Very much, then, an orientation to the social construction of learning, but crucially not one which in any way downplays the very significant contribution of more cognitively focused research to our understanding of second language acquisition. Breen is rightly very firm on this point, as indeed are several of his contributors in their other published writings, for example, Larsen-Freeman, Ellis, Lantolf, and here in their chapters. Indeed, the key weight given to the construct of *strategy* in the book, as in the chapters by Chamot and Wenden, would counter any such simplistic opposing of paradigms, with its ambiguity between the cognitive and the social. What the authors and the editor of the book are striving for, quite clearly, is a positive and creative accommodation of research positions and paradigms – a socio-cognitive position, if you like, one outlined in an exemplary way in the two major editorial contributions to the collection, the editor's Introduction and his Postscript.

This desirable accommodation notwithstanding, the emphasis of the book is very much on the social and the contextual, and it is these themes that I wish to take up, briefly, in this Preface. I do so in part because in a number of key articles Michael Breen has brought to our attention their importance for understanding the learner and the learners' contribution to language learning. In part, I want to problematise what might be taken to be too easy understandings of these terms as they relate to our study of their significance in language acquisition, and to suggest some clarifications and some points of future focus.

I begin by taking the position that language learning and teaching, like language itself, is always a social and cultural act and is always the product of socially situated participants who operate with varying degrees of licensed choice in particular settings, and are constrained individually and in various ways by specific structurings of power, by particular distributions of knowledge and by their own individual investments of energy and commitment. Although, of course, the contexts of acquisition are in no way bound to the classroom, it makes sense perhaps to argue from the canonical position of the classroom as a social site for learning, though not be at all limited to it, and to develop from that the constructs that will be needed to account for the activities and goings-on that envelop, and in part occasion such acquisition.

One first step, not always taken in the second language teaching and learning literature, is to accept, following Duranti and Goodwin (1992), that the key term *context* is differentially interpreted and used in different research paradigms, and that it needs to be explained and not self-evidently taken-for-granted. Since classroom behaviour, and quite generally the evidence for acquisition, is described in terms of *talk*, it is worth being clear first of all whether one is talking about the contexts of talk as might a linguist, where context is a feature of texts, something enduring that belongs to the text-as-entity that linguists seek to describe. On the other hand, as Mercer (2000) and Candlin and Mercer (2000) indicate, one might be talking about context as dynamic, a product of people's thinking, more the configuration of information that people use for making sense of language in particular situations. In this sense, context

> is more a mental than a physical phenomenon, something dynamic and momentary, but dependent in the classroom on the careful constructing by the teacher of a continuity and a community of shared understanding with learners.
>
> (Candlin & Mercer, 2000: 7)

Here one might say that the emotional and the affective dimensions of context take priority over the social, certainly over the linguistic. This would be a position close to that, say, of Lev Vygotsky. Again, following the work of Wertsch (1991) and of Scollon (1998), we might be talking about context as not talk-centered at all, but more as centered on action, or rather on *mediated* action, where talk is merely one among several tools that can be appropriated and used by actors in pursuance of their goals. Or, yet again, we might understand context as Hasan (2000) does, as what she calls 'discursive context... embracing Action, Relation and Contact – what social activity is being performed by persons in what social relation and what is the mode of their contact' (p. 29), and understanding context as not fixed and determined but dynamic, open to be reclassified or as she puts it 'con/textually shifted' as the text proceeds. Moving more widely, we may determine context not as particular event-bound at all, as Duranti & Goodwin (1992) suggest when they write,

> when the issue of context is raised ... the focal event cannot be properly understood, interpreted appropriately, or described in a relevant fashion, unless one looks beyond the event itself to other phenomena (for example cultural setting, speech situation, shared background assumptions) within which the event is embedded. (p. 3)

As they indicate, invoking Goffman, 'the context is thus a frame' (p. 3), a position also adopted by Cicourel:

> Verbal interaction is related to the task in hand. Language and other social practices are interdependent. Knowing something about the ethnographic setting, the perception of and characteristics attributed to others, and broader and local social organisational conditions becomes imperative for an understanding of the linguistic and non-linguistic aspects of communicative events.
> (Cicourel, 1992: 294)

Such an invocation of the *broader organisational conditions* at once introduces the political, or at least the institutional, and as in the work of James Gee, (Gee, 1999) engages us in the historically and structurally constrained conditions of production and reception of talk crucial for him to an understanding of this local context of situation.

If we wish to probe further in to these contexts of context, especially in relation to the understanding of the learners' contribution to language acquisition, what would be for me at least some useful constructs for such an explanation? Firstly, the construct of *community of practice*, as identified by Lave and Wenger (1991), and by Scollon (1998), is valuable in that it marks out communication as essentially a community matter and allows for the plurality of communities to which any person may belong. It makes an explicit connection with one reading of context's concern for *practice*, in terms of social-institutional and discursive acts, and it invokes the key construct of membership with its implications of recruitment, apprenticeship, normative behaviour, and power, as Cicourel and Gee's construction of context emphasises. In the terms of this book, not only are these communities to which learners and teachers belong in dynamic interaction with each other, as are their practices, but they also suggest that we should not attempt to explain one aspect of the practices of the members of such a community, say their language preferences in communication, and their resistance to others, in isolation from those broader and local social organisational conditions which impinge on language choice. So, as Norton, and also, more indirectly, Ellis and Oxford, evidence in their chapters here, communication and community necessarily impact on language learning practices, and vice versa.

There are two further terms which we may find helpful in our understanding of the contexts of acquisition. In any such community of practice, there will be identified, variously by particular people and at particular times and places, certain encounters which are recognisably problematic and highly charged, where persons' positions, identities, face, abilities, are placed on the line. These sites of engagement, in Scollon's phrase, (Scollon, 1998) or as I have called them, *crucial sites* (Candlin, 1990) may vary across different communities of practice or they may recur. One such might be the job interview, another, say, the application for social benefits, another the counselling interview, another the disciplining of inappropriate behaviour, another the explanation and understanding of risk. Such crucial sites can be found, as I say, across a range of communities of practice - in law, in social and health care, in medicine, in surveillance, in workplace management, and, as here, in language education. The language learning classroom of a migrant language learning community would be just such a classic case, as Norton and others have identified . Taking this, then, as a characteristic crucial site, we can identify a necessary third construct in this defining of context, what I would call *critical moments*. What I have in mind here are those instances where the themes and actions of communication touch most closely on the personalities and ideologies of the participants, such that they for a moment, often quite dramatically, reveal those ideological, social and political positions through their choices of, and responses to language. In a classroom this might be the disciplining of a student, or the handling by the teacher of unexpected reactions to stereotypical attitudes thought by the teacher to be innocuous, or responses by learners to racially motivated slurs. Not that such critical moments need be spoken. The negative comments on a piece of writing, in school or professional contexts would equally serve. They are familiar, and in the educational community of practice they have both general and specific relevance.

It is here that I run the risk of disturbing the harmonious consensus between the cognitive and the social that the editor has skillfully designed to establish. I dare to do so because it appears to me important to highlight what bids fair to become a very sharp, and ultimately wounding and counterproductive struggle in the field of second language acquisition. It is one which essentially addresses the issues posed in the quotation from Cicourel (1992) earlier. At its heart lies the issue of learner identity, and the extent to which acquisition can be separated from the contexts of that acquisition. As has been pointed out by several writers, including some in this volume, on one current orthodoxy the learner is either conceived of as an individual with various personal attributes ('more or less motivated', 'more or less intro-verted', 'more or less confident'), as it were independent of any relationship to the social, or as having some kind of group identity ('female outworker from Sri Lanka', 'young upwardly mobile male language learner from Hong Kong') that offers little scope for individual agency. An alternative position, now being canvassed strongly, especially in communities with considerable ethnic and linguistic diversity, for example, where I live in Australia, is to assert that such mainstream theories have little explanatory and critical adequacy, based in any case, as they are, on small, largely homogeneous populations in privileged learning circumstances. In this alternative position, such personality traits are held not to be fixed but dynamic, they change over time and space; the social group labels of orthodoxy serve to mask differentiation not to reveal it, and they make little if any connection to the socially and historically constituted relations of power that create the opportunities for learners to speak, and to learn. What we have, in fact, is a conflict among different constructions and interpretations of *context,* and hence the importance of deconstructing and relativising the term.

For one interpretation, then, it is not just a matter of a Vygotskyan analysis of the social bases for language learning *within* the classroom, and the con-struction of learners as *people,* as Lantolf and Pavlenko argue in their chapter, it is the necessity to 'reconceptualize the learner', in Norton's phrase, and show that the opportunities for learning are constrained by inequalities of power at home, in the workplace and in the community, inequalities marked by inequities of gender, ethnicity and class. Seen this way, language learning is not a skill, but a complex social practice, itself closely bound to the defini-tion of learner identities. Learning to communicate in another language is not just a matter of becoming a better and more autonomous language learner. It has to do with making the link between the achievement of under-standing and the achievement of access to rights and goods. The road towards exporing the topography of that territory begins with asking the critical ques-tions about the nature of learner identities, the nature of learner contributions, and how both are constructed and valued in the contexts of learning and the contexts of language use. What then turns out to be crucial, as Chamot in part indicates in her chapter, is the interplay between communication as both a socially and cognitively strategic act; understanding that communica-tion exists both as a means of asserting identity and of getting things done. It means also that we need to grasp that the constructs of self and person are frequently contested among learners and within each individual, that an individual learner's use of language serves both as evidence of solidarity with others and as a means of resistant struggle against institutions and their social practices, as Canagarajah (2000) exemplifies in the context of Sri Lanka. One way of accessing such constructs is to explore, as Wenden does in her chapter, the relation between learners' knowledge and learners' beliefs.

However, as we may have come to feel with *context,* to describe such com-municative behaviour simply in terms of language offers little explanation, although the textualisations are important. Thus, if we are to understand even partially the behaviour of learners in class, and appreciate their contributions, potential and actual, we need to explore a wider context, one which asks how the communicative practices in the crucial sites of classrooms relate to the practices in the crucial sites of the street, the workplace and the community. We may feel that learners do not act out their language learning lives as if caged in some hermetically sealed communicative compartments.

Let me now take the discussion of the importance of context further, and focus more on the data and the settings from which, and in terms of which, our understanding of learner contributions can be enriched.

If it is time to hear and listen more to the voices of the learners as individual persons it is also important to do so in terms of their interactions with others. There is a danger, not entirely avoided, of the cognitivist emphasis on individuality creeping back in through a side door where learners are seen only as quasi social beings, as it were from their own individual perspective, but not in any interaction with others. Actor is subsumed in person, just as earlier person was conflated with self. Nor is this blurring avoided in those studied encounters of learner discourse where highly controlled interactions are constructed, rather like rigidified enactments of some classic *theatre*, to produce some positivist results, which are then held to be implicative of the degree of interactionally-engendered acquisition. Breen's own chapter in this collection warns against the problems with just such conclusions . In the messy practices, sites and moments of the classroom, let alone the murky learning worlds outside the classroom, learners collaborate, or not, as well as participate, or not. Their contributions are co-constructed, as is their discourse. As selves, persons and actors, learners occupy institutional worlds where their contributions are frequently struggled over and, as Michael Breen has shown so insightfully, displayed through contradictory and contested discourses, ones which are by no means limited to classrooms, and which struggles are worked out in a myriad and not always overtly signalled ways. Classroom discourses, as evidence of learner contributions, are always reflective – whether supportively or antagonistically, whether accepted or resisted – of discourses outside the classroom. Continually, such discourses signal interdiscursively either solidarity with, or struggles against, the social practices of the institution and its members. Such practices within the crucial site of engagement of the classroom are always contested, and provide critical moments for the re- or the disconfirmation of identities. In that sense we cannot easily talk of *a* learner's contributions since learners are always in themselves plural, and their contributions similarly differentiated and heterogeneous. Such contributions also, incidentally, speak to an interpretation of context as talk *and* action. As Gee writes:

> Whos and whats are not really discrete and separable. You are who you are through what you are doing and what you are doing is partly recognized for what it is by who is doing it. So it is better, in fact, to say that utterances communicate an integrated, though often multiple or heteroglossic who-doing-what.
>
> (Gee, 1999: 14)

Learners learn to navigate these discourses, as Breen makes clear (Breen, 1998) through actions, linked principally to the discourses of negotiating and making meaning. In this process, it is not only language and learning that is negotiated, but also institutional structures and practices which are consolidated or challenged, and by all manner of semiotic means which work to reflect and reinforce their significance to the actors involved. Such processes always embodying the negotiation of different forms and values of capital. It is to this negotiation of value that the unpacking of metaphor in the chapters by Ellis and Oxford is primarily addressed, in that the metaphors that learners construct about themselves, their teachers and their learning offer powerful semiotic evidence of these processes.

'Metaphors we learn by' may not turn out then to be such a bad watchword to capture the richness of this book and also to highlight two overriding representations of the contexts of learner contribution. We may say that these contexts – however defined – in which learners make their contributions to learning, whether in the classroom or in the world outside, represent, and can be interpreted in reference to, two related but differently charged metaphors. The one, *ecological*, emphasises Cicourel's appraisal (Cicourel, 1992) of the dynamic interconnectedness between local actions within the institution and the governing historical and social structures of the broader formation, in short how learner contributions are constrained not only by the exigencies of the interaction order but by forces external to it. The other, *economic*, emphasises the classroom as a marketplace, where, following Bourdieu (1982, 1991), the values of participant contributions are measured against the perceived worth of their owners' various forms of capital: economic, cultural, social and symbolic. Here the issue of appraising learner contributions becomes one of understanding who controls and manipulates the rates of exchange, and against what kind and extent of capital. Answering that question in the light of exploring learner contributions compels us to forge a connection between the metaphors: evaluating the economy implies understanding the ecology. The major contribution of this exciting book is that it displays the ways in which such metaphors can be made to belong to one, rather than to two dissenting worlds.

Christopher N Candlin
General Editor
Centre for English Language Education & Communication Research
City University of Hong Kong

REFERENCES

Bourdieu, P. (1982) *Ce que parler veut dire: l'economie des echanges linguistiques*. Paris: Fayard.
Bourdieu, P. (1991) *Language and symbolic power*. Cambridge: Polity.

Breen, M.P. (1998) Navigating the discourse: on what is learned in the language classroom. *Proceedings of the 1997 RELC Seminar.* Singapore. RELC. Reproduced in Candlin, C.N. and N. Mercer (eds) (2000) op. cit.

Canagarajah, S. (1999) *Resisting linguistic imperialism in English teaching.* Oxford: Oxford University Press.

Candlin, C.N. (1990) What happens when applied linguistics goes critical? In Halliday, M.A.K., J. Gibbons and H. Nicholas (eds) *Learning, keeping and using language: selected papers from the Eighth World Congress of applied linguistics.* Amsterdam: John Benjamins.

Candlin, C.N. and N. Mercer (eds) (2000) *English language teaching in its social context.* London: Routledge.

Cicourel, A. (1992) *The interpenetration of communicative contexts: examples from medical encounters.* In Duranti, A. and C. Goodwin (eds) (1992) (op. cit.).

Duranti, A. and C. Goodwin (eds) (1992) *Rethinking context: language as an interactive phenomenon.* Cambridge: Cambridge University Press.

Gee, J. (1999) *An introduction to discourse analysis: theory and method.* London: Routledge.

Hasan, R. (2000) The uses of talk. In Coulthard, M. and S. Sarangi (eds) (2000) *Discourse and social life.* London: Pearson.

Lave, J. and E. Wenger (1991) *Situated learning: legitimate peripheral participation.* Cambridge: Cambridge University Press.

Mercer, N. (2000) *Words and minds.* London: Routledge.

Scollon, R. (1998) *Mediated discourse as social interaction: a study of news discourse.* London: Longman.

Wertsch, J.V. (1991) *Voices of the mind: a sociocultural approach to mediated action.* Cambridge MA: Harvard University Press.

Introduction: Conceptualization, affect and action in context

An adequate explanation of how people learn a language in addition to their first has to account for four major variables: (1) what the learners contribute to the process; (2) the language data made available to the learners in the communicative environment in which the learning occurs; (3) the inter-action between learners and environment in terms of the situated learning process; and (4) the actual outcomes from the learning. We can rephrase each of these in terms of key questions about language learning:

- What are the specific contributions of the persons doing the learning?
- Under what conditions or circumstances does the learning take place?
- How is the learning done?
- What is actually learned?

This book primarily focuses upon the first of these questions. However, as the chapters within it reveal, each of the four variables constantly interrelate. Learners work selectively within their environment of learning and upon the linguistic and communicative data made available to them in that environment. This selectivity derives from the learners' conceptualization of the conditions that they see as facilitating or hindering their learning and their conceptualization of the language to be learned. Such conceptualizations are imbued with the learners' feelings and attitudes. We may explore how the learning is done with regard to internal psycholinguistic and cognitive processes, including discrimination, attention and memory. Even these, however, are selective because of both the relative salience or accessibility of the language data made available and the potentials and constraints of the learners' internal processing. Again, it is likely that the learners' affective attributes will influence such selectivity. We may therefore regard what the learners actually learn – the outcomes from language learning – as significantly shaped by what they bring and contribute to the whole process.

The chapters in this book collectively provide a picture of the language learners as thinking, feeling, and acting persons in a context of language use grounded in social relationships with other people. The origin of these accounts of learner contributions was a colloquium at the American Association for Applied Linguistics in 1998 which addressed, from different research perspectives, the issue of how current second language acquisition (SLA) research constructs or defines the learner. Subsequently, each of the authors of the chapters that follow were invited to develop their accounts from their own research stance with regard to two main questions: (1) What contributions of the learners appear to have a significant impact upon their learning of a language? and (2) What do we remain unsure of concerning the contributions of the learners – in other words, what do we still need to discover through research? The present book therefore provides a reflection on diverse areas of research on language learners, undertaken mainly in the final decade of the twentieth century, and offers, at the dawn of the new century, a detailed agenda for future research.

All of the writers in this collection acknowledge that a full picture of learner contributions would include the psycholinguistic dimension of the process. Such a focus upon the direct interface between linguistic data and learners' internal cognitive processes has exemplified a psycholinguistic approach to SLA research. In endeavouring to account for this interface, the priority has been to uncover what may be universal in the process in terms of, for instance, a common order of acquisition or consistent developmental patterns. A concern for what is common among learners necessarily identifies as crucial those contributions that all learners share as human beings; contributions that exemplify their inherent biological and psychological capacities. Unlike the learning of a first language, however, success in learning a subsequent additional language is remarkably variable. Therefore, as several of the chapters in this book point out, a psycholinguistic focus in SLA is likely to be partial because it filters out a range of conceptual, affective, and social contributions of learners in interaction with features of the second language learning context that are more likely to account for the *different* learning outcomes among learners. An underlying theme of the present book, therefore, is how we may explain why different learners work in different ways under what appear to be the same learning conditions, with access to what appears to be the same language data, and who differentially achieve. Therefore, in also acknowledging that no single theory of language learning will fully account for the complexity of the process, the writers offer particular perspectives on learner contributions that may be seen as complementary to the psycholinguistic. (Recent exemplificatory psycholinguistic accounts are found in Bayley and Preston, 1996; Cook, 1993; Ritchie and Bhatia, 1996; White, 1989.)

Given the collective exploration of learners' thinking, affects, and actions for language learning in context, what do each of the chapters that follow specifically focus upon? By way of introduction to the perspectives offered by the chapters in this book, it is helpful to identify them by posing the main questions that each addresses. As we shall see, the chapters offer an unfolding narrative of learner contributions, each one in turn extending our perspectives from the individual to the individual in relationship to a widening context and the other people within it. We will summarize this narrative after briefly describing each of the perspectives provided in the chapters that follow.

WHICH COGNITIVE/AFFECTIVE LEARNER CONTRIBUTIONS HAVE BEEN FOUND TO RELATE TO LANGUAGE LEARNING?

In Chapter 1, Diane Larsen-Freeman explicitly addresses the major underlying theme of differential success in language learning. She focuses on particular learner contributions that have been under investigation for a good while and provides an update of an earlier review of this work (Larsen-Freeman, 1991) through an analysis of the research in the final decade of the twentieth century. She addresses these contributions in terms of her distinction between learner attributes, learner conceptualizations and learner actions. Learners' attributes include age, aptitude, personality, learning disabilities and social identity. Learners' conceptualization of the process of language learning includes motivation, attitudes, cognitive styles and beliefs. Finally, she evaluates the research on learner action in terms of learning strategies. Larsen-Freeman highlights the fact that each of these has tended to be studied in isolation. She argues that each of these facets of the learner needs to be seen in relation to the others and that research would benefit from a theoretical and investigative perspective on the learners that is more integrative. She identifies research perspectives which address the complex of learner contributions grounded in an account of the context of learning as a possible means towards this integration.

DOES LEARNERS' STRATEGIC LEARNING BEHAVIOUR MAKE A DIFFERENCE?

In Chapter 2, the focus sharpens upon what Larsen-Freeman identified as a crucial aspect of learner action – the strategies learners adopt in order to make the learning of a language more manageable to them. Here, Anna Chamot also provides a review of recent research, which is appropriately comprehensive in relation to this much explored aspect of learner action. She evaluates how strategies have been investigated, identifies influential studies of first language learning strategies, and reviews in turn what she categorizes as descriptive, longitudinal and intervention studies. She traces the descriptive work from the early focus on effective strategies, through strategies in task work, to studies comparing more or less effective strategy use. Learning strategies, like all learner contributions, are subject to adaptation and change throughout the language learning process. Recognition of the developmental dynamic of learners' strategies has led Chamot and her co-workers to trace changes in strategy use longitudinally. The third part of her review focuses on recent comprehensive research that seeks to answer a key pedagogic question as to whether effective strategies can be taught. For

Chamot, the provision of appropriate intervention depends upon the relevant expertise of the teacher. Concluding from her detailed review of this pivotal aspect of learner activity, she raises a number of questions that future research needs to address, including the teacher–learner relationship in learning strategy development.

ON WHAT BASIS DO LEARNERS REGULATE THEIR OWN ACTIONS DURING LEARNING?

In Chapter 3, Anita Wenden examines the research that explores what actually underlies learners' strategic behaviour. She identifies the characteristics of metacognitive knowledge as guiding the learners' conscious and deliberate regulatory control of how the learning is to be done. She specifies this significant conceptual contribution in terms of three superordinate areas of knowledge: person knowledge, task knowledge, and strategic knowledge. Within each of these, other forms of metacognitive knowledge are mobilized by the learners to enable them to regulate their actions. Wenden illustrates this process in detail with reference to learners' analysis of a task and its perceived demands upon them and through their ongoing monitoring of their process of language production. She argues that it is surprising that such metacognitive learner contributions appear to have been neglected in research given that they are formative prerequisites for learner self-regulation and autonomous action. They also reveal language learning as a *necessarily* reflective process in which learners constantly superimpose experientially informed meaning and purpose upon it. Wenden concludes with implications of this crucial metacognitive contribution for theory, research and practice in second language acquisition.

WHAT CONCEPTUALIZATIONS DO LEARNERS HAVE OF THEMSELVES AND THEIR TEACHERS?

The ways in which learners make sense of their experience of language learning are very likely to influence selectively both the kinds of metacognition to which Wenden draws our attention and, indeed, their whole approach to the language learning process. Such conceptualizations are both anticipatory and reflective in relation to immediate experience. They are shaped by learners' past experience of learning and by interpretations of their own role and the role of significant others, such as the teacher, in the immediate context in which they work. The psychologist George Kelly argued that we make sense of our experience in ways that would enable us to anticipate how we would act in new situations through our personal constructs (Kelly, 1955). Such constructs, although open to adaptation through new experiences, enable us to reduce the relative unpredictability of events and situations, particularly when we are learning something new, so that they become more manageable to us. The ways we construct the world in which we live and our actions within it are therefore both a potentially enabling and potentially constraining effort towards personal equilibrium. Clearly, persons' constructs are a deep and fairly resilient aspect of their conceptualization in a learning situation. More recently, there is a significant body of work which explores how our experience of the world, including scientific knowledge, is socially constructed, particularly through how we converse about it (Gergen, 1985; Harré, 1983; Potter, 1996; Shotter, 1993a, 1993b *inter alia*). The possibilities of social constructivist perspectives on the nature of language learning have yet to be fully explored in SLA research. However, as Rod Ellis explains in Chapter 4, the work of Lakoff and Johnson (1980) initiated a focus upon our everyday metaphorical use of language as one means of accessing the constructs that shape our thinking and the ways in which we act in certain situations.

Chapters 4 and 5 both address learner conceptualization in terms of metaphorical constructs and both make the important point that, just as metaphors provide clues to ways of perceiving, there is the possibility that our metaphorical constructs become the windows through which we may come to interpret things *literally*. In Chapter 4, Rod Ellis offers an interesting comparison between how a number of researchers in the field of SLA appear to be constructing 'the learner' and how a sample of adult learners appeared to construct themselves in relation to their language learning experience. He applies metaphor analysis to nine mostly recent articles by leading researchers in the field and discovers a paradox between constructs of learners as lacking agency and those of learners as having to be active problem-solvers. Some of the learners' own accounts of their key roles during language learning echo the researchers' use of language but a major contrast appears to be learners' specific emphasis upon the emotional or affective impact of their experience. Ellis concludes by identifying the potential of metaphor analysis for SLA research and pedagogy.

Relating to the notion that the language learning experience is created through social relationships and social interaction, Rebecca Oxford's account of how learners constructed their teachers confirms Ellis's discovery that the experience, from their point of view, reverberates with strong feelings. She reveals in detail the extent to which teachers have a very significant effect upon the students' definition of what it is to learn a language in the classroom context. Through a comprehensive metaphor analysis of a large sample of learner narratives she also reveals a clustering of learner accounts so that different teachers appear to be positioned in one of three ways: as autocratic, democratic/participatory, or laissez faire. Oxford suggests that learners' perceptions derive from the interface between their own self image, including cultural identity, dynamic social relationships in the classroom, and the context of learning in terms of its perceived demands upon them and their teachers. She highlights issues that she believes are insufficiently explored in language learning research: the significance of power and affect within the 'learning alliance' between teachers and students and the likelihood that students from different cultures will have different expectations of the teacher – and of themselves – in the classroom situation.

DOES THE ACTION OF OVERT PARTICIPATION IN THE CLASSROOM HAVE AN EFFECT UPON LEARNERS' ACQUISITION OF LANGUAGE?

Pursuing the significance attributed by Oxford's study to social relationships in the learning process, in Chapter 6 Michael Breen focuses upon the specific interaction of the language classroom. Pedagogic innovations such as communicative language teaching or task-based learning and current SLA theories such as the interaction hypothesis and the output hypothesis all assert that learners' productive participation in classroom talk will have a beneficial effect upon their linguistic and communicative competence in the target language. What is the evidence that we can glean from research in order to support these pedagogic innovations and these hypotheses? Breen addresses this question by evaluating the theoretical arguments and the research evidence both for and against the positive impact of learners' overt contributions to classroom and task work. Also echoing Ellis's and Oxford's discovery of the significance attributed by learners to the affective experience of language learning, Breen challenges the partiality of current research perspectives on classroom communication that appear to overlook its inherent socio-affective dimensions. He argues that the evidence derived by researchers from classroom and task interaction will remain inadequate and unconvincing until the actual nature of learners' contributions to it and the outcomes acquired from it are addressed in more subtle and context-sensitive ways. Currently, influential perspectives on SLA locate the learners' comprehension, expression and negotiation of meaning as pivotal in the process while adhering to a superficial view of what may be meaningful and significant to the learners during classroom and task interaction. He proposes that one means of accessing the meaning and significance of interaction and, crucially, their likely impact upon learning, is through a discoursal perspective on the interaction and the learners' participation within it. He concludes with a number of implications for future research that derive from adopting this perspective.

WHAT IS THE RELATIONSHIP BETWEEN LEARNERS' ACTIONS IN THE LEARNING CONTEXT, THEIR EXPERIENCE OF LANGUAGE LEARNING, AND THEIR LEARNING OUTCOMES?

Continuing the narrative of the book which, from chapter to chapter, widens the lens upon the context of learning as an arena for discovering why learners might differentially achieve, the final two chapters broaden our perspective upon learner participation. In Chapter 7, Lantolf and Pavlenko address the learning of language in terms of the learners' active engagement within activity. Offering a sociocultural perspective on learner thinking and action drawing upon activity theory, they argue that context is the *source* of mental development, including the development of a new language, and not merely a backdrop to this development. On the basis of their elaboration of the principles of activity theory, they argue that research on language learning, if it is to account for differential learner achievement, must focus upon the learners' variable exercise of agency within context. This entails seeing both the activities, in a location such as a language class, and learners' participation within them as having personal, biographical-historical *significance* grounded within particular cultural values and meanings. From this research stance, Lantolf and Pavlenko see learning a language as learning 'new ways of mediating ourselves in our relationships with others and to ourselves'. The process can be explored, therefore, as the complex transition from one linguistic identity to another. In this transition, what matters to learners is what they see as significant for them and not their 'performance' during activities or 'outputs' from them. And what is significant for the learners will shape how they act, how they define the context in which they act, and why they act in the ways that they do. Quoting from case studies, Lantolf and Pavlenko illustrate how language learners differentially exercise agency during learning on the basis of their interpretation of, access to, and participation in the target language community. Through this, they identify the possibilities of an agency of resistance as compared with an agency of engagement. From the perspective of activity theory and agency, Lantolf and Pavlenko conclude with a number of radical agendas for future research in SLA and for language pedagogy.

Bonny Norton, in Chapter 8, picks up the themes of learner agency and the transition of linguistic identity directly in terms of the possible clash of agencies as anticipated by Lantolf and Pavlenko. She does so by linking learner conceptualization, in terms of perceived or 'imagined' community identity, to learner action in terms of engaged participation or the actual withdrawal of participation. Norton introduces into our narrative the notion of learners moving between different communities of practice. She argues that different learners have different imagined communities; 'imagined' in the sense of the learners' construct of those communities. Thus, Norton also extends our account of learner conceptualizations in terms of their constructs; from Ellis's account of learner self-constructs and Oxford's account of teacher-constructs to a learner's constructs of the communities of which the self is a member or seeks to become a member.

Through the analysis of case studies of learners, Norton identifies three interweaving communities between which language learners move concurrently and with which, to different extents, language learners will identify. First, there is the learners' own biographical-historical community. Secondly, there is the learning community that language learners may choose to enter, such as a particular classroom and its unfolding curriculum, for instance. And, thirdly, there is the wider speech community which the learners may seek to join; a community immediately outside the classroom for a recent migrant, perhaps, or identified at a distance by learners in a foreign language class through, possibly, a greater exercise of the imagination. Norton argues that different learners in different circumstances will conceptualize each of these communities in different ways, particularly in terms of how they identify themselves with them. And, crucially, such conceptualizations will influence the extent to which they invest their participation in the learning of the language or, indeed, withdraw their participation completely.

WHAT OVERALL PROFILE OF THE LEARNERS' CONTRIBUTION TO LANGUAGE LEARNING IS PROVIDED BY THE CHAPTERS THAT FOLLOW?

The particular learner contributions to their language learning which are focused upon in the chapters that follow are summarized in Figure 1 (authors' names are indicated alongside the main learner contributions that they directly address). The purpose of this book is to provide a comprehensive account and evaluation of the research relating to such contributions and to identify further directions which research might take. As Figure 1 illustrates, the narrative of research that we present extends outwards from the attributes of individual learners, such as age or aptitude for example, through conceptualizations and affects that they superimpose upon the language learning experience, thence through the specific actions they undertake in the learning context, to ongoing participation as a person within and between communities. *All* of these contributions are enacted in ongoing ways and to different extents during language learning.

We have identified the language classroom as a particular context of the learning process. In Lantolf's, Pavlenko's and Norton's terms it can be seen as a specific community of practice for learners which gravitates within the wider communities from which they come, to which they currently belong, and to which they seek membership. In this sense, a language class mediates between the learners' being and becoming. Therefore, the same learner contributions that we have identified will be enacted in those other contexts in which learners seek to use and develop a new language.

What is hard to convey in diagrammatic form is the fact that these contributions will constantly interrelate with one another. As Lantolf and Pavlenko illustrate in Chapter 7, activity theory provides us with an informative means of perceiving these kinds of interrelationships. Boxes in a diagram tend to imply a lack of permeability between the things within and those without the box. We might better adopt a metaphor in terms of, for example, sound waves and their returning echoes in endeavouring to express the reverberative and iterative effect of each learner contribution in relation to others and in different contexts. Learner attributes such as, for instance, aptitude, personality or identity relate to how learners will conceptualize themselves *as learners* and the situation which they enter that provides a potential for learning – more obviously a classroom and less obviously, perhaps, other social events in wider communities. All of these, in turn, will shape their agency, participation and strategy use as a contributor to the linguistic-communicative environment available to themselves and others. Further, the engagement of all such

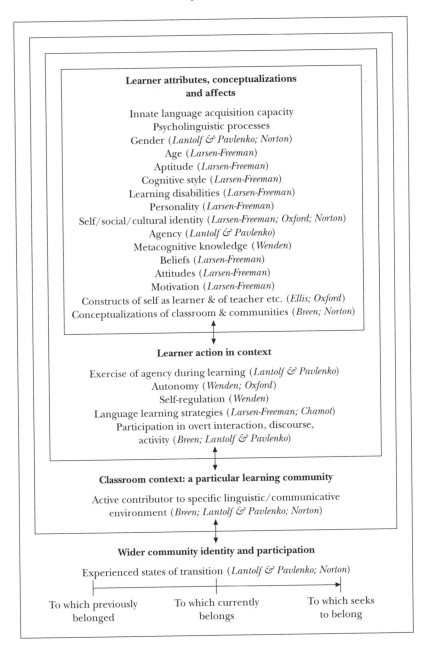

**Learner attributes, conceptualizations
and affects**

Innate language acquisition capacity
Psycholinguistic processes
Gender (*Lantolf & Pavlenko; Norton*)
Age (*Larsen-Freeman*)
Aptitude (*Larsen-Freeman*)
Cognitive style (*Larsen-Freeman*)
Learning disabilities (*Larsen-Freeman*)
Personality (*Larsen-Freeman*)
Self/social/cultural identity (*Larsen-Freeman; Oxford; Norton*)
Agency (*Lantolf & Pavlenko*)
Metacognitive knowledge (*Wenden*)
Beliefs (*Larsen-Freeman*)
Attitudes (*Larsen-Freeman*)
Motivation (*Larsen-Freeman*)
Constructs of self as learner & of teacher etc. (*Ellis; Oxford*)
Conceptualizations of classroom & communities (*Breen; Norton*)

Learner action in context

Exercise of agency during learning (*Lantolf & Pavlenko*)
Autonomy (*Wenden; Oxford*)
Self-regulation (*Wenden*)
Language learning strategies (*Larsen-Freeman; Chamot*)
Participation in overt interaction, discourse,
activity (*Breen; Lantolf & Pavlenko*)

Classroom context: a particular learning community

Active contributor to specific linguistic/communicative
environment (*Breen; Lantolf & Pavlenko; Norton*)

Wider community identity and participation

Experienced states of transition (*Lantolf & Pavlenko; Norton*)

| To which previously | To which currently | To which seeks |
| belonged | belongs | to belong |

Figure 1 The profile of learner contributions to language learning

contributions will relate to the state of transition the learners experience
in seeking membership of another speech community. And all of these interrelationships are, for the learners, imbued with significant emotions and
meanings.

The interrelationship is, of course, reflexive in the sense that people take their wider community identity and history into the classroom – as the chapters by Oxford, Lantolf and Pavlenko, and Norton reveal. This classroom context will be seen by learners to facilitate or constrain their own actions which, in turn, have an impact upon their conceptualizations, affects, and even those attributes which research tends to construct as relatively resilient or stable learner capacities, such as their psycholinguistic processes. In language learning research we have hardly commenced the investigation of the ways in which even a few of these contributions may interrelate. A further purpose of this book is to begin to identify some possible relationships and, crucially, how these may have an effect upon language learning.

There is a further important characteristic of the learner contributions on which we gradually widen the spotlight from chapter to chapter. They are dynamic both in the ways in which learners engage them in any moment of learning and they are open to change over time, especially as the language learning unfolds. This implies that virtually all of them are mutable and, thereby, susceptible to learner agency and, to differing extents, the influence of contextual variables. The relevance of this for language pedagogy is clear. Pedagogy has the capacity to provide those opportunities and conditions within which learner contributions that are found to have a positive effect upon learning may be more fully engaged. It also has the potential to constrain them or sometimes even attribute to them an assumed limitation – as in a learner's age, strategy use, classroom participation, or previous community membership, for example. Research and theory in SLA, as we have seen, seeks to identify that which is stable, consistent and common among learner contributions. For instance, it may be that our innate language acquisition capacity is immutable, although it functions in a different way when we learn an additional language, the learners' access to it being through the first language. However, the further we widen our lens from what might be described as relatively stable attributes of learners, it is more likely that we will find that their interaction reveals a dynamic which is mutual; that a change in strategy use or classroom participation, for example, can effect a change in self-identification both as learners and as potential members of a new speech community – and, of course, vice versa.

As indicated earlier, one underlying purpose of this book is to begin to explain why learners of an additional language will achieve differentially. In doing so, the chapters helpfully reveal different facets of the same key learner variables. For example, learner identity is explored in terms of personality, self-image, community and culture. Overt language learning behaviour is explored in terms of agency, engagement in joint activity, classroom and task interaction, and strategy use. And learner thinking is explored in terms of knowledge, beliefs, attitudes, constructs and conceptualizations of the learning context and community and cultural membership. We present a comprehensive and complex picture of learners, revealing them as contributing to their learning of a language in comprehensive and complex ways. A further motive, therefore, is to offer an enriched research perspective on the learner which we believe has been missing from much of the research literature in SLA to date. We acknowledge that the picture of the learner which is presented here remains itself incomplete and perceived as 'through a glass, darkly' (Corinthians, 13.1). However, to borrow Burke's concept, as quoted by Lantolf and Pavlenko in Chapter 7, the particular 'terministic screen' or investigative lens through which we have tried to understand the language learner in our narrative has been rarely used to date, and the new ways of perceiving that it allows may helpfully complement and extend theories and research that have so far preceded it.

Chapter 1

Individual cognitive/affective learner contributions and differential success in second language acquisition

Diane Larsen-Freeman, School for International Training, Vermont

INTRODUCTION

It is significant that the central theme of this book is learner contributions. For while the learner has not been ignored in second language acquisition (SLA) research, more attention has been paid to characterizing an acquisition process that is common to all learners. Thus 'mainstream' SLA research has been largely concerned with the role of the L1, acquisition orders, developmental sequences, negotiated input, the role of a biologically-specified universal grammar (UG), sequence learning, etc. From a UG perspective, the only 'contribution' of the learner is an innate predisposition for language acquisition, at least with regard to the acquisition of core grammar. From an interactionist perspective, the learner's 'contribution' is a willingness to utilize second language input, obtained usually through negotiating meaning with a more proficient speaker of the language. Of course, it is recognized by advocates of both perspectives that unlike first language acquisition, success in learning a second language is considerably more variable, and it is left to the research on individual learner factors to explain this differential success.

For some time, it seems to me, we have underestimated the significance of the learners' role in the SLA process. Unlike first language learners, second language learners can, and sometimes do, refuse to engage with the SLA process at all. Conversely, some learners will succeed when the conditions of learning do not appear conducive to success. Almost twenty years ago (Larsen-Freeman, 1983), I argued that the learner was not merely a passive recipient of customized native speaker input. I did not question the value of comprehensible input in the SLA process, but I questioned why the responsibility for increasing the comprehensibility of the input should be perceived as a unilateral process. To illustrate my point, I reported on the case of a Dutch speaker who claimed to have successfully acquired German without receiving any modified input. The Dutch speaker's sole source of input was from German radio broadcasts. Of course the learner was aided in the SLA endeavour by the similarity between the two languages; however, I cited this admittedly unusual case to support my contention that a second language learner has a great deal to do with the outcome of the process and is not merely passively dependent on some benevolent, skilful, more proficient interlocutor.

This volume signals an increased appreciation of the role of second language learners, affecting not just how much they succeed, but what they do to meet with success. In what follows, I review the largely experimental research literature of the last decade (updating Larsen-Freeman, 1991) from the perspective of individual cognitive/affective learner contributions. I am defining 'contributions' to include what learners bring, that is, who they are (*attributes*: age, aptitude, personality, learning disabilities, social identities), how they conceptualize second language acquisition (*conceptualization*: motivation, attitude, cognitive style, beliefs), and what they do (*actions*: learning strategies). After addressing these three categories in turn, I conclude by making a more global comment regarding the evolution of the construction of the learner in the second language acquisition field.

LEARNER ATTRIBUTES

Age

In my 1991 survey of the literature, I concluded that the available evidence for an age-related effect in SLA was inconsistent. However, the evidence seemed to favour the critical period hypothesis (CPH), whereby only those who begin the acquisition of an L2 before the end of a limited developmental period, coinciding about the time of the onset of puberty, can attain native-like levels of proficiency, at least for pronunciation in the L2. This position continues to receive support (Long, 1993b; Patkowski, 1994). For instance, Hurford and Kirby (1999) have used computer simulations to show how language complexity and speed of acquisition converge at puberty, demonstrating that a critical period for language acquisition is an evolutionary advantage. Then, too, Weber-Fox and Neville (1999) present evidence from event-related brain potential differences and grammatical judgement tasks to show that neural organization is different for early and late language learners. Most recently, Moyer (1999) reported that, with one exception, highly proficient L2 learners, who had begun their study of German after puberty, were not judged native-like in their pronunciation of German despite their high level of motivation and the fact that they had been immersed in the language while residing in Germany.

However, several recent studies have also challenged the CPH (see Birdsong, 1999 for a collection of papers divided evenly between supporters, for example, Eubank and Gregg (1999) and detractors of the CPH, for example, Bialystok and Hakuta (1999)). Flege (1995) and Yeni-Komshian, Flege and Liu (1997) found that L2 learners' ability to pronounce a foreign language does decline with age; however, they maintain that the ability declines linearly, that is, there is no sudden drop at puberty, which one might expect, given the CPH. Flege (1999) does acknowledge, however, that none of the 240 native Italian participants in his 1995 study, who began learning English after the age of fifteen, could be said to have learned to speak English without a detectable foreign accent. In contrast, Ioup, Boustagui, El Tigi and Moselle (1994) report on a case of an adult English learner who has apparently acquired native proficiency in Egyptian Arabic in an untutored setting. The authors account for this individual's success by arguing that the woman's language learning talent is an innate, inherited trait, associated with characteristics belonging to the Geschwind cluster such as left-handedness, twinning and allergies, among others. While not all the native speaker judges rated the woman's pronunciation as native, in a study by Bongaerts, Planken and Schils (1995), native English-speaking judges were indeed unable to distinguish ten highly proficient Dutch learners of English from a group of native speakers of English. None of the learners had begun studying English before the age of twelve. However, there was also speculation on the part of the researchers that since the learners spoke the supraregional, prestigious dialect of British English, called Received Pronunciation, the judges may have been persuaded to award higher scores than they would have had the subjects spoken a less prestigious dialect. Thus, in a follow-up study in 1997 (Bongaerts et al., 1997), judges and learners were matched in the dialect of British English that they spoke. The main result from the second study was that some, although not all, learners received ratings from judges comparable to those given the native speakers in a control group. Finally, Bongaerts (1999) reports that four of a pool of nine Dutch learners of French achieved Flege, Munro and MacKay's (1995) criterion of native-likeness on their speech samples judged by native speakers of French. Bongaerts argues that such results may be interpreted as evidence suggesting that claims concerning an absolute biological barrier to the attainment of a native-like accent in a foreign language are too strong. Having said this, Bongaerts acknowledges that native-like attainment in the domain of pronunciation seems to be a fairly exceptional phenomenon.

Research in the area of syntax, based on grammaticality judgements, also shows that native-like performance is possible in postpubertal learners (Birdsong, 1992; White and Genesee, 1996; but see Pulvermuller and Schumann, 1994). It should be noted, however, that all these learners were specially selected because of their exceptional ability. For instance, in Birdsong's study, all of the subjects, foreign language learners of French, were fluent and had been living in France for at least three continuous years prior to being tested.

Recent hypotheses about what helps some postpubertal learners succeed include brain organization (Ioup et al., 1994), high motivation and training, (Bongaerts et al., 1995; Klein, 1995; Moyer, 1999), continued access to abundant, authentic L2 input (Klein, 1995), training in speech perception (Flege, 1995), and multiple explanations, including possibly sociocultural factors and sustained access to auditory perception (Wode, 1994). Such findings remain to be corroborated when the L1 and L2 are less typologically closely related (Bialystok, 1997; Bongaerts et al., 1997; Kellerman, 1995).

Another age-related hypothesis that has been challenged is Krashen, Long and Scarcella's (1979) generalization, based on a synthesis of research studies published up to that time, that older children are initially faster than younger learners when it comes to the acquisition of morphosyntax. Slavoff and Johnson (1995) report that their subjects' age of arrival played no role in predicting the subjects' rate of acquisition. Performance was very similar between the two age groups they examined – 7–9 and 10–12-year olds upon arrival – throughout the three years of their study. Thus, there was no initial older learner advantage. They offer as an explanation for their contrary finding the fact that their learners were acquiring a language – English – that was very different typologically from the L1's of their subjects – Chinese, Japanese, Korean and Vietnamese – and of the L1's studied previously. Clearly, many questions remain to be investigated with regard to age effects and second language acquisition.

Aptitude

As I stated in 1991, it is obvious to even the most casual observer that individual learners learn at different rates. Skehan (1989) has called language aptitude 'one of the central individual differences in language learning' (1989: 25) and 'consistently the most successful predictor of language learning success' (1989: 38). What constitutes an aptitude for language learning and its precise relationship to IQ has been unclear, however, with previous research finding correlations between aptitude and IQ that varied from low to moderate (for discussion, see Skehan, 1998). After testing 160 Japanese college students studying EFL, Sasaki (1993a) found a high correlation between a general second language proficiency factor and a general cognitive or intelligence factor. But while they were correlated, they remained mutually distinct. In a subsequent qualitative study, Sasaki (1993b) observed that the general proficiency factor may be related to her subjects' ability to use the information available to them to find the correct answers to a cloze test. This observation is supported by Sasaki's (1996) factor analytic study of aptitude, showing a relationship among verbal intelligence, reasoning and foreign language aptitude.

Relevant to a discussion of research addressing the former issue, the question of the nature of aptitude, is Skehan's (1989) contention that there exist two different profiles of language aptitude – some learners possess an analytic aptitude, and others are more memory-oriented. Previous research on aptitude had tacitly assumed that the components of aptitude aggregate in cumulative fashion to influence language-learning success. Skehan speculates that analytic and memory orientations represent different routes to the same language learning success, and that success is achievable by either, provided that learners play to their strengths. The memory route to proficiency draws some support from the suggestion by N. Ellis (1996) that differences in learners' short-term memories may account for learners' differential success.

Another question that has persisted with regard to aptitude is whether components of aptitude are relevant for informal as well as formal learning environments (Krashen, 1981; Skehan, 1989). Work by Robinson (1997), who looked at individual differences in aptitude under different conditions of learning, would suggest that they are. Robinson found that when an individual's aptitude matched the demands of a task performed under any condition, incidental or instructed, rule-search or implicit, the aptitude often led to awareness, which was associated with superior levels of learning. Earlier Robinson (1995) found the highest correlations between aptitude and performance when subjects' focus was away from form and towards meaning.

Although strictly speaking distinct from language aptitude, Howard Gardner's concept of multiple intelligences is relevant here. Gardner (1983) grouped human capabilities into seven categories which he called 'intelligences': verbal-linguistic, logical-mathematical, visual-spatial, body-kinesthetic, musical-rhythmic, interpersonal, and intrapersonal. According to Gardner, each person possesses all seven intelligences to varying degrees. While I am unaware of any SLA research that relates multiple intelligences to individual differences in language learning outcomes, I agree with Schmidt (1997) that it would seem that this area warrants further investigation, especially since it has attracted a great deal of attention in language teaching circles.

Personality

In my 1991 review of the research literature, I discussed many different individual personality traits thought to facilitate or inhibit SLA: self-esteem, extraversion, anxiety, risk-taking, sensitivity to rejection, empathy, inhibition, and tolerance of ambiguity. Since then, although a great deal of research has been conducted, most has centred on learners' reactions to anxiety. Perhaps this should not be surprising for Gardner and MacIntyre claim that 'the single best correlate of achievement is language anxiety' (1993: 183). Anxiety not only causes difficulty in oral performance, but also in second language reading (Saito et al., 1998) and writing (Cheng et al., 1999). Its influence also seems to extend to different contexts. Aida (1994) found that consistent with research using western languages, language anxiety was found to be significantly negatively related to American students' performance in Japanese. Its effects are so pervasive that one research study has shown that it even interferes with students' estimation of their L2 competence, with anxious students underestimating their competence relative to less anxious students (MacIntyre et al., 1997).

In fact, it may be that the study of language anxiety no longer belongs in a discussion of general personality factors at all. For while it was once thought that anxiety was a trait factor, indicative of a person's tendency to become anxious in any situation (MacIntyre and Gardner, 1991a), a more likely explanation according to MacIntyre and Gardner (1991b) is that there is a special form of anxiety, language anxiety, or 'the feeling of tension and apprehension specifically associated with second language contexts', which MacIntyre and Gardner (1994) claim can be discriminated reliably from other types of anxiety and which many people experience.

One of the interesting issues debated in the research on the effect of anxiety on second language achievement is the controversy sparked by Ganschow, Javorsky, Sparks, Skinner, Anderson and Patton (1994) and Ganshow and Sparks (1996), raising the now familiar question of directionality: 'Does anxiety impair second language performance as MacIntyre and Gardner claim, or does poor performance lead to anxiety as a consequence?' (1994: 42). In MacIntyre's (1995) response to Ganschow et al.'s challenge, he affirms his beliefs that the evidence supports a strong initial influence of affective factors on student performance, not only in the learning of a second language, but also in demonstrating what he or she has learned. He also adds, however, that 'the cyclical relation between anxiety and task performance suggests that as students experience more failure, their anxiety level may increase even more' (MacIntyre, 1995: 97).

Another personality trait which has received some recent attention in the research literature is extraversion (for a review, see Dewaele and Furnham, 1999). Dewaele and Furnham (2000) discovered a significant positive correlation between extraversion, as measured by the Eysenck Personality Inventory, and the fluency of French–English bilinguals, especially in interpersonally stressful situations. However, other research conducted by Carrell, Prince and Astika (1996), Ehrman (1993, 1995, 1996), Ehrman and Oxford (1995), and Oxford and Ehrman (1993), in which the Myers-Briggs Type Indicator has been used to assess personality type and learning style, has found that extraversion is not an especially good predictor of language learning success.

There were very few other direct relationships between personality traits and language performance measures in this research, although in their sample of 855 language learners, mainly adult learners of varying languages from the US Department of State, Ehrman and Oxford found that 'students who reported themselves as defiant were slightly ahead of their compliant classmates in both speaking and reading' (Ehrman and Oxford, 1995: 80). For the same two skills, 'thin' ego boundaries (an operationalization of the concept of tolerance of ambiguity, as determined by the subjects' answers on the Hartmann Boundary Questionnaire (Hartmann, 1991)), were associated with proficiency outcomes. Interestingly, in support of Skehan's (1989) claim, far more robust correlations held for the aptitude measures (the MLAT) than for any personality traits.

A personality trait that was not mentioned in the earlier review is 'willingness to communicate'. Willingness to communicate is said to reflect a stable predisposition to talk in various situations and is therefore essentially a personality trait (MacIntyre et al., 1998). Using path analysis, MacIntyre and Charos (1996) concluded that each of the 'Big Five' personality traits (extraversion, agreeableness, conscientiousness, emotional stability and openness to new experiences) contributes to developing motivation for language learning or to willingness to communicate, or to both. They argue, though, that the effect of personality seems to be channelled through more specific variables, such as intergroup attitudes and confidence in the second language.

Learning disabilities

Since the 1991 review, much has been written in the general education literature on learning disabilities. Among students who have foreign language learning difficulties, no differences have been found between the L1 skills and foreign language aptitude of students classified as learning disabled and students not classified as learning disabled (Sparks et al., 1998). Whether or not such students with learning disabilities achieve differentially in an L2 from students without learning disabilities is an empirical question (Sparks and Javorsky, 1999). However, it is the case that learning disabilities can manifest themselves as language (decoding/encoding) difficulties (Ganschow and Sparks, 1993, 1995). And this might well have repercussions for differential achievement, unless certain modifications to instruction are made (Arries, 1999).

Social identities

This review thus far has focused on factors which have received most of the attention in SLA research on individual differences until recently. We are more aware now, though, of the importance that social identity plays in affecting learner performance. Norton Peirce (1995) and Norton, in Chapter 8 of the present volume, argues that a comprehensive theory of social identity which integrates the language learner and the language learning context is needed in SLA research. For Norton, community membership and learner transitions between communities of speakers is a crucial aspect of social identity. She also maintains that SLA research has not paid sufficient attention to the issue of power relations between language learners and target language speakers. Siegal (1996) examines the intersection of learner identity, social position and SLA in a white woman learning Japanese in Japan. She points out that both native and non-native speakers engage in the act of 'impression management' as they interact in the target language. Recent discussions on the effect of social identity include Ibrahim (1999) on the relationship between racial identity and learning, Nelson (1999) on sexual identity, and Carrier (1999) on social status.

LEARNER CONCEPTUALIZATIONS

Motivation

Motivation continues, rightfully, to receive a great deal of respect among SLA researchers. True to this point, Pulvermuller and Schumann (1994), in their parsimonious neurobiological model of language acquisition, attest to the importance of learner motivation by considering it as the only other factor besides grammatical acquisitional ability that will account for the difference between L1 and L2 acquisition and variable success in SLA. Schumann (1998), however, proposes that L2 motivation, in turn, is multifaceted, consisting of various permutations of five stimulus appraisal patterns: novelty, pleasantness, goal/need significance, coping potential, self and social image.

Many researchers today acknowledge that our current conceptualizations of motivation are too simplistic. While some research has supported Lukmani's observation (1972) that instrumental motivation can be just as powerful as integrative motivation for explaining learners' differential success (Gardner and MacIntyre, 1991; see also Samimy and Tabuse, 1992), other research has called into question the simple binary distinction between instrumental and integrative motivation. Gardner and Tremblay (1994a, 1994b), for instance, make the case for a contrast between integrative and instrumental orientations, an orientation being a class of reasons for studying a language which includes, but is not the same as, motivation. Clément, Dörnyei and Noels (1994) report an association, rather than an independence, between instrumental and integrative motivation based on an analysis of factors accounting for the success of foreign language learners of English in Hungary. And Belmechri and Hummel (1998) also provide evidence that orientations among francophone high school students learning English in Quebec are context dependent, not exclusively instrumental nor integrative.

But beyond challenging the simple binary distinction with regard to motivation and second language acquisition, work by Crookes and Schmidt (1991), Dörnyei (1994, 2001), Fotos (1994), Oxford and Shearin (1994), Schmidt, Boraie and Kassabgy (1996), Tremblay and Gardner (1995), and Williams and Burden (1997) has observed in general how narrow our view of motivation has been. Dörnyei, for example, has argued that in determining the motivation of second language learners, we need to take into account not only social group factors (for a review see Dörnyei, 1998), as important as they may be, but also personal factors such as the need for achievement and self-confidence, and situational factors such as the interest and relevance of course-specific materials. Another example of the influence of local factors comes from Noels, Clément and Pelletier's (1999) recent study demonstrating that students' perceptions of their teachers' communicative style were related to intrinsic motivation, such that the more controlling and less informative students perceived their language teacher to be, the lower students' intrinsic motivation was. One thing that is clear is that motivation is multifaceted and that no available theory has yet managed to represent its complexity.

Attitude

This same general concern for inclusivity has characterized the work on the influence of learner attitudes on second language learning success. For instance, in the earlier review (Larsen-Freeman, 1991), I pointed out that it was not sufficient to look at the attitudes of the learners alone, especially in the case of young learners; we needed also to examine the attitudes of influential others such as parents, peers and teachers. When they looked at parental attitudes, Lambert and Taylor (1996) found that the social class of parents of language learners affected their attitudes towards their children's language learning, which in turn affected issues of language maintenance. Working-mothers of Cuban heritage living in the United States encouraged their children to learn English in order to succeed in America, an attitude that led to advances in English at the expense of the children's Spanish fluency. In contrast, for middle-class mothers, success was associated more with the encouragement of Spanish competence, not English, resulting in their children's enjoying an additive, rather than a subtractive, bilingualism. Then, too, Flowerdew, Li and Miller (1998) found that despite the rather ambi-valent attitude towards the study of English indicative of the sociolinguistic tensions currently within the Hong Kong society at large, parents still desire their children to be educated in English-medium schools in order to maxim-ize their career prospects.

Another issue that begs for further attention is the question of the direc-tion of the influence: Does a positive attitude underlie better achievements, or do better achievements contribute to a more positive attitude, or is there a reciprocal relationship (Hermann, 1980; Larsen-Freeman and Long, 1991)? This question motivated a recent study by Kuhlmeier, van den Bergh and Melse (1996). What these researchers found was that students who entered a first-year German course with a positive attitude rated higher in achievement than those having a negative attitude both at the beginning and at the end of the school year. Direct effects of students' attitudes on achievement (and vice versa) could not be established, however, still leaving us with the ques-tion of reciprocity.

One of the contributions of the Kuhlmeier, van den Bergh and Melse study is to remind us of the importance of measuring learner factors at more than one point in time. So far research designs have often included self-report measures administered once during the study. A longitudinal perspective should be encouraged in order to obtain a better picture of how different motivational or attitudinal influences evolve. Mantle-Bromley (1995), for ex-ample, showed how students' attitudes and misconceptions about the language learning process could be altered by a systematic instructional program, so that they would not hinder students' progress and persistence in language study. It is conceivable that as we search for an enhanced conceptualization of learner factors, we will also find that they are not only mutable but that they also vary in their influence, depending on the learners' stage of acquisition. We have yet to determine, for instance, if Spolsky (1989) was right that aptitude has more of an effect in early language acquisition than at later stages.

The final point I will make relevant to the discussion of the socio-psychological factors stems from the need not only to assess the impact of these and other factors longitudinally, sensitive to their mutability, but also to recognize that the variables do not likely operate independently of one another. We clearly need more integrative research on learner factors. Looking at one factor at a time obscures relationships among them. For example, Harley and Hart (1997), integrating the first two learner factors in this review, found that there was a statistically significant relationship between age and the components of aptitude. They discovered a positive relationship between L2 outcomes and an analytic dimension of language aptitude for adolescent (Grade 11) learners of French and a positive relationship between L2 outcomes and memory ability for younger learners (Grade 1). Noels and Clément (1996) and Noels, Pon and Clément (1996) have also conducted studies examining the interrelationship among various types of variable: social context variables, attitudinal/motivational factors, self-confidence, and L2 acquisition/acculturation processes.

Simple univariate, and even multivariate correlations, are misleading in that they do not distinguish direct from indirect paths of causation. More powerful causal modelling techniques exist today that will allow specification of indirect paths of causation, with one variable (e.g., attitude) influencing another (such as motivation), which in turn influences the final dependent variable (e.g., achievement) (Skehan, 1991). For example, Wen and Johnson (1997) were able to establish a hypothetical causal model for sixteen L2 learner variables that have been assumed to account for some of the variance in English achievement among Chinese EFL learners. Of the sixteen, only three unmodifiable variables (sex, and previous L1 and L2 proficiency) and three modifiable variables (strategies of vocabulary acquisition, tolerating ambiguity and mother-tongue avoidance) were found to be direct. Gardner, Tremblay, and Masgoret (1997) were also able to evaluate the contributions of a number of affective measures to second language achievement using a causal model. Such models permit one way of understanding how the variables interrelate and complement one another.

Cognitive style

Another significant challenge in working on individual difference factors has been operationalizing and measuring the factors. The difficulty in doing so has meant that research on learner factors has sometimes been suspect. Oller and Perkins (1978), for example, attacked Gardner's methods of measuring motivation, claiming that instead of detecting motivation, subjects' scores on Gardner's scales reveal such characteristics as language proficiency and verbal intelligence. While Oller and Perkins's criticism has been countered by Gardner and others (see, for example, Gardner, 1980), contention around measuring learner factors has been renewed, this time with regard to cognitive style. Articles by Chapelle (1992), Chapelle and Green (1992), Griffiths and Sheen (1992), and Sheen (1992) have all centred on whether or not subjects' performance on the Group Embedded Figures Test is a valid measure of field independence, ironically the one cognitive style factor that has been demonstrated in the past to correlate with language learning success. The controversy centres around whether the GEFT is really a test of cognitive style or simply an ability test.

What perhaps best sums up what we are left with at this point is Chapelle's (1992) statement that the existence of cognitive styles remains a matter of opinion. In actual fact, the argument over what the GEFT measures may prove irrelevant since research by Elliott (1995), who used the same Group Embedded Figures Test to measure 66 undergraduate Spanish learners' phonological acquisition, showed that students' GEFT performance was not a significant predictor of improvement in pronunciation.

Beliefs

During the past decade, researchers have begun to investigate learners' beliefs about the nature of language and language learning in an attempt to account for individual differences (Cotterall, 1995; Elbaum et al., 1993, Grotjahn, 1991; Kern, 1995). Educational research consistently indicates that students' epistemological beliefs can have significant influence on learning and comprehension (Jehng et al., 1993). For instance, Schommer (1990) demonstrated that a strong belief in quick all-or-nothing learning predicts oversimplification of complex knowledge and failure on the part of students to integrate new information with existing knowledge.

Mori (1999a) explored the relationship between language learners' beliefs and the strategies they use to deal with new words. More specifically, Mori examined whether there is any connection between the beliefs of native English-speaking college students learning to read Japanese and their ability to infer meaning from component Kanji characters and information from context. Mori found modest, but statistically significant, correlations to suggest that language learners' word inference strategies at least partially reflect their beliefs about learning in general and language learning in particular. Mori (1999b) noted that learners who consider a foreign language easy are more likely to outperform those who view it as being difficult. Then, too, Williams and Burden (1999) discovered that a language teacher can play a significant role in the development of students' conceptions of language learning success and failure and how these are judged. Oxford's detailed account of students' perceptions of their teachers, in Chapter 5 of the present volume, suggests that the teacher effect upon language learners' beliefs about themselves as learners and how they actually undertake learning may be highly significant.

LEARNER ACTIONS

Learning strategies

The chapter that follows this one is devoted entirely to the theme of learning strategies. As such, I will be brief here. Much of the research on learning strategies continues to be descriptive. For example, work by Green and Oxford (1995) found that overall strategy use varied significantly by proficiency level, with more strategy use by more successful students and more strategy use by females than by males. On the other hand, Huda (1998) reports that good language learners use fewer learning strategies than less proficient learners. The incongruence with previous research is explained by speculating that good language learners may learn a second language more efficiently and may better know what works and doesn't work for them.

In addition to describing strategy use, the other thrust of the research that has been conducted in this area has been on whether or not learners at varying levels of instruction can learn how to improve their comprehension and production of a foreign language through strategies-based instruction (Chamot and O'Malley, 1994a; Cohen et al., 1998; Dörnyei, 1995; McDonough, 1995; Mendelsohn, 1994; Nunan, 1996; Oxford, 1993). Results have been somewhat positive. Cohen, Weaver and Li, for example, reported that on one of three post-tests, the experimental group who had received instruction in learning strategies outperformed the comparison group (Chamot, in the following chapter, provides a detailed review of this kind of intervention). Contradictory findings exist though, suggesting that strategy use does not relate strongly to proficiency (cited in Oxford 1996a) and that proficiency differences may have more to do with appropriate choice of strategies than sheer strategy use (Vann and Abraham, 1990). Wenden, in Chapter 3 of the present volume, addresses the important question of the influence upon strategy choice of students' metacognitions. Questions have also been raised about whether findings concerning strategy use apply to other cultures (LoCastro, 1994; M. Richards, 1997; Wenden, Chapter 3).

With regard to the last point, Donato and McCormick's (1994) research on language learning strategies should be singled out. These researchers bring a sociocultural perspective to the study of language learning strategies. In so doing, they argue that the development of language learning strategies is mainly a by-product of mediation and socialization into a community of language learning practice. As such, strategies are situated in a particular context and are continually under development. According to these researchers, since language learning strategies are particular to a given context, it makes no sense to expect that they can be directly exported from one context into another and implemented with uniform success.

CONCLUSION

To what extent individual difference factors are altered by contextual factors is, of course, an enormously important, yet vexing, question. A similar concern has been raised recently with regard to the SLA process. Charges that 'mainstream' SLA fails to take into account the social reality of SLA (see, for example, the Fall 1997 and Spring 1998 issues of *The Modern Language Journal*) call into question how truly universal the SLA process is. The critics not only object to the decontextualization of SLA research, they also object to the etic view of the language learner, a view represented by much of the research I have reviewed here. Breen (1996), for example, suggests that only part of the variation in learning outcomes is due to the diversity of learner contributions. He adds, 'variation will also have to be explained with reference to the context in which the learning occurred so that input, process, and outcomes are seen as extensions of how the learners variously defined that context and acted in it' (Breen, 1996: 86).

Such a view of the language learner, represented by several of the chapters in this volume, clearly needs to be taken seriously, as there will be far-reaching consequences if learners' construal of the context and their action is what determines the course of second language development. That the very human process of language acquisition itself varies according to contextual factors is a large claim. Ironically, those calling for a more *social* perspective on SLA may actually contribute to foregrounding the uniqueness of *individual* learners engaged in SLA in different contexts.

As I wrote in 1991, we need more ethnographic research that takes the social context into account. With this review, I add that it is not likely that we can overlay learner factors on some common understanding of the acquisition process, should we ever endorse one (Larsen-Freeman, 1997). In my opinion, we need more holistic research that links integrated individual difference research from emic and etic perspectives to the processes, mechanisms and conditions of learning within different contexts over time (Larsen-Freeman, 1998).

Chapter 2

The role of learning strategies in second language acquisition

Anna Uhl Chamot,
The George Washington University

INTRODUCTION

An important contribution that learners make to acquiring a second language is their use of learning strategies – the techniques or procedures that facilitate a learning task. Learning strategies are directed towards a goal and, as mental procedures, are not directly observable, though some learning strategies may result in specific behaviours. For example, an individual might decide to attend to certain aspects of incoming information, such as listening for a specific event or time, or scanning a text to find a particular piece of information. This selective attention is a learning strategy that has the goal of understanding, storing or retrieving information. During the process of selective attention, the individual may also decide to write down important information for future reference or as a memory aid. Thus, note-taking is an observable learning strategy paired with the unobservable strategy of selective attention. Students who try to take notes without deciding to attend selectively to specific aspects of input quickly fall behind as they try to write down everything they are listening to or copy everything they are reading.

Learning strategies are important in second language acquisition for two major reasons. First, in investigating the strategies used by second language learners during the language learning process, we gain insights into the cognitive, social and affective processes involved in language learning. These insights can help us understand these mental processes as they relate to second language acquisition, and can also clarify similarities and differences between language learning and general learning processes. The second reason supporting research into language learning strategies is that it may be possible to teach less successful language learners to use the strategies that characterize their more successful peers, thus helping students who are experiencing difficulty in learning a second language become better language learners. Therefore, two major goals in language learning strategy research are to (1) identify and compare the learning strategies used by more and less

25

successful language learners, and (2) provide instruction to less successful language learners that helps them become more successful in their language study.

In order to achieve these goals, the first step is to gain a clear understanding of the learning strategies used by language learners and differences between learning strategies of more and less effective learners. The second step is to find the most effective approach to teaching language learning strategies. Finally, we need to discover whether instruction in language learning strategies actually has an impact on proficiency and achievement in the second language.

This chapter first provides a brief overview of methods used by various researchers to identify language learning strategies and discuss the strengths and weaknesses of each. The second section presents representative learning strategies studies in first language contexts, and discusses aspects of this body of research that have applications to second language learning. This is followed by an overview of major studies of learning strategies in second language acquisition research (see also Chamot, Barnhardt et al., 1999, for an earlier version of sections two and three of this chapter). The final section is a summary of what we have learned about language learning strategies, and suggestions for moving forward in this area of research.

HOW ARE LEARNING STRATEGIES INVESTIGATED?

In the more than twenty years of investigation of language learning strategies, researchers have used a variety of approaches for identifying the mental processes used by learners as they seek to understand, remember and use a new language. Observation of students in language classrooms has proved singularly fruitless as a method of identifying learning strategies (Cohen, 1998; Naiman et al., 1978, 1996; O'Malley and Chamot, 1990; Rubin, 1975; Wenden, 1991a). The reason why classroom observation yields little information about students' use of learning strategies is that most learning strategies are mental processes and as such are not directly observable in terms of outward behaviour. Therefore, research in this area has relied for the most part on learners' self-reports. These self-reports have been made through retrospective interviews, stimulated recall interviews, questionnaires, written diaries and journals, and think-aloud protocols concurrent with a learning task. Each of these methods has limitations, but at the present time the only way to gain any insight at all into the unobservable mental learning strategies of learners is by asking them to reveal their thinking processes.

In retrospective interviews, learners are asked to reflect on a learning task and recall what strategies or 'special tricks' they used to carry out the task (see O'Malley et al., 1985a). The task may be a recently completed one or a typical task with which the learner is familiar, such as learning and remembering new vocabulary words or reading a story in the target language. The questions asked may be open-ended ('What do you do when you are reading and you see an unfamiliar word?') or specific ('When you are reading and see an unfamiliar word, do you make inferences about the meaning or just read on?'). The advantages of retrospective interviews are that they provide a great deal of flexibility, as the interviewer can clarify the questions if necessary, ask follow-up questions, and comment on the student's responses. In addition, if the retrospective interview is conducted with a small group of three or four students, one student's comments can spur the memories of other students about their uses of learning strategies. The disadvantages of retrospective interviews are that students may not report their strategy use accurately, that they may report what they perceive as the interviewer's preferred answers, or that they may claim to use strategies that have been encouraged by teachers rather than actually used by students.

A stimulated recall interview is more likely to accurately reveal students' learning strategies because it is conducted immediately after the student has engaged in a learning task. The actual task is videotaped, the interviewer then plays back the videotape, pausing as necessary, and asks the student to describe his or her thoughts at that specific moment during the learning task (Robbins, 1996). Studying learning strategies through stimulated recall interviews can produce task-specific strategy descriptions with corroborating evidence of their use. However, this method is time-consuming and only yields the strategies used on one occasion for a specific task. It does not reveal the range of students' strategies or their frequency across tasks.

Questionnaires are the easiest way to collect data about students' reported use of learning strategies, and questionnaires such as Oxford's Strategy Inventory for Language Learning (SILL) have been used extensively to collect data on large numbers of language learners (Oxford, 1996c). The SILL is a standardized measure with versions for ESL students and students of a variety of foreign languages and, as such, is extremely useful for collecting and analysing information about large numbers of students. Other studies have developed questionnaires focused on particular learning activities in which their subjects were engaged (Chamot and Küpper, 1989; O'Malley et al., 1985a). One of the advantages of questionnaires, aside from their ease of administration, is that students are asked to rate the frequency with which they use a particular strategy, rather than only indicating whether they use it at all. The drawbacks of questionnaires are that students may not understand the intent of a question, that they may answer according to their perception of the 'right answer', and that the questionnaire may not fully elicit all of a student's strategies.

A think-aloud protocol involves a one-on-one interview in which the language learner is given a target language task and asked to describe his or her thoughts while working on it. The interviewer may prompt with open-ended questions such as, 'What are you thinking right now? Why did you stop and start over?' Think-aloud interviews are recorded and transcribed verbatim, then analysed for evidence of learning strategies. While think-aloud procedures often provide a very clear picture of a learner's on-line processing strategies, they also have shortcomings. These include the presence of the interviewer and the somewhat artificial situation, which may affect the learner's responses. For example, the learner may not engage in his or her usual amount of planning before engaging in the task because of a perception that the interviewer wants the task to be completed quickly. Similarly, once the task is completed, the learner may not (without a direct prompt) take the time to look back on the task and evaluate his or her performance. An additional drawback of think-aloud procedures is that individual interviews, transcription, and analysis are extraordinarily labour-intensive. In spite of these difficulties, however, data collected through think-aloud protocols provide rich insights into language-learning strategies.

Research on self-reports of the use of learning strategies has provided important information about learners' understanding of their own learning processes. However, a weakness in learning strategy research is that all data collection methods are subjective in nature, depending as they do on self-report from the learner. A second area of research on learning strategies has examined approaches to teaching students effective strategies for a variety of learning tasks. This second area has been most thoroughly investigated in first-language contexts.

WHAT DO WE KNOW ABOUT LEARNING STRATEGIES IN NATIVE LANGUAGE CONTEXTS?

A substantial body of research supports the explicit teaching of learning strategies for academic achievement in different content areas in native language contexts (Pressley et al., 1995; Weinstein and Mayer, 1986). For example, teaching students to use problem-solving strategies has had a positive effect on their mathematics achievement (Carpenter et al., 1989; Silver and Marshall, 1990). Instruction in reading strategies has significantly improved students' comprehension, especially for poor readers (Brown et al., 1994; Collins, 1991; Duffy et al., 1987; Gagné et al., 1993; Palincsar and Brown, 1986). Reading strategies that have been successful in these first language settings include *using prior knowledge, predicting, inferencing, visualizing, self-questioning, verifying one's understanding,* and *summarizing.* Similarly, improvements in writing performance have been reported in several studies in which learning disabled students were explicitly taught strategies for planning, composing and revising their writing (Englert et al., 1991; Harris and Graham, 1992; Schumaker and Deshler, 1992).

Learning strategy instruction studies in native language contexts have shown that students can learn to use strategies and that the use of the instructed strategies results in more effective learning and school achievement (see Pressley et al., 1989 for a review). Such validations of learning strategy instruction inspired the development of instructional models that incorporate learning strategies for content instruction for native English-speaking students (Bergman, 1992; Gaskins and Elliot, 1991; Jones and Idol, 1990; Palincsar and Brown, 1986; Snyder and Pressley, 1990). Further research examined how these instructional models were implemented in the classroom (see, for example, Derry, 1990; Dole et al., 1991; El-Dinary et al., 1995; Idol and Jones, 1991; Palincsar and Klenk, 1992; Pressley et al., 1995; Wood et al., 1995). This literature extended the scope of learning strategies instruction and revealed the many complexities involved in trying to understand how learners process information and skills.

WHAT DO DESCRIPTIVE STUDIES OF LANGUAGE LEARNING STRATEGIES REVEAL?

Research on language learning strategies has focused mainly on descriptive studies that have identified characteristics of 'the good language learner' and compared the strategies of more effective and less effective language learners. These studies have been important in understanding how language learners use strategies, and they have provided important information to guide experimental studies to identify the effects of learning strategies instruction on students.

Descriptive studies of language learning strategies have taken several forms. This line of research began with studies of the characteristics of effective language learners. As the role of strategies became clear, researchers began developing instruments for measuring students' strategies use. Other studies have used individual, group, or think-aloud interviews to characterize how students apply strategies while working on language learning tasks. These descriptive studies include comparisons of learning strategies used by more and less effective language learners and, more recently, studies of how learning strategies develop over time.

Who is the 'good language learner'?

In 1975, Rubin suggested that a model of 'the good language learner' could be identified by looking at special strategies used by students who were successful in their second language learning. Stern (1975) also identified a number of learner characteristics and strategic techniques associated with good language learners. Hosenfeld (1976) further elaborated these characteristics, using think-aloud protocols, to investigate students' mental processes while they worked on language tasks. These studies were followed by the work of Naiman, Fröhlich, Stern and Todesco (1978, 1996), which further pursued the notion that second language learning ability resided at least in part in the strategies one uses for learning. Taken together, these studies identified the good language learner as one who is an active learner, monitors language production, practises communicating in the language, makes use of prior linguistic knowledge, uses various memorization techniques, and asks questions for clarification.

How do we measure strategy use?

The cataloging of characteristics of the good language learner made it possible to develop instruments for measuring the use of learning strategies. Oxford (1986) used more than sixty strategies identified from the literature on second language learning to develop the Strategy Inventory for Language Learning (SILL), a Likert-type instrument which classifies strategies as cognitive, compensation, metacognitive, social or affective. The SILL has versions in seventeen languages and has been administered to about 10,000 language learners in mainly foreign language contexts (e.g., French or Spanish in the United States, English in Japan) both in the United States and internationally (Oxford, 1999). The SILL studies have revealed correlations between learning strategies and other variables such as learning styles, gender and culture (Bedell and Oxford, 1996; Green and Oxford, 1995; Oxford and Burry-Stock, 1995). In one such study, the SILL was administered to 1,200 university students studying various foreign languages (Nyikos and Oxford, 1993). The analysis of responses revealed that language students may not use the strategies that research indicates would be most effective – such as strategies that promote self-regulated learning and strategies that provide meaningful practice in communication.

The SILL has been used in Japan in a number of studies of students learning English as a foreign language (EFL). For example, Takeuchi (1999) conducted a series of studies of 2,683 college students of EFL and twenty-five of their instructors, using their responses on the SILL to determine which types of strategy were used most frequently and which were considered important for language learning. Kimura (1999) also used the SILL with 1,399 Japanese college students of EFL to compare reported strategy use of students who had not lived outside Japan and 'returnees', or students who had had at least two years' residence in an English-speaking country. He found that the returnees in general used significantly more learning strategies, especially communicative strategies, than their peers without overseas residence.

The large number of SILL studies have yielded important information about the reported language learning strategy use of a large number of language learners around the world, and provide useful insights about learning strategies that might help students become better language learners. Other questionnaires designed to measure frequency of learning strategy use have been developed for various studies and books for language learners and teachers (e.g., Chamot and O'Malley, 1994a; Chamot, Barnhardt et al., 1999; G. Ellis and Sinclair, 1989; O'Malley and Chamot, 1990; Padron and Waxman, 1988; Rubin and Thompson, 1994; Weaver and Cohen, 1997). These instruments have been developed to assess students' use of learning strategies for specific contextualized tasks, rather than the more general approach taken by the items in the SILL.

What strategies do learners use during language tasks?

While questionnaires such as the SILL are useful for gathering information from large numbers of subjects for quantitative comparisons, in-depth interview studies have elicited rich descriptions of students' use of learning strategies. For example, in a longitudinal EFL study, Robbins (1996) investigated the learning strategies of Japanese college students as they developed their ability to carry on conversations in English. Paired with a native speaker of English, the Japanese students were videotaped before and after an eight-month period of language exchange. The students watched videotapes of their conversations and provided a verbal report on their thoughts during them. Despite their reputation for reticence, the students reported their thought processes, and therefore their learning strategies, in great detail. It was found that fewer learning strategies were reported as the students progressed towards being more at ease with conversation in English; probably because of fewer challenges and pauses to recall the problem when reviewing the conversation. Some students mentioned that the experience of watching themselves converse on video made them more aware of what aspects of their speaking ability they needed to improve.

An early study of seventy high school ESL students identified the range and variety of learning strategies used for different tasks by successful students. The study revealed that these good language learners were active and strategic, and could focus on the requirements of a task, reflect on their own learning processes, and transfer previously learned concepts and learning strategies to the demands of the English as a second language (ESL) or general education content classroom (Chamot, 1987; O'Malley et al., 1985a).

Do more and less language effective learners use strategies differently?

A follow-up investigation to O'Malley, Chamot, Stewner-Manzanares, Küpper and Russo (1985a) compared the learning strategy profiles of more and less successful students in ESL classrooms and discovered significant differences in the listening approaches of the two groups (O'Malley et al., 1989). The more effective students *monitored* their comprehension by asking themselves if what they were hearing made sense, they related new information to their own *prior knowledge*, and they made *inferences* about possible meanings when encountering unfamiliar words. In addition, the more successful students were able to transfer their prior academic knowledge in Spanish to the requirements of the English-language classroom. Thus, these more effective ESL listeners were displaying a number of learning strategies that are typical of good readers in native English-speaking contexts (e.g., Pressley et al., 1995).

The body of research on second language reading and writing processes also includes descriptions and comparisons of strategy use by more and less effective readers and writers (see, for example, Barnett, 1988; Cohen and Cavalcanti, 1990; Devine, 1993; Krapels, 1990). This research indicates that good second language readers are able to monitor their comprehension and take action when comprehension falters, and that composing strategies are more important than language proficiency in good second language writing.

A study of high school foreign language students used individual, group, and think-aloud interviews in which students identified the learning strategies they used for a variety of language tasks, including listening, reading, grammar cloze, role-playing and writing (Chamot et al., 1988a; Chamot, Dale et al., 1993). Differences between more and less effective learners were found in the number and range of strategies used, in how the strategies were applied to the task, and in whether they were appropriate for the task. In these studies, students' understanding of the task's requirements and whether they could match a strategy to meet those requirements seemed to be a major determinant of effective use of learning strategies.

Other studies comparing more and less effective language students have revealed a recurring finding that less successful learners do use learning strategies, sometimes even as frequently as their more successful peers, but that the strategies are used differently (Abraham and Vann, 1987; Chamot and El-Dinary, 1999; Chamot et al., 1988b; Keatley et al., 1999; Padron and Waxman, 1988; Vandergrift, 1997a, 1997b; Vann and Abraham, 1990). These studies confirmed that good language learners demonstrated adeptness at matching strategies to the task they were working on, while the less successful language learners seemed to lack the metacognitive knowledge about task requirements needed to select appropriate strategies. This trend was apparent with children in foreign language immersion classrooms, high school ESL and foreign language students, and adult language learners.

How do learning strategies develop over time?

More recently, as we have seen, think-aloud research has been used to understand the development of language learning strategies. A study of elementary school language immersion students revealed a developmental sequence in the acquisition of learning strategies for reading and writing tasks, in that younger language learners resemble older, less effective learners (Chamot, 1999; Chamot and El-Dinary, 1999; Chamot, Keatley et al., 1996; Keatley et al., 1999). In fact, these young readers and writers in immersion programs develop reading and writing abilities in much the same way that children do in non-immersion native language programs. Many children (even some first graders) were able to describe their thinking processes, demonstrating metacognitive awareness in their ability to describe their own thinking, usually in the second language. As further evidence of metacognition, students often had thoughtful responses about when and why they think in L2 or in L1.

In summary, the descriptive studies of language learning strategies exemplified here have revealed some differences between successful and less successful learners. These differences tend to be not so much in number of strategies used, but in the choice and flexible application of strategies that are appropriate to the learning task at hand. Can less successful students be taught to use learning strategies in ways that can contribute to higher achievement levels? This is the basic question addressed by intervention studies in language learning strategies.

CAN LANGUAGE LEARNING STRATEGIES BE TAUGHT?

Most learning strategy research conducted with language learners has sought to identify learner's strategies through questionnaires and other self-report measures. These descriptive studies have provided us with an understanding of the types of learning strategy generally used by language learners and have also revealed differences between more and less effective learners. A number of intervention studies have also been conducted, often as a follow-up to descriptive studies. Intervention studies have sought to teach language learning strategies and to measure their effects on students. Most of the intervention studies have been either quasi-experimental (treatment and control groups not selected randomly) or non-experimental (no control group), although a very few have attempted a true experimental design. These studies have taken place in classroom settings in which teachers and/or researchers have provided more or less explicit instruction to students on strategies to help them become better language learners. The effects investigated include performance on language tests, increase in reported use of learning strategies, attitudes and self-efficacy.

A number of researchers have also suggested approaches and developed models for teaching language learning strategies and for helping teachers teach learning strategies, as reviewed by Wenden (1998b). This section reviews examples of intervention research in which students were taught to use learning strategies for various types of language learning task, including vocabulary learning, listening comprehension, reading comprehension, speaking, writing and learning content subjects.

What strategies can help students learn vocabulary?

Techniques abound for learning vocabulary, both in one's native language and in a second language. For instance, the effectiveness of the keyword method, in which learners pair the word to be learned with a similar-sounding word in their native language, then link the two with a visual image, has been investigated in a series of nearly fifty experimental studies (reviewed by Pressley et al., 1982). This body of research has revealed that the keyword method is particularly effective for vocabulary recognition, especially of readily imageable words, but is less effective in helping students learn accurate pronunciation or spelling (Ellis and Beaton, 1993).

Other strategies have also proven quite useful for vocabulary learning. Cohen and Aphek (1981) taught students of Hebrew to remember vocabulary words by making paired mnemonic associations and found that those who made associations remembered vocabulary words more effectively than students who did not make associations. In the first experimental study of language learning strategies instruction, O'Malley and his colleagues (1985b) taught high school ESL students how to apply learning strategies to three different types of task, and compared their performance to that of students in a non-strategies control group. In the vocabulary task, students had to make their own groupings of words to be learned and then make a mental image of each group of related words. These strategies (*grouping/classification* and *imagery/visualization*) were effective for students who had not developed alternative strategies, but not for those who already had strong memorization strategies. A similarly designed study was conducted with Arabic-speaking students at a university intensive English program, in which students received different types of strategy instruction for vocabulary learning. On post-test, the group receiving a combination of strategies designed to provide depth of processing through visual, auditory and semantic associations had a significantly higher rate of recall (Brown and Perry, 1991). In his review of vocabulary intervention studies, N. Ellis (1994) concluded that the most effective strategies for vocabulary learning are: 'inferring word meanings from context, semantic or imagery mediation between the FL word (or a keyword approximation) and the L1 translation, and deep processing for elaboration of the new word with existing knowledge' (1994: 263).

How have learners been taught listening strategies?

Instruction in learning strategies for listening comprehension has been the focus of a number of language learning studies (for a review, see Chamot, 1995a). In many of the studies on listening, the task was listening to and viewing a video, then completing a comprehension measure. In the O'Malley et al. (1985b) study described above, another of the three tasks was listening to and viewing a video, then answering comprehension questions about it. Students in the intervention group were taught to *use selective attention, take notes* and *cooperate* with a classmate to review their notes after listening. Results showed that the strategies were helpful for the videos that students found personally interesting, but not for those that were less interesting or for which students lacked appropriate prior knowledge.

Additional studies have revealed other aspects of learning strategy instruction, suggesting implications for teaching. Rubin, Quinn and Enos (1988) taught high school students of Spanish to use learning strategies while listening to/viewing a video, and compared three different types of strategy instruction to the control group, which had no strategy instruction. This study documented many of the problems associated with classroom-based experimental studies. For example, teachers often had difficulty in implementing the learning strategy lessons, and students used the instructed strategies only when the video was challenging. The implications of these problems are that teachers need to design their own learning strategy lessons, and they need to teach students to use strategies for tasks that cannot be accomplished otherwise.

Ross and Rost (1991) used a ground-up approach to developing instruction in their listening comprehension study of communication strategies used by Japanese college students learning English. Researchers first identified differences in clarification strategies used by higher and lower proficiency level students. Then students were randomly assigned for learning strategy training to one of three different videos and taught the strategies previously identified for higher proficiency students. The results showed that lower proficiency level students could successfully learn to use the same questioning strategies that were used by more proficient students to increase listening comprehension.

Another study of listening comprehension measured for transfer of the strategies taught (Thompson and Rubin, 1996). Third-year college students of Russian viewed a variety of authentic Russian video clips over the course of an academic year. One class was taught metacognitive and cognitive strategies for improving comprehension of the video material, and the other class viewed the same videos but had no strategy instruction. Students receiving strategy instruction showed significant improvement on the video comprehension post-test compared to the students in the control group. A standardized audio-only listening comprehension test was also administered to participating students, and on this measure (which did not test what had been taught), the improvement of the experimental group approached, but did not reach, significance. In addition, students in the strategies group demonstrated metacognitive awareness through their ability to select and manage the strategies that would help them comprehend the videos.

Does instruction in reading strategies improve comprehension?

Reading comprehension strategies have been the focus of several instructional studies in foreign language learning. In an early study, high school students of French were taught explicit reading strategies which improved their reading comprehension (Hosenfeld et al., 1981). An experimental study of metacognitive reading strategy instruction for college-level ESL taught students in the experimental groups to use either semantic mapping or an explicit technique for relating prior knowledge to the text (Carrell et al., 1989). Students in both experimental groups showed significant comprehension gains over the control group when answering open-ended questions, though not for multiple choice questions.

In another experiment, third-grade Spanish-speaking children who were taught reading strategies in Spanish improved in reading performance on standardized tests in both Spanish and English, and they were able to transfer the instructed metacognitive strategies to their second language (Muñiz-Swicegood, 1994). A recent study with seventh-grade native Spanish-speaking low-level readers involved a number of strategic interventions (Jiménez and Gámez, 1998). First, students' metacognitive awareness of their own thinking was developed by teaching them to think aloud (in either Spanish or English or a mixture) about a Spanish text. Next, the researchers provided culturally relevant stories in English and taught students how to use strategies for unknown vocabulary, how to ask themselves questions about the text, and how to make inferences. Statements by students after the intervention indicated that they had more metacognitive understanding of their own reading processes and were aware of strategies they could use to assist comprehension.

Can speaking and writing strategies be taught successfully?

Learning strategy intervention studies for speaking and writing are few in number, as much of the research in these areas has been descriptive and has tended to focus on communication strategies or composing processes (for example, Cohen and Cavalcanti, 1990; Cohen and Olshtain, 1993; Leki, 1995; Robbins, 1996; Zamel, 1983).

In the first experimental study on the effects of language learning strategies instruction on student achievement described earlier (O'Malley et al., 1985b), strategies-trained students performed significantly better on a transactional speaking task than students in the control group. This study was conducted with seventy-five high school ESL students who were randomly assigned to experimental or control groups. For two weeks the experimental group students were taught various strategies for academic tasks (vocabulary, listening and speaking). Significant differences in oral proficiency favouring the strategies-trained groups were found for the transactional speaking task, in which students had to prepare a brief oral report on a topic of their choice and present it to a small group of classmates. All practice sessions as well as pre- and post-tests were tape-recorded and evaluated on preestablished criteria by outside judges. The experimental groups were taught *organizational planning* for their reports and techniques for *cooperating* with classmates to elicit feedback. The experimental groups were judged to be significantly more comprehensible and organized in their reports than control group students. Almost all students wrote out their reports before presenting them orally, so it is likely that instruction in these same strategies would be equally helpful for writing reports.

The effectiveness of learning strategies instruction for speaking was also investigated in EFL settings in Egypt and Japan (Dadour and Robbins, 1996). Learning strategies were explicitly taught to college-level EFL students in both countries. The study in Egypt was experimental, with students randomly assigned to intervention or control groups. The experimental groups participated in a special strategy instruction course, and the results on post-test showed that their speaking skills and use of the strategies were significantly superior to those of students in the control groups. The intervention study in Japan taught a variety of strategies for speaking to students for three months, then assessed the value of the instruction through a student questionnaire. The results showed that most students understood the value of strategies instruction and wanted to learn more strategies for speaking.

Cohen and his associates (1998) investigated the impact of strategies-based instruction on college students of French and Norwegian during ten weeks of instruction. The intervention groups received instruction in learning strategies that focused on using speaking strategies, while the comparison groups received language instruction only. Students were pre- and post-tested on three different speaking tasks in the target language: a self-description, retelling of a fairy tale they had read, and a description of a favourite city. After each task, students completed a checklist reporting the strategies they had used. Students were also pre- and post-tested with the Strategy Inventory for Language Learning (SILL). In addition, a sample of students at differing levels of proficiency were asked to describe their reasons for their choices on learning strategy checklists, thus providing think-aloud data as they were completing the checklists. The results indicated that integrating strategies instruction into the language course was beneficial to students, though the relationship of reported strategy use to performance was complex. For example, some students in the comparison group reported using strategies, even though they had not received strategies instruction and, in some instances, the increase in reported strategy use by comparison students seemed to be detrimental to performance. The reasons suggested for these findings were that (1) some students are able to acquire effective learning strategies without instruction; and (2) systematic instruction and practice with learning strategies is needed for many students in order to learn how to apply strategies effectively.

An experimental study involving writing in conjunction with reading comprehension investigated the effects of learning strategy instruction on third- and fourth-grade limited English proficient children (Bermudez and Prater, 1990). Strategies taught to the experimental group were *brainstorming* and *clustering*. Before reading an expository text (story), children used the title and illustrations to brainstorm or predict what it might be about, and the teacher recorded the results on a graphic organizer. After reading, experimental children were taught to cluster connected ideas in the text by colour-coding similar ideas. Finally, all students wrote a paragraph about the text. The results showed that the strategies group produced significantly more elaborations in their essays, and that their paragraphs tended to be better organized than those of the control group.

Can learning strategies be taught in a content-based language program?

Learning strategy instruction in content-based ESL has been investigated in a number of studies based on the Cognitive Academic Language Learning Approach (CALLA), an instructional model that integrates content subjects, academic language and learning strategies instruction (Chamot and O'Malley, 1994a). Evaluations of the CALLA model were conducted for five different CALLA programs, and though all reported the successful use of learning strategies by students, reliable assessment of the effect of learning strategy instruction was provided in only two (O'Malley and Chamot, 1998). In the first, teachers in ESL-mathematics classrooms implemented learning strategy instruction to assist students in solving word problems (Chamot, Dale et al., 1993). Students were taught to use *planning, monitoring, problem-solving* and *evaluating* strategies in a sequential order for solving word problems. Students in high-implementation classrooms (in which teachers had provided explicit and frequent strategy instruction) performed significantly better on a word problem think-aloud interview than students in low-implementation classrooms (in which the instruction was mainly implicit and infrequent).

In the second study, Varela (1997) recently investigated the effects of CALLA learning strategy instruction in a middle school ESL-science classroom compared with a similar classroom that received equivalent instruction without the learning strategies component. This study was based on the transactional speaking component of the O'Malley et al. (1985b) study. In the Varela (1997) study, students in the intervention classroom were taught strategies to assist them in presenting an oral report on their science fair projects. The strategies included *using graphic organizers, selective attention, self-assessment* and *self-talk*. After two weeks of instruction, students in the strategies group not only reported using significantly more strategies than control group students, but their videotaped performance of their science fair reports showed significant improvement over their performance prior to the strategies instruction.

How do teachers become expert in teaching learning strategies?

Until recently, the preparation of language teachers has not included instruction and practice in the teaching of language learning strategies. A focus of my own research has been the development of effective procedures for helping teachers incorporate learning strategy instruction in their own classrooms (Chamot, Barnhardt et al., 1999). A series of studies has been conducted with foreign language teachers in the United States at both the school and university levels.

In the first of these studies, researchers and teachers developed a learning strategies curriculum which was then pilot-tested in high school and university Russian and Spanish classrooms (Chamot and Küpper, 1989, 1990; Chamot et al., 1988a, 1988b). The curriculum was then revised according to feedback from teachers and, in a follow-up study, was implemented by different teachers and for different languages. Findings from these two studies indicated that learning strategies instruction calls for a special type of teaching and that teachers may need support in its implementation. In addition, student responses to the instruction indicated that they enjoyed learning strategies activities and had individual preferences for different strategies, but that they were confused when too many strategies were introduced at once. These studies revealed some of the practical realities and challenges of learning strategy instruction.

In two subsequent parallel studies, high school teachers and university foreign language instructors implemented learning strategies instruction in Japanese, Russian and Spanish foreign language classrooms (Chamot, 1993, 1994; Chamot, Barnhardt et al., 1996; Chamot and O'Malley, 1994b). Researchers developed resource guides for teaching learning strategies and provided ongoing professional development workshops and conferences to help teachers implement the instruction. After implementing the sample lesson plans developed by the researchers, teachers then began to develop their own learning strategy lessons. The teacher-developed lessons were integrated into their regular course of study and were focused on the needs of the particular group of students. The learning strategy instruction was evaluated through interviews and questionnaires with teachers and students. Teachers reported that the strategies instruction helped their students, especially their weaker students, make greater achievements in the language class. Most students reported that the strategies instruction had had a positive effect on their language learning, and some (but not all) students indicated that they also used the strategies outside class. Students' metacognitive awareness of their own approaches to learning was reflected in their comments on the strategies they used or did not use, and reasons for using or not using them.

This research direction was continued in another instructional study conducted with foreign language teachers in the United States (Chamot, Barnhardt et al., 1996). The objective of this particular study was to investigate how to best support instructors of Chinese, French, German, Japanese, Russian and Spanish so they could effectively teach language learning strategies in classes of different levels ranging from elementary immersion programs through higher education. Researchers worked with participant teachers for three years to provide professional support for teaching learning strategies. Classroom observations, student group interviews, and teacher interviews and questionnaires were the methods of evaluation. While workshops motivated teachers to try learning strategy instruction, follow-up support such as model lessons, one-to-one coaching, and peer discussions were invaluable in integrating learning strategies into language instruction. Several aspects of learning strategy instruction proved to be especially troublesome for teachers. First, most teachers believed that they were actually teaching strategies when in fact they were not providing explicit instruction by naming, modelling or describing the strategies. Although it was difficult for teachers to move from implicit to explicit strategy instruction, those who did reported that their students seemed to be much more aware of the purpose of the strategies. A second area of difficulty for teachers was in integrating learning strategy instruction into their regular course work. Many teachers saw learning strategy instruction as a separate activity from their normal teaching, and tended to use learning strategy activities as something fun to do when time permitted or as a break from the regular course work. Teachers also struggled with determining an appropriate scope and sequence of strategies to teach at various levels, and they wanted guidance in how to scaffold strategies effectively at upper levels and for high achievers.

Overall, however, the coaching that was provided enabled teachers to adapt instruction to their own languages and levels. Teachers in the study cited a variety of positive impacts that strategies instruction was having on their students, including improving understanding of the target language, helping students become more responsible and active learners, improving motivation for language learning, and building independent use of strategies. Several teachers also said that strategies instruction had improved their teaching in general.

In summary, the effectiveness of learning strategies instruction has been well established in first language contexts and shows promise in second language learning. Research in first language contexts has moved from validating instruction in individual strategies to identifying elements of effective strategies instruction integrated into a curriculum. Many of the same learning strategies that have been identified and successfully taught in first language contexts have also proven useful in second language learning. Studies in second language learning began by focusing on the strategies that distinguish effective language learners. Research is now moving towards an understanding of strategies development, validations of language learning strategies instruction in the classroom, and an understanding of the professional support teachers need for developing effective learning strategy instruction.

WHAT ARE THE NEXT STEPS FOR LANGUAGE LEARNING STRATEGIES RESEARCH?

The study of language learning strategies will continue to develop as second language acquisition researchers seek to understand different learner characteristics and the complex cognitive, social and affective factors involved in processing language input and using the language for a variety of purposes. Likewise, language educators and methodologists will continue their quest for more effective instructional approaches and, with the increasing emphasis on learner-centred instruction and learner empowerment in all areas of education, instruction in learning strategies will assume a greater role in teacher preparation and curriculum design. How successful future research in language learning strategies will be depends in large part on the development and adaptation of instruments that are reliable and valid in identifying the strategies (whether acquired independently or through instruction) that learners use, and on the design of research studies that address questions that as yet have not been answered. Weaknesses in current research on language learning strategies include those related to research methodology and to unanswered questions about developmental stages and individual and cultural variations in the acquisition and use of strategies.

How should research methodology be improved?

As described earlier in this chapter, the instruments used to collect data on language learning strategies are all based on learners' self-reports. At present there does not seem to be any other possible approach, since behavioural observation is not an effective way to identify internal mental processes. However, the instruments used to collect verbal reports can certainly be strengthened. Questionnaires, for example, can be made more context-specific to include questions about language learning tasks that students are actually engaged in. Questionnaires that include a large number of items referring to unfamiliar learning experiences are difficult for respondents to understand and answer accurately. In a communicative language classroom, students would provide more accurate information on a questionnaire that asks questions about learning strategies framed within descriptions of typical communicative activities. Similarly, students from different language and cultural backgrounds would probably respond with greater understanding to questions that reflect their own learning experiences and educational or cultural values. In addition, learning strategy questionnaires need to be developed for different developmental stages and ages of students, including adaptations for students with low levels of literacy in both the L1 and the L2. Once such learner and context-specific learning strategy questionnaires are developed, they need to be standardized on a large group of the types of student for whom they are intended. Similar types of standardization procedure need to be developed for interview protocols that reflect factors such as age, L1 and type of language program.

Another methodological challenge in much of the research is the establishment of a correlation between the use of learning strategies and increased proficiency and achievement in the target language. Many researchers have had to rely on teacher or researcher-constructed tests of language proficiency to show that students who use learning strategies learn more effectively than students who do not use strategies. Often the reason is that the research is conducted on beginning-level students, and standardized tests do not distinguish small differences in proficiency in beginning-level students. Another difficulty with language tests is that the test-taking or language proficiency interview situations may actually discourage the use of learning strategies, as these typically call for responses that have been learned to the point of automaticity and there is little time available to applying learning strategies (rapid recall strategies might be the exception). A better language test might be one in which the learner is given time to solve a language learning problem rather than having to perform quickly and correctly on a language task.

In addition to refining the instruments used in learning strategy research, research designs need to include multiple sources of data, both quantitative and qualitative, as the convergence of evidence strengthens claims to causal effects. Since language learning is a slow process, studies of the effects of learning strategies need to be conducted over a long enough period of time for language gains to be demonstrated unequivocally. Finally, intervention studies need to include frequent observations of both the experimental and control classrooms to make certain that the teachers are indeed teaching the strategies, and that the control teachers are not in fact also teaching strategies! This type of sustained research effort brings with it a host of difficulties, but the results are more credible than very short studies and studies in which no control is exercised over instructional implementation.

What questions still need to be answered?

Although we have learned a great deal about language learning strategies in the last twenty or more years, there is a need for further studies that describe learners' current strategies, that teach learners new strategies, and that develop teachers' ability to provide learning strategy instruction in the language classroom.

Even though the bulk of language learning strategies research to date has been descriptive, there still remain some tantalizing puzzles. For example, descriptive research is needed with young language learners in a variety of settings, including children in bilingual, second language, and non-immersion foreign language programs. Additional studies are needed to confirm differences in learning strategy use between younger and older children identified in the foreign language immersion study described earlier (Chamot, 1999; Chamot and El-Dinary, 1999; Keatley et al., 1999) and to discover whether similar developmental features are found in children in other types of language learning program. In general, studies of the development of learning strategies over time in both children and older learners would provide needed information about changes in use of strategies related to age and to increasing proficiency in the target language.

Another aspect of descriptive research that would have implications for learning strategy instruction is the investigation of the transfer of learning strategies from the L1 to the L2 – and from the L2 to additional languages and even back to the L1. In native language contexts, transfer of learning strategies learned in one context has proven difficult to achieve, though explicit instruction has been beneficial in assisting transfer.

More descriptive research is needed on students from different language and cultural backgrounds. Promising work has begun in this area (see, for example, Oxford, 1996c), but additional information is needed about the actual relationship between learning strategies and cultural beliefs and values. For example, are learning strategies that seek to develop learner autonomy perceived as valuable universally or only in some cultures? Are collaborative social strategies valued in competitive societies? Do metacognition and metacognitive strategies play an important role in language and general learning for all individuals, regardless of their cultural, linguistic and educational background? These are important questions that have direct implications for learning strategy instruction and curriculum development.

Finally, a crucial issue in investigating the strategic behaviour of learners is learner choice and control of specific strategies, and Wenden, in the following chapter, addresses this in examining the role of learners' metacognitive knowledge in relation to ongoing strategy use.

Relatively few intervention studies have been conducted on the effect of learning strategies instruction on language learning and proficiency. Further rigorous intervention studies like those conducted by Cohen et al. (1998), O'Malley et al. (1985b), Thompson and Rubin (1996), and Varela (1997) would provide information about the effects of learning strategy instruction. Most intervention studies have been conducted with high school or college students (Varela's study is the only one conducted with middle school students). Similar studies need to be conducted with different ages of language students. For example, the effect of learning strategies instruction on children in different second and foreign language learning contexts (immersion, non-immersion, bilingual, ESL, EFL) is as yet unknown. We do not know which learning strategies could be taught successfully to younger students or, indeed, at what age language learning strategy instruction could be success-fully initiated.

In addition to younger students, strategy intervention studies need to be conducted with adolescent and adult immigrant students with limited aca-demic backgrounds in their native language. Are learning strategies a func-tion of schooling, or can they also be applied successfully to functional and occupational language learning contexts? Can students of any age learn to use effective language learning strategies or is there an upper age limit to learning new strategies? The need for older individuals to learn a new lan-guage becomes urgent when wars and civil unrest displace people from their native countries to seek asylum in Western Europe, the United Kingdom, the United States, or other countries. How does learning strategy instruction apply to these refugees? These are questions that need to be explored through learning strategies experimental intervention studies.

A third area for future research is in the development of language teacher expertise for integrating learning strategies into their classrooms. What type of professional development activities are most useful to novice language teachers? Are the same or different activities of greatest use to experienced teachers? On average, how long does it take for a teacher to become success-ful in teaching language learning strategies? The evaluation of different models for teacher preparation in learning strategies instruction could lead to refin-ing and improving such models. In addition, studies need to be undertaken to identify the relationship of effective learning strategy instruction to teacher characteristics such as teaching approach, attitude and teacher beliefs, amount and type of pre-service and/or in-service preparation in learning strategies instruction, and years of teaching experience, including length of time teach-ing learning strategies. The purpose of such studies would be to discover whether effective learning strategy instruction is closely tied to specific teacher characteristics. A first step in undertaking this type of research should be the development of an operational definition of what constitutes effective learning strategy instruction. Is it merely instruction that results in both greater variety and higher frequency of strategy use by students? Or, should the definition of effective learning strategy instruction also consider the achievement of higher levels of proficiency in the target language in a shorter period of time than average? Once effective strategy instruction has been defined, information about effective teaching of strategies could be gathered through classroom observations and videotapes, teacher interviews, and use of existing measures of language teacher beliefs. The relationships between teacher and learner in the area of language learning strategies has only begun to be explored, and much remains to be accomplished in this area.

It is important that learning strategies research continue, both in these and other directions, for only through a better understanding of the learn-ing and teaching process can more language learners achieve the level of success that currently characterizes only a small proportion of all of the students studying a foreign or second language around the world.

Chapter 3

Metacognitive knowledge in SLA: the neglected variable

*Anita L. Wenden, York College,
City University of New York*

INTRODUCTION

Most of the theories that have been developed to explain second language acquisition acknowledge the influence of learner differences on the process. Referring to child language acquisition, proponents of Universal Grammar (UG) note that a learner's developing perceptual abilities and memory capacity will limit the rate of acquisition (see McLaughlin, 1987; L. White, 1989). The impact of age on language learning has been considered from the perspective of neurolinguistic (e.g., Beebe, 1988) and cognitive theory (e.g., Ellis, 1986), while creative construction theory introduces the notion that personality and experience may influence both affective and cognitive processes (e.g., Dulay and Burt, 1977). The role of affective factors – attitudes, motivation, ethnic identity – have been highlighted by social psychological theories (e.g., Gardner and Lambert, 1972; Giles, 1977) and though not explicitly linked to cognitive theory, language aptitude, intelligence and cognitive style are cognitive factors that have been put forth to explain differences in the rate and success of SLA (e.g., Genesee, 1976; Wesche et al., 1982; Willing, 1988). Finally, emphasizing the role of social setting and the interaction which takes place within a setting, sociocultural theory provides an explanation of the manner in which learners acquire the ability to regulate their learning (see Lantolf and Appel, 1994). While focusing on different learner variables, all of these theories refer to cognitive and affective factors that operate below consciousness.

In contrast, with the introduction of learning strategies, cognitive theory introduced into the discourse on learner differences the notion of deliberate and autonomous action on the part of the learner (Naiman et al., 1978; O'Malley and Chamot, 1990; Rubin, 1981). Implying that consciousness plays a role in SLA, this notion of language learners engaged in the conscious regulation of their learning was controversial at the outset. However, as Chamot makes clear in the previous chapter, learning strategies have now become an accepted field of research and is included as one type of learner difference in SLA texts used as standard references by students and instructors (Brown, 1994; Cook, 1996; R. Ellis, 1986, 1994; Larsen-Freeman and Long, 1991; Lightbown and Spada, 1993; McLaughlin, 1987; *inter alia*). On the other hand, the metacognitive knowledge learners bring to the task of learning, which the cognitive literature recognizes as essential to the effective use of learning strategies (Wenden, 1998a offers a review of this literature) and which foreign/second language teachers agree is key to the regulation of learning (see Wenden, 1998b), remains unrecognized in the SLA literature.

The purpose of this chapter, therefore, is to enhance our understanding of this relatively unknown learner difference: metacognitive knowledge. After defining the term, I will briefly summarize what studies have documented about the metacognitive knowledge of FL/SL language learners. In the body of the chapter, I will illustrate and explain the role that metacognitive knowledge plays in the self-regulation or self-direction of language learning and in the conclusion, I will briefly outline what the insights on metacognitive knowledge provided by this discussion implies for theory, research and practice in SLA.

CHARACTERISTICS OF METACOGNITIVE KNOWLEDGE

Metacognitive knowledge is a *specialized portion of a learner's acquired knowledge base* (Flavell, 1979). It is that part of long-term memory that contains what learners know about learning. Thus it is a *stable* body of knowledge though, of course, it may change over time. It *develops early*. Research has shown that elementary and secondary school children (e.g., Chinn and Brewer, 1993; Paris and Byrnes, 1989) and even pre-schoolers (e.g., Kreutzer, Leonard and Flavell, as cited in Brown et al., 1983) have developed some knowledge about learning. This knowledge may be acquired unconsciously, the outcome of observation and imitation, or it may also be acquired consciously. Learners remember what their teachers or parents tell them about how to learn, or they may reflect on their process and make generalizations about it. The research has shown that learners are capable of bringing this knowledge to consciousness and talking about it. It is *statable*. Moreover, while learners may make some statements about language learning that appear arbitrary, in fact, their acquired knowledge consists of *a system of related ideas*, some accepted without question and others validated by their experience.

The characteristics of metacognitive knowledge outlined above also define the nature of learner beliefs about language learning. In addition, beliefs are value-related and will be held more tenaciously, one characteristic which distinguishes them from metacognitive knowledge (Alexander and Dochy, 1995; Wenden, 1998a). Research findings on the metacognitive knowledge of language learners are more frequently referred to as beliefs. However, since the latter are considered a subset of the former (Flavell, 1987), in the discussion that follows, metacognitive knowledge will be used to refer to both.

TYPES OF METACOGNITIVE KNOWLEDGE

The different types of metacognitive knowledge referred to in the cognitive and FL/SL literature usually focus on either learner, task or process variables. Flavell (1979, 1981) refers to these three categories respectively as person, task and strategic knowledge.

Person knowledge (PK)

Person knowledge is knowledge learners have acquired about how cognitive and affective factors, such as age, language aptitude, personality, motivation, may influence learning. In addition, it includes specific knowledge about how the above factors apply in their experience. For example, is it their view that they do or do not have the aptitude for learning another language? Or that their type of personality will inhibit or facilitate language learning? Person knowledge also refers to knowledge learners have acquired about their proficiency in a given area, for example, how well they read or write, what they know or don't know about a certain subject.

Task knowledge (TK)

Task knowledge refers, first of all, to *knowledge of task purpose* – what learners know about the pedagogical intent of a task and their expectations of how it will serve their language learning needs. Will it improve their writing skills? Expand their vocabulary? Develop their fluency in oral communication? It also includes *knowledge about task types*, that is a recognition of the similarity and/or the differences between the demands of a new language learning task and tasks previously done, for example taking notes while reading and while listening to a lecture; an open-ended task vs a structured task. *Knowledge about a task's demands* is the third and most complex facet of task knowledge. It includes knowing what knowledge and skills are required to do a particular task; how to go about doing it; its anticipated level of difficulty; and awareness of the learning plan that is the outcome of this analysis of the task's demands. Task knowledge should be distinguished from *domain knowledge* (DK), which is not a category of metacognitive knowledge. Rather, domain knowledge is conceptual and factual knowledge about the subject matter of learning.

Strategic knowledge (SK)

Strategic knowledge refers to general knowledge about what strategies are, specific knowledge about when and how to use them, and their effectiveness. It also includes knowledge about how best to approach language learning, that is general principles about language learning that can guide a learner's choice of strategies. An example would be that practice is important.

METACOGNITIVE KNOWLEDGE IN SECOND
LANGUAGE LEARNING

In contrast to the body of research on learning strategies, the research on the metacognitive knowledge of language learners has been relatively scant although recent interest in the topic has begun to make up for the lack. Most of this research has documented the content of learners' metacognitive knowledge. Generally, the subjects of the studies have been students of high school and college-age learning English or a foreign language in formal settings and, to a lesser extent, adults acquiring English in informal settings. The most common approach to data gathering has been semi-structured and open-ended interviews and structured questionnaires. The latter have been devised through focus group interviews and/or by adapting instruments devised for the same purpose in other fields. Most use a Likert Scale, requiring learners to indicate to what extent they agree or disagree with some aspect of language learning represented in the statements that make up the questionnaire. A few researchers have utilized an ethnographic approach, including participant observation and informal discussions with informants as well. Some form of content analysis has been applied to findings from the more qualitatively oriented data while the structured surveys have been reported in terms of descriptive statistics and, in some cases, factor analysis has been used to identify how subsets of beliefs were organized. Table 3.1 provides a listing of these studies.

While also documenting the content of learners' metacognitive knowledge, other studies have further attempted to establish a relationship between this knowledge and learners' approach to learning, specifically their readiness for autonomy, choice and use of learning strategies, setting of goals, and evaluation of their learning. A few have also demonstrated the link between knowledge and learning outcomes, for example reading comprehension, writing and effective completion of other learning tasks. These studies are listed in Table 3.2.

While Tables 3.1 and 3.2 outline what has been typical in the research, there have been a few studies which have made original contributions to this small, but growing body of knowledge. Among this smaller group, some have sought to demonstrate how metacognitive knowledge develops and evolves (e.g., Enkvist, 1992; Hosenfeld, 1999; Shaw, 1998; White, 1999). There have been two intervention studies which implemented procedures to revise and expand learners metacognitive knowledge (Ho, 1996), and a specialized survey instrument which focuses exclusively on language learners self-efficacy beliefs has been developed (Huang et al., 1998).

In addition, some researchers have addressed the question of methodology. Sakui and Gaies (1999) report on a process to develop and validate a structured questionnaire that focuses on a wide range of beliefs, while Tittle (personal communication) reports on a similar validation process that draws upon sources from both language learning and general education to develop a structured questionnaire that focuses on epistemological beliefs of language

Table 3.1   Metacognitive knowledge in language learning: content and instrumentation

Researcher(s)	Content of metacognitive knowledge	Instrumentation
Barcelos, A.M. 1995	nature of language teacher role/student role TL setting vs NL setting	interviews questionnaire classroom observation
Elbaum, B. et al. 1993	Efficacy of strategies	rating tasks
Horowitz, E. 1987, 1988	language learning aptitude/process difficulty of language learning effective approaches	structured questionnaire
Horowitz, E. 1999	cultural & situational differences	structured questionnaire
Kern, R.G. 1995	language learning aptitude/process difficulty of language learning effective approaches	structured questionnaire
Mantle-Bromley, C. 1995	language learning aptitude/process difficulty of language learning effective approaches	structured questionnaire
Mori, Y. 1999a	epistemological beliefs and their relationship to LL beliefs	structured questionnaire factor analysis
Richards, J.C. and Gravatt, B. 1998	nature of language learning, language aptitude, strategies	structured questionnaire
Sakui, K. and Gaies, S. 1999	language teaching methodology quality & sufficiency of classroom instruction foreign language aptitude	structured questionnaire interviews
Tumposky, N.R. 1991	aptitude, process, difficulty, effective approaches	structured questionnaire
Victori, M. 1995	strategic, task, person knowledge in writing	structured questionnaire interviews, think-aloud protocols
Wenden, A. 1986, 1987	nature of language, personal factors, effective approaches	focused interviews
Wenden, A. 1991b	task and person knowledge in writing	introspective reports
White, C. 1999	relationship between learner & setting, tolerance of ambiguity, locus of control	interviews, open-ended questionnaire, ranking & scenario exercises, yoked subject procedures

learners. White (1999) describes a longitudinal study which utilized a five-phase approach to data collection that chose, developed and adapted appropriate instruments (i.e., interviews, ranking exercises, questionnaires, scenarios and yoked subject procedures) during the research cycle in response to the

Table 3.2 Metacognitive knowledge in language learning: content, relation, instrumentation

Researcher(s)	Content of knowledge	Relationship to learning	Instrumentation
Benson, M.J. 1989	conception of learning	approach to learning	interviews, response to taped lectures, student notes, observation
Benson, P. and Lor, W. 1998	conceptions of language & language learning	readiness for autonomy	classroom observation informal discussion interviews
Carrell, P.L. et al. 1989	metacognitive awareness in reading	reading outcomes	structured questionnaire focused interviews
Cotterall, S. 1995	role of teacher/feedback approaches to studying learner confidence/independence experience in language learning	readiness for autonomy	structured questionnaire factor analysis
Cotterall, S. 1999	role of teacher, feedback, sense of self-efficacy, effective strategies & attitudes towards strategy use	autonomy	structured questionnaire
Elbaum, B. et al. 1993	nature of language learning	choice of strategies	rating tasks
Holec, H. 1987	student/teacher roles function of materials	goal setting	interviews
Park, G. 1994	aptitude, learning process, nature of language	self-direction	structured questionnaire factor analysis
Vann, R. and Abraham, R. 1990	task knowledge	effective task completion	focused interviews
Victori, M. 1999	strategic, task, person knowledge in writing	effective writing	interviews think aloud protocols
Wenden, A. 1987	theories of language learning	goal setting, strategy choice, evaluation	focused interviews
Yang, N.D. 1999	self-efficacy beliefs, value & nature of LL, language aptitude, formal structural study	use of learning strategies	structured questionnaire, interviews, factor analysis

kinds of information that emerged in a previous phase. Another contribution to the methodology of researching learner beliefs and knowledge is an approach to classification developed by Benson and Lor (1998) which distinguishes conceptions of learning from language learners' specific beliefs and, further, organizes these conceptions according to whether they imply a quantitative or qualitative view of the nature of language and of language learning.

THE FUNCTION OF METACOGNITIVE KNOWLEDGE IN THE SELF-REGULATION OF LANGUAGE LEARNING

The theory and research in the cognitive literature maintain that metacognitive knowledge is critical to the self-regulation of learning (Wenden, 1998a). It is maintained that while metacognitive strategies, such as planning, monitoring and evaluating are essential to self-regulation, if these strategies fail to make contact with a rich knowledge base, they are weak (Perkins and Salomon, 1989). Furthermore, the research has shown that self-regulated learners are distinguished by their ability to use metacognitive knowledge in a flexible manner (Brown et al., 1981; Pressley et al., 1987). This literature supports results from the L2 research cited above which has shown a relationship between what learners know about language learning and their approach to the task (Benson and Lor, 1998; Elbaum et al., 1993; Holec, 1987; Park, 1994; Wenden, 1987; Yang, 1999).

To provide further insight on the function of language learners' metacognitive knowledge in learning, the analysis to be presented in this chapter intends to clarify the nature of the interaction that defines the relationship between what learners know and how they self-regulate their learning. Excerpts from introspective and retrospective learner accounts will be analysed to illustrate how the three main categories of metacognitive knowledge – person, task and strategic knowledge – come into play in the operation of two key self-regulatory processes: task analysis, and monitoring. The introspective Excerpts that follow (1, 2, 4, 5, 6) have been taken from data collected for an exploratory study reported in Wenden (1991b) and the retrospective Excerpts (3, 7, 8) are from data reported in Wenden (1982). Self-regulation, a term used in the cognitive literature, refers to the processes by which learners plan how they will approach a task, their task analysis and how they actually monitor its implementation. The L2 literature on learner autonomy refers to the same processes as self-direction.

TASK ANALYSIS

Task analysis is the planning that takes place prior to task engagement as learners:

1. Consider the *task's purpose* – determine what they expect to learn from the task and its relevance to their learning needs and goals.
2. Classify the *task type* – identify the nature of the problem it poses and consider whether it is similar to tasks they've already done.
3. Assess a *task's demands* – consider how to do the task, that is what to do and in what order, the knowledge and skills they will need to do so, and the anticipated difficulty of the task.

The outcome of a task analysis is a learning plan that will guide the implementation of the task. (For a more extended discussion, see Wenden, 1995.)

Excerpt 1: Dina

In Excerpt 1, Dina, a language learner of intermediate proficiency, illustrates how task knowledge and subject matter knowledge are brought into play as she performs a task analysis prior to writing an essay.

Composition topic: Should immigrants be expected to return to their native countries?

[She had looked at the list of topics, selected one and quickly had written the first sentence of her composition, 'One of the biggest problems that exists today in the US is the problem of ILLEGAL IMMIGRANTS.' She stopped and looked at the sentence. I said 'You started writing right away. You didn't have to think about it?']

'. . . . .*I was thinking of the way how to write and everything. . .I was thinking before of the topic. . .*
I was thinking about the title. I decided it's a big problem and my ideas is that I . . . .think they don't have to go back to their native countries. But I'm going to give first why is the problem and then I'm going – uh – you know – the against – the plus and against but my opinion I will try to support my opinion that they don't have to go back to their countries. But now I'm just trying to put it in the way that I am thinking to give first a general idea to put everything that I want . . .and maybe I'm going to change. Usually I change them you know. I wrote something then I put all the corrections that I want..'

In this task analysis, completed after the first sentence of the essay had been written, Dina is analysing the task's demands – how to go about writing the essay – the knowledge she draws upon to do so being implicit in the decisions she makes. First, she decides what her view is on the stated question – whether illegal immigrants should be allowed to stay in the United States or return to their native countries. The basis for this decision is her *subject matter knowledge,* that is what she knows about the topic. Then, guided by her *rhetorical knowledge,* she outlines the procedures she will follow in writing the essay. She will state the reason for the problem. Then, she will argue for the pros and cons of allowing immigrants to stay and provide supporting information for her opinion. Finally, referring explicitly to her *strategic knowledge,* she indicates the strategy she usually uses to complete a first draft: first to write down everything she's thinking and then to make changes. The final outcome of this analysis is new knowledge: of a writing plan which will guide her as she proceeds with the task. The following summarizes the metacognitive knowledge and subject matter knowledge Dina uses in Excerpt 1:

Task analysis	*Metacognitive and domain knowledge*
Analysing task demands – Dina's view on the topic *I was thinking before of the topic. . .I was thinking about the title. I decided it's a big problem and my idea is that I . . . .think they don't have to go back to their native countries.*	subject matter (DK)
Analysing task demands – how to do the task *I'm going to give first why is the problem then I'm going – uh – you know – the against – the plus and against, but my opinion I will try to support my opinion that they don't have to go back to their countries.*	rhetorical (TK)
Choosing a strategy *but now I'm just trying to put it in the way that I am thinking to give first a general idea to put everything that I want . . .and maybe I'm going to change. Usually I change them you know. I wrote something then I put all the corrections that I want.*	strategic (SK)

Excerpt 2: Jen

In Excerpt 2, Jen, a language learner of intermediate proficiency, also illustrates how task knowledge is brought into play as he performs a task analysis prior to writing an essay.

Composition topic: Why people steal?

'. . . . .Now I start writing my composition [pause] I've never written this composition before. . . .this topic. . . .I'm thinking how to start [10 seconds]. . . I think maybe I suppose there are three factors make people steal. . . I suppose. . .so I say [types] "there are three factors that make people steal. ."'
I have a topic sentence here. . .OK that's good. .that's a requirement. . . .

What will be the three factors I will think about? eh . . .maybe education, the first one (uh huh) Ok. . .the second factor might be the family and, the third factor (15 seconds) friend (uh huh). . . .no friends (uh huh) OK . . . . .this is my topic sentence. . .I have to write about these three factors. .'

[I asked him why he wrote down three factors, that is if he had education, family and friends in mind when he decided on three. He responded:]

'. . . . . .No I want to write a good composition that has several paragraphs. Two is more common, but three is good. . . . .I suppose three, so I say family, education and friends.'

In his task analysis, Jen begins by classifying the task. When he says 'I've never written this composition before. . . .this topic. . . .', it may be inferred that he has referred to his *knowledge of (writing) task types* and attempted to see if this one was similar to others he had written about. Jen, then considers how he will tackle writing about this topic, referring explicitly to the *rhetorical knowledge* that guides the writing of his first sentence 'There are three factors that make people steal.' That is, an essay needs a 'topic sentence', which determines the length of the essay, that is the number of paragraphs. In addition, a good essay has several paragraphs and three is better than two. The metacognitive knowledge Jen has used in this Excerpt is summarized below.

Task analysis	Metacognitive knowledge
Classifying the task	
I've never written this composition before. . . . this topic. . . .	task types (TK)
Analysing task demands: how to approach the task	
I'm thinking how to start [10 seconds]. . . I think, maybe, I suppose, there are three factors make people steal. . . I suppose. . .so I say [types] "there are three factors that make people steal. . ." I have a topic sentence here. . .OK that's good.. that's a requirement. . . .	rhetorical (TK)
I want to write a good composition that has several paragraphs. Two is more common, but three is good.	rhetorical (TK)
What will be the three factors I will think about? eh . . . maybe education, the first one (uh huh) OK the second factor might be the family and, the third factor (15 seconds) friend (uh huh). . . .no friends (uh huh) OK . . . . .this is my topic sentence I have to write about these three factors. .	rhetorical (TK)

Excerpt 3: Oshi

In Excerpt 3, Oshi, a language learner of intermediate proficiency, refers to the task and strategic knowledge that is associated with his analysis of how to read the *New York Times*.

'I read the Japanese newspaper and then when I read the summary on Sunday (i.e., the New York Sunday Times), it's easy for me. . . . .Reading the paper is like an English comprehension test. If I read the questions first and then read the passage, I can complete it in half the time. But if I read and then look at the questions it takes longer. It's the same if I read the news first in Japanese and then in English.'

Oshi's statement, 'reading the paper is like an English comprehension test', suggests that he has referred to his *knowledge of (comprehension) task types* and perceived the similarity between this reading task and reading comprehension tests in English. Then, drawing upon his *strategic knowledge*, he has chosen a strategy similar to the one he uses when he does an English reading comprehension test: advance preparation. First, he will read the news in a Japanese newspaper; then he will read the *Times*. Finally, it may be further inferred that *knowledge of this strategy's effectiveness* has led him to anticipate that reading the *New York Times* will be easy. The following summarizes the metacognitive knowledge Oshi refers to in Excerpt 3.

Task analysis	Metacognitive knowledge
Classifying the task	
Reading the paper is like an English (reading) comprehension test.	task type (TK)
Analysing task demands: how to do the task	
I read the news first in Japanese and then in English. I read the questions first and then read the passage (reading comprehension test).	task appropriate strategy (SK)
Analysing task demands: level of difficulty	
I read the Japanese newspaper and then when I read the summary on Sunday, it's easy for me. . . . If I read the questions first and then read the passage, I can complete it in half the time.	strategy effectiveness (SK)

MONITORING

Monitoring consists of five sub-processes: self-observation, assessment, deciding whether to take action, deciding how and when to take action, implementing the action (Wenden, 1997). *Self-observation* refers to the ongoing attention learners must pay to various aspects of the task they are completing, their progress in completing it, and to the factors that may facilitate or impede this progress.

Assessment refers to the evaluations learners make about:

- what they know and understand;
- the effectiveness of a learning method or strategy;
- whether or not their pre-set goals are being met;
- whether or not they expect that they will be.

As a result of their evaluation learners must determine if it is necessary to *take action and if so how and when*. Then having made a plan learners must act to *implement* it. New remedial strategies may be deployed; strategies already in use may be modified; new goals may be established; the cognitive task may be redefined.

Excerpt 4: Dina

Excerpt 4 points to the strategic and task knowledge that is the basis of the monitoring process that accompanied Dina's writing of sentence 2 of her composition on immigrants.

Thousands people of different nationality enter every day in the U.S. and that makes the citizens very confused to wonder if all those new people should be stay or returned to their native country.

Speaks outloud as she types the sentence; rereads it outloud and says: '*I always try to say outloud. I like to hear my ideas. . . . . . . .In a minute I'm going to change something. But then I'm going to go over it and I'm going to change it again. . . . I like my ideas but I don't like the place. I'm going to change the place. . . . but now I'm just want to put down my ideas in the right order.*'

In monitoring the writing of this sentence, Dina's report suggests that she has been attending to her ideas and order (i.e., the place), implicitly revealing her *rhetorical knowledge*: that these are aspects of written prose that one must attend to. She assesses what she has written. Her positive evaluation of the ideas suggests that she has drawn upon her *knowledge of her writing plan* devised during the task analysis (Excerpt 1) to note whether they convey the meaning she intended. Implicit in her assessment of place as needing to be changed is *rhetorical knowledge* regarding the organization of ideas. Then, based on this latter assessment, she decides to take remedial action later and to continue writing her ideas down in the right order. The former decision, it may be inferred, will be based partly on the same *rhetorical knowledge* that provided the criteria for her earlier assessment of this problem (inappropriate order). The second decision appears to be based on *knowledge of her writing plan* (Excerpt 1): first to put everything down as she thinks about it and then make revisions. The Excerpt also reveals her *knowledge of a strategy* that she always uses to attend to her ideas, that is she auditorializes. The metacognitive knowledge Dina used to monitor her writing of sentence 2 is summarized below.

Monitoring processes	Metacognitive knowledge
Self-observation	
I always try to say outloud.	task appropriate strategy (SK)
I like to hear my ideas.	
Assessment	
I like my ideas	writing plan (TK)
– but I don't like the place.	rhetorical (TK)
Decision to take action	
I'm going to change the place. In a minute	rhetorical (TK)
I'm going to change something	
– but now I'm just want to put down my	writing plan (TK)
ideas in the right order.	

Excerpt 5: Dina

Excerpt 5 points to the task and person knowledge that is the basis of the monitoring process that accompanied Dina's writing of sentences 5 and 6 of her composition.

The biggest immigrant's number is also uneducated people who try to find any kind of job and they don't offer anything in the American society. They don't pay any taxes and they don't vote. In other words they don't meet the responsibilities of an American citizen.

[writes sentences 5 and 6, pauses, rereads them outloud and in response to my question, 'What were you thinking?']
'I was just thinking, you know, if I had to add something. . . Because really I'm not with this side. But I have. . . .you know. . . the illegal immigrants must stay. .I have more, but I don't want to say more because then I change another meaning that I (don't) want to give. I'm not going to say more than this. . .Now I'm going to say the other side. . . . . '

In monitoring the writing of these two sentences, Dina's report suggests that she is attending to the supporting ideas she's written to make a case against illegal immigrants. She is assessing the adequacy of these supports, trying to decide whether or not she could and should add more. Implicit is her *rhetorical knowledge* that an adequate number of supporting details are necessary to support a main idea. At the same time, she refers to her *person knowledge*, that is what she knows about the topic and concludes that she has the knowledge required to add more details should she decide to do so. However, referring to her writing plan – that she will argue in favour of immigrants remaining in the United States – and realizing that supports are intended to influence readers (*rhetorical knowledge*), she decides not to add more supports as it would change the meaning she intends to convey. Finally, again, referring to her writing plan, she decides to proceed with the development of the other point of view on immigrants. The following is a summary of the metacognitive knowledge Dina used to monitor her writing of sentences 5 and 6.

Monitoring processes	Metacognitive knowledge
self-observation/assessment *I was just thinking, you know, if I had to add something.*	rhetorical (TK)
Decision regarding adding supports *I have more*	what she knows about the topic (PK)
I'm not with this side. . . . the illegal immigrants must stay	writing plan (TK)
I don't want to say more because, then, I change another meaning that meaning I (don't) want to give. I'm not going to say more than this.	rhetorical (TK)
Decision to continue *Now, I'm going to say the other side.*	writing plan (TK)

Excerpt 6: Dina

Excerpt 6 points to the person knowledge that guided Dina's monitoring of sentence 8.

They came here and the work very hard with all the news and strange situations trying to understand how the things are going in the 'new home' and what the new society expect for them.

[writes sentence 8 to *situations*, rereads it with a gesture of disgust and continues to 'new home', which she has put in quotes]
'. . . . . *I don't know. . . . . you don't use those things (i.e. the quotation marks) but I can't use my words when I want to emphasize something. . . . .So I try to find – you know – all those things I find on the computer. .the punctuation to emphasize my idea because I don't have the words to give you or somebody what I want to say . . . In my language I don't use so much because I can express all the things that I want to say. In this language I can't.'*

In monitoring the writing of sentence 8, Dina's report suggests that she is attending to the meaning she wishes to emphasize and becomes aware of an obstacle preventing her progress, that is her inability to find a word to express her meaning (the gesture of disgust). She, therefore, decides on a production strategy to deal with the problem: she puts quotation marks around the idea she wanted to emphasize. In this Excerpt Dina refers to *person knowledge* to explain the problem that is encountered in completing the writing task. Her English linguistic proficiency is inadequate – she does not have the vocabulary necessary to emphasize her ideas. This same knowledge explains her choice of production strategy. In addition, it brings to awareness her knowledge of her superior ability in her language (*person knowledge*). The following summarizes the metacognitive knowledge Dina used to monitor her writing of sentence 8.

Monitoring processes	Metacognitive knowledge
assessment of reason for problem *I can't use my words when I want to emphasize something.*	proficiency in English (PK)
decision to take action and how *. . . . .so I try to find – you know – all those things I find on the computer. . the punctuation to emphasize my idea.*	
I don't have the words to give you or somebody what I want to say. .	proficiency in English (PK)
In my language. . . . I can express all the things that I want to say. In this language I can't.	proficiency in native language (PK)

Excerpt 7: Oshi

While it is true that the monitoring of a task can only be captured through introspective reporting, retrospective reports can reveal some of the knowledge that has guided the process. Thus, in Excerpt 7, Oshi reveals the person and task knowledge that, it may be inferred, influences the selection of a strategy in response to problems encountered as he monitors his conversations with an employee.

(a)

'If he uses new words, I ask the meaning – stop the discussion. Then he uses another word – easier, and the discussion continues.'

[What do you do about the word?]

'I am very old. My ability to learn by heart becomes worse. But I'm trying to. . . It's better to write it down and try to use it.'

(b)

[When you talk do you worry about making mistakes?]

'There are several ways to say things. I'm very careful because I don't want to disturb relations between people. I don't want to offend them.'

(c)

[Referring to his employee]

'. . . . .when he corrects me. . . . .I try to understand the reason and check the reason and if it's not satisfactory, I ask him for the reason. He explains. That discussion is helpful to understand grammar.'

In Excerpt (a), Oshi reveals the *person knowledge* – that age affects one's memory – which guides his choice of a learning strategy for remembering new words encountered as he talks with his employee. In (b), it is his understanding of the social appropriateness of language – his *task knowledge* – that influences his choice of production strategy when communicating with him and other Americans. He is very deliberate in choosing the socially appropriate word. Finally, in (c), he provides the reason for the strategy he uses to deal with corrections of his spoken English made by his employee. When he cannot determine the reason for the explanation himself, he asks for an explanation, noting that this feedback is very useful for understanding grammar (*task knowledge*). The metacognitive knowledge Oshi uses to select these strategies is summarized below.

Monitoring processes	*Metacognitive knowledge*
Choosing a plan of action, i.e. a strategy	
If he uses new words, I ask the meaning – stop the discussion.	
Then he uses another word – easier, and the discussion continues.	
[What do you do about the word?]	
I am very old. My ability to learn by heart becomes worse. But	effect of age on
I'm trying to. . .It's better to write it down and try to use it.	learning (PK)
[When you talk do you worry about making mistakes?]	
There are several ways to say things. I'm very careful because I don't	social appropriateness
want to disturb relations between people. I don't want to offend them.	of language use (TK)
[Referring to his employee]. . . . .*when he corrects me*. . . . .*I*	importance of
try to understand the reason and check the reason and if it's not	feedback (SK)
satisfactory, I ask him for the reason. He explains. That discussion	
is helpful to understand grammar. . .	

Excerpt 8: Oshi

In contrast to Excerpts 4–6, the monitoring process suggested by the Oshi's report in Excerpt 8 extends beyond one instance in time and beyond one discrete task to a series of instances extended over a period of time and consisting of multiple language learning activities. In this Excerpt, Oshi makes explicit the strategic and task knowledge he used to evaluate these activities.

(a)

'I went to a language school in Germany. . . . .the teacher came from England. If I tried to use a new word in class, the teacher told me you'd better use it in this way and she wrote it on the blackboard. That was very helpful.'

(b)

[Referring to an English course in the US] *'I must be able to write essays to complete my admission form to get into an MBA program. After classes I have exercises to do. They teach grammar. That's helpful.'*

'. . .my job requires that I make telephone contacts and arrange interviews to sell my products. My business clients are not too well educated. They speak very quickly and if I don't understand, they become angry and hang up and I lose a client. The people in the class also have that type of English and so I have an opportunity to practice.'

(c)

[Referring to a GMAT course] *'Studying GMAT is good cause I must compete with American people not foreigners. If I get into an MBA class, I must say something. Otherwise, I can't graduate. That's very hard to argue with American people to understand the argument going on between American people, then get into the conversation . . .very hard but helpful.'*

In example (a), Oshi refers to the importance of feedback (*strategic knowledge*) to explain why he found his teacher's style of teaching useful. In the other two examples, Oshi explains how his English class in the United States and the GMAT course consist of activities and/or opportunities for language use that are relevant to his language learning needs and goals. That is, his knowledge of task purpose (*task knowledge*) provides the criteria for judging the utility of these self-selected language learning activities. Summarized below is the metacognitive knowledge Oshi uses to evaluate these activities.

Monitoring processes	Metacognitive knowledge
assessing a chosen strategy/activity	
[referring to language school in Germany]	
the teacher came from England. If I tried to use a new word,	importance of feedback (SK)
the teacher told me you'd better use it in this way and she	
wrote it on the blackboard. That was very helpful.	
[referring to an English course in the US]	
After classes I have exercises to do. They teach grammar.	task purpose/utility (TK)
That's helpful. My business clients are not too well educated.	
They speak very quickly. . . . The people in the class also have	task purpose/utility (TK)
that type of English and so I have an opportunity to practice.	
[referring to a GMAT course]	
Studying GMAT is good cause I must compete with	task purpose/utility (TK)
American people not foreigners. That's very hard to argue	
with American people to understand the argument going on	
between American people, then get into the conversation.	

SUMMARY

The purpose of this chapter has been to clarify the nature of the relationship between metacognitive knowledge and self-regulation in language learning. The analysis of the learner accounts has shown that metacognitive knowledge is a prerequisite to the implementation of two sets of regulatory processes in language learning: the task analysis which guides pre-task engagement planning and the monitoring which oversees task completion. The relationship between the specific sub-types of metacognitive knowledge and the individual processes that constitute task analysis and monitoring, which were illustrated, explained, and summarized in the body of the chapter, are outlined in more general terms in Table 3.3.

According to the summary outline in Table 3.3, task knowledge appears to be the most complex of the three main categories of metacognitive knowledge – the reports of the three learners together illustrating five sub-types. Knowledge of task types and rhetorical knowledge were utilized in the *task analysis*, the former to classify a task and the latter to determine a task's demands, that is how to do the writing task. To *monitor* the completion of their tasks, the learners drew upon (1) rhetorical knowledge to determine what aspects of the task to observe, to assess their progress and to decide whether or not to take action; (2) metalinguistic knowledge to choose a strategy; (3) perception of a task's purpose to assess the effectiveness of a language learning activity; and (4) awareness of their writing plan to assess their progress and decide whether to take action and how.

In addition, three sub-types of person knowledge were illustrated in the Excerpts, each one utilized in monitoring: to determine the choice of a strategy (age and learning; linguistic proficiency); to assess the cause of a

Table 3.3 Metacognitive knowledge and regulatory processes

Metacognitive knowledge	Regulatory processes	
Types and sub-types	Task analysis	Monitoring
TASK KNOWLEDGE		
knowledge of task types	classifying a task	
rhetorical	analysing task demands: how to do the task	self-observation assessment of progress decision to take action
metalinguistic		decision how to take action: choice of strategy
task purpose		assessment of a language learning activity
writing plan		assessment of progress decision to take action decision how to take action
PERSON KNOWLEDGE		
age and learning		decision how to take action: choice of strategy
linguistic proficiency in L1 and L2		assessment of problem decision how to take action: choice of strategy
subject matter knowledge		decision to take action
STRATEGIC KNOWLEDGE		
task appropriate strategy	analysing task demands: choice of strategy	self-observation decision how to take action assessment of an activity
strategy effectiveness	analysing task demands: level of difficulty	
guidelines for learning		decision how to take action: choice of strategy

problem (linguistic proficiency); and to determine whether to take action (subject matter knowledge). The learners' Excerpts also pointed to three sub-types of strategic knowledge. This knowledge was used as learners analysed a task's demands – providing insight on the difficulty of a task (strategy effectiveness) and guiding the choice of a strategy to complete it (task appropriate strategy). In addition, while monitoring, strategic knowledge was used by the learners to facilitate the self-observation process and to assess the effectiveness of a language learning activity (task appropriate strategy); to decide how to take action (task appropriate strategy and guidelines for learning).

In sum, the analysis of these eight Excerpts illustrates how metacognitive knowledge was utilized by learners to self-regulate their completion of an assigned writing task (Jen and Dina) and of self-selected language learning tasks, that is reading the newspaper, conversing with an employee, taking language courses and college preparatory courses (Oshi). At the same time, it should be noted that, in her task analysis (Excerpt 1), Dina also used knowledge she had acquired about immigration, the topic of her composition. This suggests that other than metacognitive knowledge, subject matter or domain knowledge is also necessary in the regulation of learning and communication tasks.

CONCLUSION

This chapter has summarized research on the metacognitive knowledge of language learners and analysed selected Excerpts from learner accounts to illustrate how this knowledge functions in the self-regulation of language learning. To conclude I would like to suggest briefly what this implies for theory, research and practice in SLA.

Theoretical implications

As noted at the beginning of the chapter, thus far SLA theories have not included metacognitive knowledge among the learner differences proposed as influencing the process of acquiring another language. The developing body of research summarized in this chapter suggests that it is a cognitive variable that should be acknowledged. Beyond providing data that may be used to correlate what learners know with learner outcomes, the analysis of the eight learner accounts suggests an added benefit. The manner in which metacognitive knowledge influences the self-regulation of learning, illustrated by such accounts, can provide an explanation for a learner's approach to SLA, thus enhancing conclusions drawn from the correlations.

Secondly, a recognition of the function of metacognitive knowledge in the self-regulation of learning should contribute to a clearer understanding of learner autonomy, specifically how it can be developed and enhanced. As indicated in the literature on adult learning, autonomy is a potential and a goal towards which all humans strive in their various life roles, for example as children, parents, professionals and as learners (Knox, 1977). The realization of this potential for language learners is in part dependent upon their ability to self-regulate or self-direct their learning (see Holec, 1981). This means being able to conduct a task analysis that contributes to the overall planning of a task and, then, monitoring the task's implementation; a set of sub-processes which includes the evaluation of progress and means of learning. As illustrated in this chapter, metacognitive knowledge is a prerequisite to the deployment of these self-regulatory processes. It is the basis for planning and monitoring. Thus, it is essential to the development and enhancement of a learner's potential for autonomy. It is the possession of and the ability to apply such a body of knowledge that is one characteristic of autonomous learners (Benson, 2000). As the Excerpts have suggested, such learners are *reflective* in their approach to learning. They draw upon acquired metacognitive knowledge to better understand themselves as language learners. They reflect upon their experience to form their own theories about the nature of language and effective approaches to language learning, that is to develop further their body of metacognitive knowledge. Furthermore, they are *self-directed*, drawing upon the knowledge that is the outcome of their reflective process to analyse a task, devise a learning plan, and to monitor its implementation.

Research implications

To refine and expand our understanding of the function of metacognitive knowledge in language learning further, research on metacognitive knowledge in language learning needs to be expanded and diversified in content. Thus far, most studies have documented general knowledge language learners hold about various aspects of their language learning. There is a need for research which documents the metacognitive knowledge learners bring to specific tasks of language learning and language use (e.g., reading, listening in formal and informal settings, acquiring vocabulary).

Insights gained from the analysis of the eight Excerpts in this chapter suggests a second area for research. Task-based studies should also document how metacognitive knowledge comes into play as learners self-direct their learning. What kind of knowledge is utilized as learners plan to do a task (conduct a task analysis) and implement it (task monitoring)? How is the knowledge utilized? The outcome of such research should also contribute to our understanding of learning strategies. To date most learning strategy research has been isolated from the processes of self-regulation that deploy them and the metacognitive knowledge that motivates and guides these processes. Research on the use of metacognitive knowledge in the self-regulation of learning should also explain which strategies are selected, when they are, and why. How metacognitive knowledge is acquired and changed is a third research area that needs expanding. How does this knowledge change over time? Why does it change? To what extent and how might teacher interventions lead to these changes? How can changes in metacognitive knowledge lead to learners' more active involvement in the regulation of their learning?

Pedagogical implications

Finally, FL/SL instruction should benefit by acknowledging this hidden variable. First of all, the recognition of metacognitive knowledge as a learner difference and of its role in the self-regulation of learning should remind teachers that there is a rationale underlying learners' approach to language learning. There is a reason for what they choose to learn, the strategies and learning activities they prefer, and the manner in which they approach and complete a task.

It is to this rationale that they can turn in order to understand better how learners approach the completion of language learning tasks and, ultimately, why some learners are successful and others are not. Teachers should attempt to discover this rationale, through their learners' metacognitive knowledge. Applying to this enterprise the various techniques used by researchers to elicit introspective and retrospective reporting, they can expect to gain insights that will enhance their attempts to facilitate the process of second language learning within the classroom and to provide learners with guidance for pursuing their learning independently in informal settings.

Chapter 4

The metaphorical constructions
of second language learners

Rod Ellis, University of Auckland

INTRODUCTION

How do second language acquisition (SLA) researchers construct second language (L2) learners? How do L2 learners construct themselves? The aim of this chapter is to explore these two questions and, in particular, to high-light differences in the constructions of researchers and learners. Such a comparison is compatible with the postmodernist conviction that the study of L2 acquisition is a highly complex phenomenon that can best be under-stood by examining its multiple realities. This chapter, then, reports an ini-tial study of how SLA researchers construct L2 learners and how L2 learners construct themselves.

In order to undertake such a study it is necessary to address two problems – one conceptual and the other methodological. As evidenced by some of the classic papers in SLA (e.g., Corder, 1967), it is clear that SLA researchers do not so much talk about learners as about learning. Lantolf (1996) recently reached a similar conclusion, noting that SLA talks of 'systems and processes' that 'are independent of the very people who are trying to learn a second language' (1996: 717). Furthermore, as Tollefson (1991) has pointed out, even when SLA does acknowledge that learners exist, it adopts the neo-classical view that they make choices by weighing up personal benefits and costs and, typically, ignores how social context structures these choices. Learners, then, are not so much constructed by SLA researchers as both deconstructed and decontextualized! However, it is also apparent that there are indeed implicit constructions of learners in the models and theories of SLA and that these implicit constructions were precisely what need to be teased out.

The second problem concerned the kind of methodology for achieving this. One intriguing possibility was to examine the metaphors that SLA researchers have used to write about language learning. Such an approach is warranted in part by Lantolf's demonstration that SLA theory, contrary to the claim of some researchers, is inherently metaphorical and in part by the practical need for a tool to compare the constructions of researchers and learners.

This chapter will begin, therefore, with a brief discussion of metaphor and the use of metaphor analysis in applied linguistic research. It will then examine some of the key metaphors that have figured in SLA research and in so doing attempt to identify researchers' implicit constructions of L2 learners. Next, a number of journals kept by a group of L2 adult learners will be analysed to examine the metaphors they used to talk about language learning. Finally, the chapter will consider to what extent the researchers' and learners' constructions are similar and different and consider the relevance of this kind of enquiry for SLA research.

METAPHOR ANALYSIS IN APPLIED LINGUISTICS

What Steen (1994) calls 'metaphorology' has undergone a remarkable revolution in the last twenty years or so. Traditionally, metaphor was viewed as a unique form of linguistic expression associated with literature, in particular poetry. It involved 'fancy language' that was in some way unusual or deviant. As such, it was largely ignored by linguists. At the end of the 1970s, a number of publications, in particular Lakoff and Johnson's *Metaphors We Live By* (1980), convincingly argued the case for metaphor as central to not just language but to human cognition as well. Lakoff and Johnson's arguments, subsequently repeated and developed in a series of publications throughout the 1980s (e.g., Lakoff, 1986, 1987; Lakoff and Turner, 1989), are based on two principal contentions.

The first is that metaphorical use far from being special and rare is in fact very ordinary and commonplace. Lakoff and Turner (1989) argue that 'metaphor is a tool so ordinary that we use it unconsciously and automatically, with so little effort that we hardly notice it' (1989: xi). They note that people have the potential to construct and understand an infinitely large range of metaphors but, in fact, draw on a fairly well-defined and limited set. They refer to these as 'conventionalized metaphors', some of which are 'basic' in the sense that they are conceptually well-established, very widely used, and often realized linguistically by means of formulaic expressions. Basic metaphors are 'conceptually indispensable' according to Lakoff and Turner. Examples of such metaphors, of which we will find versions operating widely in SLA, are PEOPLE ARE CONTAINERS and PEOPLE ARE MACHINES.

Lakoff and Turner's second contention is that metaphors are 'a matter of thought not language' (1989: 107). That is, people store metaphorical mappings as mental schemata which they draw on automatically in order to process metaphorical expressions in understanding and production. Such metaphors, therefore, are reflective of the modes of thought of the members of the linguistic community that employ them. Metaphor, then, is not just a linguistic embellishment, but a primary means by which people make sense of the world around them. Metaphor helps us to construct reality, to reason about it and to evaluate it.

These contentions are not uncontroversial. It is not clear, for example, whether expressions such as 'input', a term in common usage in SLA, is best seen as metaphorical (i.e., a slot in the particular form of the PEOPLE ARE

MACHINES metaphor) or as polysemous, with the specific meaning attached to it in SLA as just one of several possible meanings. Glucksberg, Keysar and McGlone (1992) have argued that many conventionalized metaphors cease to function as metaphors (i.e., they are no longer processed analogically). The 'analytic' methods used by Lakoff to investigate metaphor only demonstrate the existence of two semantic domains in a metaphor, not two conceptual domains. It is a moot point, then, whether a semantic mapping corresponds to a conceptual mapping. However, this is not the place to pursue this controversy here. The position adopted in this chapter is that linguistic metaphors are potentially conceptual metaphors and that, even with overuse, the metaphorical value of an item such as 'input' is potentially still available to us.

Of much greater interest here is how metaphors structure cognition and, most importantly, how the study of metaphor can serve as a tool for investigating the way we construct reality. Conceptual metaphors, particularly the conventional kind, demonstrate how we view reality – how we cognize matters of vital concern to us. In western thought (and perhaps in other cultures as well), for example, 'life' is viewed as a 'journey', 'love' as 'fire', and death as 'night'. Shortly, it will be shown that the metaphors that SLA researchers and L2 learners use to talk about language learning, many of which are highly conventionalized, reflect their particular orientations to this phenomenon – that they function as windows through which we can view the mental constructs they work with. But conventional metaphors do more than construct particular realities; they also channel and constrain thought. As Lakoff and Turner (1989) put it, 'anything we rely on constantly, unconsciously, and automatically is so much a part of us that it cannot be easily resisted, in large part because it is barely noticed' (1989: 63). Highly conventional metaphors tend to lose their metaphorical power and be understood directly without awareness of their non-literal nature (Hoffman and Kemper, 1987); they become 'literalized'. The danger, here, as Lantolf (1996) has pointed out, is that we lose sight of the metaphorical origins of our theories, and treat them as literal statements about reality. Of course, new metaphors have the potential to expand one's thinking. Metaphor can liberate as well as constrain.

It follows that metaphor analysis can serve two primary functions in the epistemological study of SLA. First, it can help to clarify the nature of the constructs that SLA researchers work with. Secondly, it can assist in the process of demythologizing SLA by revealing what has become hidden as metaphors are literalized. In particular, as we will see, it can serve to show how deeprooted the assumption is in SLA that the learner functions as some kind of computer, processing input and producing output in a machine-like way. A metaphorical analysis can also help to demonstrate the dubious nature of the often-made distinction between analogical and scientific thought (Leary, 1990).

In fact, metaphor analysis has become an accepted tool in both educational and applied linguistic enquiry. Briscoe (1991), for example, shows in a case study of a science teacher struggling to change his style of teaching that 'the metaphors teachers use to make sense of their roles have a substantial affect on classroom practice' (1991: 197). The images teachers use metaphorically help to organize their belief sets and serve as an aid to reflection-on-practice. Block (1997) reports clear differences in the metaphors used by teachers and L2 learners to conceptualize what language learning involves and their roles in the classroom. Koch and Deetz (1981) show how an analysis of the metaphors used by people to talk about organizational systems reveals how they perceive such systems and their roles in them. They identify two main metaphors; ORGANIZATION AS MACHINE and ORGANIZATION AS LIVING ORGANISM and note that the former implicitly downplays the role of human ideation in organizations, a point we will find relevant later when we examine the PEOPLE AS MACHINE metaphor which is so prominent in SLA. Koch also makes the important point that it is valuable to identify the entailments latent in key metaphors in order to discover which options afforded by a metaphor are or are not exploited. More recently, Cameron and Low (1999) have collected a number of papers illustrating the use of metaphor analysis in applied linguistic fields, including SLA (Block, 1999) and teaching and teacher education (Cortazzi and Jin, 1999).

Metaphor analysis has also been seen as important in English for Specific Purposes. Salager-Mayer (1990) reports the results of an analysis of metaphorical usage in medical texts in English, French and Spanish. Interestingly, she finds the same metaphors occurring in all three languages and suggests that this supports Widdowson's (1979) claim regarding the universality of scientific discourse. Lindstromberg (1991) adapts Corson's 'lexical bar' theory to suggest that L2 learners from a non-Germanic background are likely to experience difficulty in understanding conventional metaphor in English. He points out that metaphor introduces 'extraneous and unpredictable lexis' into field-specific discourse which may pose a greater problem than technical lexis. He argues that TESOL has been neglectful in viewing metaphor as 'a feature of poetry and somewhat extravagant prose' (1991: 218).

A number of researchers have noted the role that metaphor plays in SLA. In a discussion of the 'discourse problem' that arises in communication between researchers and teachers, Kramsch (1995) notes that 'each domain has its own metaphors' and that this creates misunderstanding. She focuses on the 'input-black box-output' metaphor, so dominant in SLA and notes that the choice of a metaphor drawn from the source domain of electrical engineering was expeditious because it linked SLA to an upcoming and prestigious field and thus ensured both respectability and funding. The metaphor was also useful to researchers in that its entailments led them to ask important questions such as 'what is the *nature* of input?' and 'what *counts* as input?' But Kramsch also notes that the metaphor soon took on 'a life of its own' (1995: 11) with the result that it limited the scope of SLA research and, also, ultimately reinforced the divide between researchers who study input and teachers who mediate it. Lantolf (1996) sees all theories as inherently metaphorical. He points out that while the traditional view of scientists is that discourse (including metaphor) is a process of putting thoughts into words, an equally tenable (and from Lantolf's perspective more convincing) view is that discourse imposes structure on the mind. Like Kramsch, he sees what he calls the 'mind-as-computer' metaphor as having achieved an unhealthy dominance in the field of linguistics and SLA. He also warns against the dangers of literalized metaphors restricting thought and limiting theory development. He argues, as I have done (R. Ellis, 1994), for an acceptance of plurality of theories in SLA, and suggests that to keep the field fresh and vibrant it is necessary continually to create new metaphors. Block (1999) also uses metaphor analysis to show how SLA has been 'framed' as 'monotheistic'. His analysis indicates that SLA has been characterized as problematic and anarchic because of the existence of multiple theories (as opposed to a single, widely-accepted theory), of the application of multiple criteria for evaluating theories, and of the absence of replication studies. Block argues the need to study the 'framing' function of metaphors.

The general drift of these arguments is that SLA has become narrowly psycholinguistic because of the power of metaphor to direct and constrain the field. The same point is made by Firth and Wagner (1997). However, they draw attention to a different metaphor which has characterized the thinking of SLA researchers – the metaphor of the learner-as-defective communicator. They note that learners are typically viewed as non-native speakers who are 'handicapped' by the 'problem' of an underdeveloped competence. They suggest that this metaphor has enabled researchers to ignore the contextual and interactional aspects of language use and acquisition in favour of psycholinguistic aspects. Like Lantolf, they call for a widening of the research agenda to include approaches that view the learner more holistically by taking into account the social context in which learners learn, that adopt an emic perspective (i.e., take the learner's perspective) and that are more critically sensitive to fundamental concepts such as 'native speaker' and 'interlanguage'.

From this brief review of some of the work based on metaphorical analysis, we can see clearly that the study of metaphor provides a basis for identifying the mental constructs that underlie our thinking about the world and, importantly, for evaluating them. In the eyes of some, SLA has become myopic as a result of its domination by a restricted set of metaphors, in particular those of the LEARNER AS A MACHINE and LEARNER AS DEFECTIVE COMMUNICATOR.

THE METHODOLOGY OF METAPHOR ANALYSIS

None of the commentators on SLA referred to above comment explicitly on the methodology they used to identify and analyse the metaphors they describe. One is left with the impression that they adopted a rather *ad hoc* approach, relying primarily on their own general understanding of what SLA is about to select metaphors for analysis. Thus, while their account of these metaphors is convincing, their general comments about the state of affairs in SLA, as it stands today, may be somewhat partial. A more rigorous approach to metaphor analysis is desirable.

Following standard definitions of metaphor (see, for example, Cameron, 1999), an expression will be considered metaphorical if it contains an explicit and implicit comparison involving an attempt to express some kind of anomalous relationship between a Topic and a Vehicle. Metaphor can take many linguistic forms. Cameron notes that verb metaphors may be more common than noun metaphors. Following Lakoff and Johnson (1980), it is assumed that metaphors are not just linguistic expressions but are reflections of the ways in which people (researchers and learners) conceptualize language learning.

The approach to be followed here is that outlined by Koch and Deetz (1981), which is summarized as follows:

1. Choose a representative corpora of texts.
2. Isolate metaphorical expressions in the texts and list them.
3. Decide which metaphors are worth analysing in accordance with the research purpose.
4. Reduce the metaphorical expressions to the metaphors they display by identifying the source and target domains.
5. Sort these metaphors into coherent groups, thereby establishing the 'main metaphors' in the corpora.
6. Consider the possible entailments of each main metaphor and examine to what extent these are or are not expressed in the corpora.

This approach will be followed to examine, first, the metaphors in common use in SLA and, secondly, the metaphors employed by a group of learners to talk about their own learning of an L2.

THE METAPHORICAL CONSTRUCTIONS OF LEARNERS IN SLA

A total of nine articles were selected as the corpora of texts (see Table 4.1 for a list). The choice was motivated by several concerns. (1) The articles should be written by leading researchers in SLA – Corder, Gregg, Kasper, Krashen, Long, Norton Peirce, Pica, Schmidt, Swain. (2) They should reflect a variety of theoretical orientations, including those that were psycholinguistic and those that were more social. However, a decision was taken not to include any article dealing with individual learner differences, partly to economize on the size of the corpora but mainly to ensure that the articles reflected the metaphors in use in 'mainstream SLA', which has been primarily concerned with the universal aspects of L2 acquisition. (3) The preponderance of articles should be recent (i.e., published since 1990) so that the corpora reflected current metaphors and, thereby, current conceptualizations in SLA.

Many of the key terms found in SLA, and therefore in the corpora, are, in fact, metaphorical in origin, a testimony to the power of metaphor to shape a field of enquiry. Two such terms are *transfer* and *interlanguage*. However, these will not be considered here as they have become so literalized that they no longer function metaphorically. It is worth noting, however, that, as metaphors, both are problematic. The notion of transfer implies that something (a feature of the learner's L1) is moved to somewhere else (into the L2), but, as we well know, this is not what happens; learners do not generally lose their L1 when they learn an L2 so nothing is in fact transferred. This was one reason why Kellerman and Sharwood Smith (1986) suggested an alternative term – *crosslinguistic influence* – a suggestion that has not caught on. The *interlanguage* metaphor is problematic too. It suggests that the grammar which a learner mentally constructs lies in between something. But in between what? And what exactly is the starting point for the learner's construction of a mental grammar? Interestingly, these questions, which originate directly from the metaphorical value of *interlanguage*, have aroused considerable attention among SLA researchers (see, for example, Selinker, 1992).

Determining exactly what was metaphorical in a text did not prove easy. This was because it is was often not clear whether a particular expression was metaphorical or polysemous. For example, does 'construct', as used in phrases like 'construct an interlanguage grammar', draw on a building metaphor or is it simply a lexical item, one whose literal meanings is 'to put together'? Following Lakoff and Turner (1989), a linguistic expression was deemed metaphorical if it was linked conceptually to an obvious source domain. Therefore, 'construct' can be considered metaphorical because it is associated strongly with the idea of 'building construction'; interlanguage (the target domain) was in effect being compared to a building. In practice, however, it was not always so easy to classify expressions. For this reason, no statistical breakdown of the metaphorical expressions identified in the texts will be provided. Instead, a more interpretative account will be provided by describing and discussing the 'main metaphors' that were identified. These metaphors will be referred to using the frame LEARNER AS X, even though in many cases the target domain of the metaphors used in the corpora was learning (or, in some cases, language use) rather than learners. Table 4.1 summarizes the basic metaphors used by the nine SLA researchers.

Learner as container

This metaphor figures in Corder's seminal paper in his reference to 'the capacity of the learner'. It is maintained in many of the more recent publications (e.g., in Gregg, Krashen, Long and Schmidt). Long, for example, refers to 'processing capacity' and 'attentional space'. This metaphor has three obvious entailments, all of which are exploited. The first is that a container must contain something. In Gregg's case this is 'linguistic competence'. In Schmidt's case it is 'memory' and 'primary consciousness'. Secondly, a container presupposes that things can be put into and taken out of it. Thus, Schmidt talks about 'unattended form entering memory' and 'retrieval from memory'. In this respect, the LEARNER AS CONTAINER metaphor can be

Table 4.1   Basic metaphors used by nine SLA researchers

Researcher	Date of Publication	1	2	3	4	5	6	7
Corder	1967	*	*		*			
Gregg	1989	*	*					
Kasper	1996b		*	*				
Krashen	1994	*	*					
Long	1996	*	*	*	*	*		
Norton Peirce	1995		*				*	*
Pica	1994		*	*	*	*		
Schmidt	1994	*	*		*			
Swain	1995		*	*	*	*		

Key to metaphors:
1. LEARNER AS CONTAINER
2. LEARNER AS MACHINE
3. LEARNER AS NEGOTIATOR
4. LEARNER AS PROBLEM-SOLVER
5. LEARNER AS BUILDER
6. LEARNER AS STRUGGLER
7. LEARNER AS INVESTOR

seen as related to, and perhaps part of, the more general conduit metaphor discussed by Reddy (1993). The third entailment is that a container has a fixed, limited capacity. Schmidt talks quite explicitly of the 'limited resource metaphor of attention'.

The LEARNER AS CONTAINER metaphor presents learners as passive and restricted. Learners are passive in the sense that they have things done to them rather than do things themselves. They are restricted in the sense that they have limited capacities for learning, both in the sense of what they can attend to and what they can remember. There are other possible entailments of this metaphor, for example a container can be damaged, broken, thrown away, but there were no metaphorical expressions relating to these entailments. The metaphor, then, was fairly narrowly developed.

An extension of the LEARNER AS CONTAINER metaphor is, perhaps, the LEARNER AS A PLACE. Long, for example, frequently refers to learners 'accessing' L2 data while Schmidt and Long talk of 'gaps'. This idea of the learner as a place finds its clearest expression in Bialystok and Sharwood Smith's (1985) use of an extended library analogy in their discussion of interlanguage in terms of 'knowledge' and 'control'.

Learner as machine

The LEARNER AS MACHINE metaphor proved by far the most ubiquitous in the corpora, thus bearing out the observations of Kramsch (1995) and Lantolf (1996). Frequent use of it occurred in all the articles, the one exception being Norton Peirce. Long's account of acquisition as involving 'input, internal learner capacities, particularly selective attention, and output' is typical.

There are numerous entailments of this metaphor, one reason, perhaps, for its popularity. We can talk about what goes into the machine (input) and, of course, how this must be prepared to suit the way the machine works (environmental conditions). We can consider how the machine starts up – Long's frequent mention of a 'trigger'. We can refer to the actual parts of the machine (internal structure; components; mechanisms; devices; filters) and how they work (functions; operations; systems; processes; procedures). We can speak of what comes out of the machine (constructions; products; by-products; output). What comes out can also have things done to it (we can reprocess or modify output). Also, of course, we can control machines by speeding them up or slowing them down (processing control).

There is also the question of what kind of machine it is. Lantolf (1996) specifically sees it as a computer. So too does Schmidt when he notes that 'the computer is the dominant metaphor' (1994: 13). However, in many of the articles I examined the machine seems to exist more generically as something that takes in material, processes it and comes out with a product. It can be a computer, a gun (as with the reference to a 'trigger') or even some kind of lathe. There are advantages in this kind of vagueness. It removes any need to specify in any precise way what the machine consists of or how it works. In the case of theories like Krashen's Input Hypothesis this has obvious advantages; Krashen's interest does not lie in telling us how the machine works on the input.

Like the LEARNER AS CONTAINER metaphor, the LEARNER AS MACHINE metaphor positions learners as lacking control over what they do and how they learn. They have no say in the components of their machines or in the processes these components are capable of performing. They have to learn in accordance with how the machine works. Of course, they are not entirely powerless. They can influence the input that goes into the machine and they can, if they so choose, decide to 'reprocess output' from the machine. But the machine itself remains a black box that they can do nothing about. They are not even in charge of switching it off, this being something that happens automatically when they reach a certain age (Long, 1990). One wonders whether mainstream SLA researchers (among whom I include myself) really do wish to position learners as so unempowered and whether the time has come to free ourselves from this metaphor, as Kramsch (1995) and Lantolf (1996) suggest. Of course, such a step would require the use of alternative metaphors, which, as a number of commentators (e.g., Firth and Wagner, 1997) have pointed out, are not readily available.

Learner as negotiator

The notion that learners function as negotiators has figured prominently in those branches of SLA that treat L2 acquisition as a social phenomenon. Reference to 'negotiation' was found in Kasper, Long, Norton Peirce, Pica and Swain, although the precise meaning attributed to it varied somewhat, reflecting the particular theoretical orientations of these writers. Kasper talks of learners engaging in 'the joint negotiation of illocutionary goals'. Norton Peirce refers to a learner who 'negotiates a sense of self'. Pica and Long, as might be expected, talk about the 'negotiation of meaning' and how this assists learners to access form. Swain refers to the 'negotiation about form'. What gets negotiated, then, in this metaphor is highly variable.

Apart from what is negotiated, other obvious entailments of the LEARNER AS NEGOTIATOR metaphor are who does the negotiating, how the negotiation takes place and what is accomplished via negotiation. In SLA, the negotiators are L2 learners (more often than not referred to as 'non-native speakers') interacting with either other learners or with native speakers. Researchers commonly speak of 'joint negotiation', thus emphasizing the collaborative nature of negotiation. Negotiation is not something that is done to learners but rather something that they do themselves with others. As Long puts it, it involves 'work'.

The way in which negotiation takes place is itself conceptualized metaphorically, particularly by Pica. In her review article, she views negotiation at one time or another as a 'commodity' ('negotiation appears to be a powerful commodity'), as some kind of container out of which linguistic information can be 'extracted' and as some kind of machine equipped with an 'indicator', 'signal' and 'trigger'. Similar terms are found in Long. A more pervasive metaphor in Pica's article (but not Long's) is of negotiation as a journey down a river or along a road. She talks of 'the flow of interaction', 'longer stretches of input', 'the smooth flow of an even exchange'. On this journey the travellers can be 'rerouted by a new topic' and experience 'breakdowns' which need to be 'repaired'. Pica, then, seems to vary between viewing negotiation as an object, reflecting perhaps the chunks of transcribed conversation that serve as her data, and as a process that is accomplished through 'work'. Long more consistently treats negotiation as involving 'work' in 'repairing the discourse'.

What is achieved by negotiation varies according to the purpose of the negotiation. Thus, in Norton Peirce, learners negotiate identities they feel comfortable with and in Swain they negotiate an understanding of how a grammatical form works. In the case of Long and Pica, negotiation has two outcomes. It is the means by which learners can successfully comprehend others and it is a means by which they come to attend to particular grammatical properties of the input. Negotiation in interactionist theories of the kind Long and Pica adhere to serves to provide input for the acquisition machine to work on.

Clearly, the LEARNER AS NEGOTIATOR metaphor puts the learner in a much more active role than the two previous metaphors. Moreover, contrary to Firth and Wagner's (1997) claim that SLA has characterized learners as defective communicators, this metaphor, potentially at least, treats the learner as someone who contributes equally to the process of making meaning in an L2. However, the LEARNER AS NEGOTIATOR metaphor is probably best seen not as an alternative to the LEARNER AS CONTAINER and LEARNER AS

MACHINE metaphors. Rather, it is complementary and, in some cases, even ancillary to them, for as we have seen, negotiation serves as the means by which 'data' becomes available for the learner's internal mechanisms to work on.

Learner as problem-solver

It is perhaps not so surprising that another very common metaphor is that of the LEARNER AS PROBLEM-SOLVER. It was prominent in Corder, Long, Pica, Schmidt and Swain. In this respect, researchers are perhaps creating learners in their own image. Just as they seek to solve problems *about* learning so learners solve problems *in order to* learn.

The entailments of this metaphor concern (1) what the problem consists of and (2) how the problem can be solved. In fact, (1) is often specified very generally as 'difficulties' (Corder), 'communicative trouble' (Long), 'linguistic limitations' (Swain), 'a linguistic problem' (Swain), 'difficulties in producing' (Swain) and 'noticing target language forms' (Pica). Schmidt refers to two general problems: the 'matching problem' (i.e., the problem of identifying how output differs from input) and 'the problem of control' (i.e., the problem learners face in accessing and using what they know).

The methods by which learners can solve their learning problems are dealt with more fully. The learner is frequently seen as a kind of scientific investigator who tests out hypotheses. Thus Corder talks of the learners 'investigating the systems of the new language' by 'testing hypotheses'. Long refers to the learners' use of 'positive' and 'negative evidence', terms that have become widely used in SLA. Pica also sees learners as 'discovering rules through hypothesis testing'. In general, these authors are neutral as to whether an obvious entailment of the LEARNER AS HYPOTHESIS-TESTER metaphor applies, namely that the process of testing hypotheses is intentional and conscious. However, Schmidt talks of 'forming and testing *conscious* hypotheses, while Swain argues that learners' hypothesis-testing is both implicit ('output as the hypothesis itself') and explicit as when learners consciously identify linguistic problems and seek solutions.

The LEARNER AS PROBLEM-SOLVER metaphor also entails the notion of the actions that the learner performs to solve a problem. As Swain notes, 'to test a hypothesis learners need to do something'. Here, of course, is where the idea of 'strategies' fits in. In fact, the literature on learner strategies typically views them as means for solving problems, either of communication or learning (see, for example, Færch and Kasper, 1983; Oxford, 1990; Chamot in Chapter 2 and Wenden in Chapter 3 of this book).

It is also possible to see current ideas about the role of 'noticing' in SLA as an extension of the LEARNER AS PROBLEM-SOLVER metaphor. Swain, for example, talks about 'noticing a problem'. The metaphorical nature of the idea of 'noticing' is evident in the fact that it commonly appears in citation form in the texts. Noticing can be seen as an action performed by learners that enables them both to construct new hypotheses and to test them out ('noticing-the-gap'). These references to 'noticing' might also be seen as belonging to the very general metaphor, SEEING IS KNOWING (see Lakoff and Turner, 1989). Schmidt, for example, talks of 'not only hearing a grammatical marker but also "noticing" it' (1994: 17). The 'problem' of how to get learners to notice linguistic features in the input is what motivates current work on focus-on-form in L2 classrooms (see, for example, Doughty and Williams, 1998).

The LEARNER AS PROBLEM-SOLVER metaphor casts learners in a very different light from the first two metaphors we considered. It positions them as cognitively active in shaping both what they learn and how they learn it. It credits learners with agency. Also, it potentially acknowledges learner differences both with regard to what particular problems individual learners choose to focus on and how they set about solving them.

Learner as builder

Learners 'construct' and 'restructure' their interlanguages. They engage in 'syntax building' (Pica); they 'build syntactically' (Long). The metaphor of the LEARNER AS BUILDER is a common one in SLA but it remains relatively undeveloped. The obvious entailments are the materials and tools a builder works with and the kinds of buildings that get constructed, but with one exception these go unmentioned. The exception is Swain when she draws on sociocultural theory (e.g., Vygotsky, 1986) to explain how learners arrive at a metalinguistic understanding of grammatical rules in the course of carrying out communicative tasks. Here she resorts to the metaphor of 'scaffolding'. This metaphor is central to the Vygotskyan notion of inter-mental activity as a source of intra-mental consciousness. Swain, borrowing from Vygotskyan vocabulary, talks of 'the construction of co-knowledge' which is achieved by means of the 'collective scaffolding' that arises out of interaction. One learner offers another 'scaffolded help'.

It is somewhat surprising that the LEARNER AS BUILDER metaphor remains so under-represented in SLA. It would seem capable of representing some of the key features of L2 acquisition – the developmental aspects of interlanguage, the active contribution of the learner, the importance of technical skills, the need for support, etc. The LEARNER AS BUILDER metaphor would in many ways seem better suited to conveying what SLA has found out about the way people acquire a language than the more fully developed LEARNER AS CONTAINER and LEARNER AS MACHINE metaphors. The LEARNER AS BUILDER metaphor may have failed to mature because it is not a favourite in the primary source disciplines of SLA – generative linguistics and cognitive psychology.

Learner as struggler

The analysis concludes with two metaphors found only in Norton Peirce. The Norton Peirce article was included because of the wish to include at least one article that directly addressed how learners acquire an L2 and yet lay outside the mainstream of SLA. It was anticipated that the critical social perspective that Norton Peirce espouses would be reflected in the metaphors she works with. Indeed it is.

Norton Peirce exploits the LEARNER AS STRUGGLER metaphor fully. English, the target language of the learners she was investigating, becomes 'a means of defence'. The social contexts in which the learners find themselves are 'sites of struggle'. The learners have rights ('the right to speak') which they need to defend. To do so they must be prepared to show 'resistance to inequitable forces' and find ways of 'resisting the subject position' they are often assigned in communication with native speakers. They must be prepared to 'challenge and transform social practices'. Furthermore, taking on the role of fighter is no easy option; learners need 'courage'.

Norton Peirce is, of course, talking about immigrant learners who face the need to learn an L2 to survive. The LEARNER AS STRUGGLER metaphor seems particular appropriate for such learners but it may be less well-suited to many classroom learners of foreign languages. This observation suggests that we may need rather different metaphors to describe the learning experiences of learners in different social contexts. Whereas it may prove possible to identify a number of core metaphors to reflect the universal aspects of L2 acquisition, SLA researchers will also need to employ more specific metaphors to characterize the kinds of learners found in different settings.

Learner as investor

Norton Peirce's other main metaphor is the LEARNER AS INVESTOR. This is also quite substantially exploited. Learners need to make an 'affective investment' in the target language by drawing on their symbolic and material 'resources'. Such investment does not take place in a vacuum but is connected to the 'ongoing production of a language learner's social identity'. Sometimes 'investments may conflict with a desire to speak'.

Norton Peirce's choice of this metaphor is somewhat surprising. The idea that learners are investors seems ironic in the context of an article about the impact that the inequities which learners face in a capitalist society has on acquisition. Is this irony intentional? Or is the metaphor simply borrowed from the literature Norton Peirce draws on (e.g., Bourdieu (1977) makes extensive use of metaphors drawn from the field of economics, such as 'cultural capital'). No matter, it is a powerful metaphor, capturing the ideas of sacrifice and risk learners must face as well as the idea of the benefits that accrue when they are successful. Unlike the LEARNER AS STRUGGLER metaphor, this metaphor may be universally applicable.

The basic metaphors so far described are, of course, not the only metaphors evident in the corpora. A multitude of metaphors occur, some quite idiosyncratic. For example, Swain, whose style of writing proved to be particularly rich in metaphorical expressions, employs a LEARNER AS CHEAT metaphor ('learners can fake it' and they 'pass themselves off'). Long seems to view the learner's mental representations of the L2 grammar as diseased. Thus he talks of 'overgeneralization from which it is impossible to *recover*', of 'the prognosis for recovery', of 'premature IL stabilization' and, more optimistically, of negative evidence as a 'remedy'. The metaphor is a surprising one given the emphasis SLA in general has attached to recognizing interlanguage systems as natural languages in their own right and errors as tools for learning (see, for example, Corder, 1967). Gregg has a taste for extended metaphors. In his article he draws on chess-playing, digestion and the liver in his analogies. This taste for metaphor sits somewhat uneasily with Gregg's (1993) dismissal of theories in SLA as mere 'metaphors' (i.e., they are not real theories). Krashen employs metaphors to describe the field of SLA itself. He sees this as a kind of competitive game involving 'rival hypotheses' and 'consistent winners'.

What then does this analysis show us about how SLA constructs L2 learners? A number of generalizations are possible. The first is the obvious tendency of mainstream SLA to view L2 learners as objects that have learning done to them rather than as agents responsible for their own learning. This is the message conveyed by the dominant LEARNER AS CONTAINER and LEARNER AS MACHINE metaphors. Secondly, some metaphors that are apparently very different are, in fact, compatible with each other. For example, the LEARNER AS NEGOTIATOR metaphor was found to be compatible with the LEARNER AS CONTAINER and LEARNER AS MACHINE metaphors in so far as learners do not negotiate learning but can negotiate the data they need for learning. This is reflected textually in the interweaving of one set of metaphors with another to produce quite complex patterns, as in Pica's and Long's articles. Thirdly, it is also clear that some of the metaphors in use in SLA are conflictual. Thus, the same researchers can conceive the learner as a passive (or even sick) object and as an active investigator forming and testing hypotheses. The obvious question arises as to how a learner can be at one and the same time a container or a machine and a problem-solver. SLA researchers failed to explain this paradox – in fact, they have not even addressed it. Fourthly, the metaphor analysis has shown that psycholinguistic and social accounts of L2 acquisition are indeed conceptually very different. Thus although Gregg and Norton Peirce share a taste for metaphor as a method of argument, there is an enormous divide in the metaphorical worlds they inhabit. Thus, whereas the psycholinguistic perspective constructs learners as machines who are acted upon, the social perspective views learners as human beings who can function as agents in their own learning. Such different conceptualizations would seem to be irreconcilable. Metaphor analysis, then, may constitute a tool for helping to decide which theories are indeed complementary and which ones are oppositional (see Long, 1993a).

LEARNERS' METAPHORICAL CONSTRUCTIONS OF THEMSELVES

In order to investigate how learners construct themselves metaphorically as language learners the diaries kept by six adult learners of German as a foreign language in two tertiary colleges in London were analysed. The learners were enrolled in intensive *ab initio* courses designed to develop a high level of proficiency within one academic year. At the end of the year the learners were able to choose whether they wished to continue with or drop German. Four of the learners were female and two male. Two of them were bilingual (English and Spanish), another spoke Creole French as her native language, while the other three were native speakers of English. All six learners were complete beginners of German.

The learners were members of a group of thirty-nine learners, who were part of a larger study of classroom language learning (see Ellis and Rathbone, 1987). Five of the learners were chosen as diarists because they evinced a positive attitude to learning German (as shown in their responses to a pre-course questionnaire) and because they expressed an interest in keeping a journal. The sixth learner (Monique) volunteered.

The six learners were asked to keep a journal of their reactions to the course, their teachers, their fellow-students and any other factors which they considered were having an effect on their language learning. They were issued with an exercise book and a set of guidelines about how to keep their journals and what to look out for and were assured that their journals would be treated in full confidentiality. The diaries were collected in at regular intervals for photocopying and then returned immediately to the learners. They wrote their journals for approximately seven months.

The analysis of the diaries was carried out using the same procedure as that for the research articles. It resulted in the identification of five main metaphors. In the discussion of these metaphors, the learners will be referred to using fictitious names.

Learner as sufferer

Five of the learners referred to learning as suffering in the sense of experiencing anxiety, pain or hardship. They used a variety of metaphorical expressions to do so. Maria talks of her brain being 'wrecked' while at another time she says she was 'literally pulled to pieces'. Monique found herself frequently 'quite at a loss', 'panicked', 'trapped' and 'bemused'. Robert was 'swamped' and frequently 'not comfortable'. Caroline talks of the 'pressure' which she found 'almost too much to bear' and comments that she has been 'pushed too hard'. Manuel found 'the whole experience a shock to the system' and also refers frequently to 'pressures'. Only Maggie did not seem to suffer. In contrast, she refers to her learning experience as a 'comfortable' and 'relaxed' one.

The agents and instruments of this suffering are varied. Sometimes it is the teachers who go too fast, make fun of their students, ask questions of them in class, or set too much homework. More often, however, it is the learners' sense of not being able to understand a grammar point, not being able to do a learning activity, a failure to remember vocabulary or a poor performance on a test. With some learners, Monique and Caroline in particular, it was the conviction that they were not as good as the other students in their class.

The LEARNER AS SUFFERER metaphor emphasizes a dimension of language learning which is clearly very salient and important to language learners – the affective dimension. Learners think of their learning experiences in terms of how they feel in class and, more generally, how they feel they are coping. In this respect, then, the metaphorical analysis supports the findings of previous diary studies which emphasize affective factors such as anxiety and competitiveness (see Bailey, 1983). What the metaphorical analysis revealed is the intensity of the inhibitive feelings that are often aroused.

Learner as problem-solver

All six learners saw learning German as a problem or a puzzle to be tackled and overcome. Maria sees language learning as a 'test', talks of 'obstacles' to her progress and of 'mental blocks'. Monique refers to the need to 'decipher' the language. Maggie is concerned that German is 'illogical' and therefore 'confusing'. Robert had 'grammatical problems'. Caroline sometimes found German 'really confusing'. Like Maria, Manuel experienced 'mental blocks' and struggled to discover 'how German works'.

The learners also all had ways of talking about their success in overcoming their problems. They struggled to 'get to grips' with a problem, they 'sorted out' things, they 'grasped' something or 'got the hang of' something that was difficult for them, they 'cracked' a problem. Sometimes, however, problems seemed to solve themselves. As Manuel put it, 'words are beginning to fall into place'. 'I'm beginning to click into how German works', he comments. Caroline talks of a grammar rule 'starting to come naturally'. In general, though, solving problems needed conscious application and perseverance.

The main problem for these learners was grammar. In part, this was because the course they were taking was quite traditional in emphasizing explicit grammatical explanation, but also it seems to reflect the learners' preferred orientation. They all felt a strong need to understand how the grammar of German worked. They all refer to quite specific areas of grammar – such as prepositions, cases, verb tenses and word order rules – and displayed considerable metalinguistic knowledge. All of these learners worked with the assumption that consciously knowing a grammatical rule was a necessary part of language learning.

Whereas the LEARNER AS SUFFERER metaphor emphasizes the affective dimension of language learning, the LEARNER AS PROBLEM-SOLVER metaphor views learning as a cognitive challenge. These two aspects are related; the problems of understanding how German worked was a major source of suffering for these learners.

Learner as traveller

All the learners except Maggie view learning German as a kind of journey or voyage. Manifestations of this metaphor are in fact extremely common in the journals. Maria, for example, talks of 'sailing through' a lesson, of having 'shot off in the wrong direction' and, at another time of 'being miles away'. Robert, in particular, draws extensively on this metaphor. He refers to 'covering a great deal of ground', 'catching up', 'not being able to keep up', 'lagging behind', 'being left behind' and 'grinding to a halt'. Manuel, too, uses the metaphor to describe his sense of lack of progress: 'I'm not getting anywhere', he wrote. In contrast, Caroline, uses it to refer to her own sense of success. 'I'm getting there', she writes at the end of the first term. Several learners refer to the speed of the journey. For example, Manuel complains 'we have been going too fast'. In referring to lessons where students who have been absent suddenly reappear, Caroline says 'the pace slows down when they decide to turn-up so they can catch up'. This metaphor clearly affords a rich number of entailments which learners can exploit to refer to different aspects of the learning process. The learners in this study used it to refer to their own ability as learners, their sense of progress or lack of it through the teaching syllabus, their speed of learning, their misunderstandings, the students they are learning with (fellow travellers) and barriers to learning. The LEARNER AS TRAVELLER metaphor can be seen as an adjunct of the more general LIFE IS A JOURNEY metaphor, which Lakoff and Turner (1989) claim is one of the major ways in which we conceptualize goal-oriented behaviour.

Learner as struggler

Three of the learners employ this metaphor. Mostly, the references are not so much to what they do as to what is done to them, however. For example, Manuel talks of his 'pride being bashed'. He writes about 'the injuries that learning German caused me'. Referring to a particular lesson, Robert complains that he 'got grilled' by being 'bombarded with questions'. Caroline stubbornly insists 'I'm not going to be defeated'. Thus, the learners see themselves as fighters who 'struggle' to stave off 'injuries' and 'defeat'. In this respect, the ground of this metaphor is similar to that of the LEARNER AS SUFFERER metaphor.

Learner as worker

Two of the learners make use of the LEARNER AS WORKER metaphor. Maria talks about the 'extra work' she put in 'paying off'. She sees the teacher as a kind of boss who 'pushes' the students to their 'limits'. Caroline also sees learning a language as work. She notes that her sense of competing with other students obliged her to work harder, that for her 'work is very important', and sadly, when she eventually decided that she would not continue with German that there was 'no point in working hard anymore'.

However, this metaphor is not fully exploited by even those learners who employ it. It seems to be used to refer to the idea of self-directed effort in learning and as such is clearly closely related to the technical construct of motivation (which the learners never refer to directly). Potential entailments,

Table 4.2   Basic metaphors occurring in the learners' journals

Learner	Metaphors				
	1	**2**	**3**	**4**	**5**
Maria	*	*	*		*
Monique	*	*	*		
Maggie		*			
Robert	*	*	*	*	
Caroline	*	*	*	*	*
Manuel	*	*	*	*	

Key to metaphors:
1. LEARNER AS SUFFERER
2. LEARNER AS PROBLEM-SOLVER
3. LEARNER AS TRAVELLER
4. LEARNER AS STRUGGLER
5. LEARNER AS WORKER

like different kinds of work, work tasks, work positions, salary, promotion, are not referred to at all or are exploited only weakly.

A summary of the distribution of the five basic metaphors in the learners' journals can be found in Table 4.2. Other metaphors also figure in the journals of individual learners. Two of the learners make passing use of the LEARNER AS MACHINE metaphor. Interestingly, though, they refer to their own agency in relation to the machine – 'I switched off totally' – which contrasts with the view taken by the researchers. Monique sees learning in terms of a harvest metaphor – she talks of 'reaping the seeds' of her studies during the vacation. Three of the learners make occasional metaphorical reference to the idea of learners as risk-takers. Monique talks of how she 'adventured' into using new vocabulary. Maggie talks about how she believes she should volunteer in class even if it means 'making an idiot' of herself. The image schema metaphor of 'up an down' is used by Manuel to describe the changes in his affective orientation to learning German. In general, however, the metaphorical expressions found in the six journals belonged to the five main metaphors described above.

   Two general points can be made about the learners' choice of metaphors. First, most of the metaphors characterize the learners as agents in their own learning (the LEARNER AS PROBLEM-SOLVER, LEARNER AS TRAVEL-LER and LEARNER AS WORKER metaphors) but there are also metaphors which construct them as patients who undergo experiences of which they have no control (the LEARNER AS SUFFERER and LEARNER AS STRUG-GLER metaphors). Thus, although the learners in this study learned in what were by and large very teacher-centred classrooms (i.e., the interactions were teacher controlled, with little opportunity for small-group work), they constructed themselves as self- as well as other-directed. They knew the journey was mapped out for them but they also knew they had to make it themselves. Interestingly, they are as critical of themselves as learners as they are of their teachers. Secondly, the metaphors show the learners' awareness of the two dimensions of learning – the affective and the cognitive – and of the relationship between the two. They were very aware of their feelings and how these affected their progress. They were also constantly monitoring their conscious understanding of how German worked as a language.

CONCLUSION

To summarize, this study has examined the metaphors used by SLA researchers in a number of key publications and those used by adult classroom learners of L2 German in their diaries. The dominant researcher metaphors were those of the LEARNER AS CONTAINER and the LEARNER AS MACHINE. In contrast, the dominant metaphors in the learner diaries were the LEARNER AS SUFFERER, the LEARNER AS PROBLEM-SOLVER and the LEARNER AS TRAVELLER. There were two metaphors in common – the LEARNER AS PROBLEM-SOLVER and LEARNER AS STRUGGLER – although only one researcher (Norton Peirce) employed the latter. There were also a number of less widely used metaphors that were specific to the researchers and the learners (e.g., LEARNER AS NEGOTIATOR was used by the researchers and LEARNER AS TRAVELLER by the learners).

Two questions arise out of this study. The first is to what extent the metaphorical constructions of researchers and learners are the same or different. The second is whether metaphorical analysis of the kind I have employed is a useful addition to the tools available for SLA research.

How similar are the metaphorical researchers' and learners' constructions of L2 learning? One similarity is that both researchers and learners view language learners as problem-solvers; both see learners as 'discovering' the rules of the grammar. However, whereas most of the researchers generally viewed this discovery as an automatic and unconscious process, all the learners conceptualized it as a highly conscious mental activity. The other similarity is more apparent than real – the learners saw learning as a struggle, a view that just one of the researchers (Norton Peirce) shared. Overall, it is the differences between the researchers and the learners that are apparent. Mainstream SLA, as Kramsch and Lantolf have pointed out, constructs the process of language acquisition mechanistically – something that is seen to happen automatically when the right conditions prevail. It depicts learners as containers and as machines who are acted on by data with little acknowledgement of the role of human ideation and affective states in learning. In contrast, the six adult learners constructed themselves primarily as sentient beings who experienced fear, frustration and sometimes personal gratification as they struggled to learn German. They saw themselves as travellers on a long journey, coping with the affective and cognitive problems that confronted them. The journey was mapped out for them but they are the ones that must make it and in this respect they were the agents of their own learning. Perhaps the researcher construction of learners that most closely matches that of the learners themselves is Norton Peirce's. However, Norton Peirce was more concerned with the social identity of learners and there is no evidence that the classroom learners showed much concern for this. What Norton Peirce's and the learners' visions do share is a sense of the importance of learners' agency in their learning.

Of course, these differences may not matter. Researchers and learners have different agendas – learners to learn and researchers to describe and explain learning. At the very least, however, information about the ways in which learners conceptualize language learning constitutes one kind of data that researchers would do well to consider. As Block (1997) has pointed out, 'listening to learners' should be an essential part of both teaching and research. In the previous chapter, Wenden revealed how learners' metacognitive knowledge guides how they work during learning. Minimally, accessing learner perceptions can therefore lead to a greater awareness of how learners think and, maximally, it can result in changes in research practices. One such change might be to pay more attention to the metacognitions of learners, as revealed through metaphor analysis. Oxford's account, in the following chapter, of learners' metaphorical constructions of their teachers is an example of this. It is less clear, however, that learners have much to gain by 'listening to researchers'. To do so would entail viewing themselves as containers or machines! However, there may be more benefit if learners are encouraged to see themselves as negotiators and fighters, as Norton Peirce proposes. Making learners aware of the metaphors they use to conceptualize their learning may be one way of increasing their control over learning.

How useful is metaphorical analysis as a methodological tool? Koch and Deetz (1981) claim that 'by isolating the predominant metaphors and their entailments, the current reality and conceptions of the members of an organization can be described in varying degrees of detail' (1981: 13). The analyses reported in this chapter go some way to demonstrating the validity of this claim. It has proved possible to identify the main metaphors used by both SLA researchers and a group of L2 learners and to show how these metaphors reveal the underlying conceptualizations of the worlds they inhabit. The main doubts, however, centre not so much on validity, although as Steen (1994) rightly points out, analysis cannot demonstrate that linguistic metaphors have a conceptual basis in the minds of the people, as on reliability, an issue not discussed by Koch and Deetz. The key procedure in metaphor analysis is the identification of metaphorical expressions in a text. How can researchers ensure that this is done accurately and comprehensively? Accuracy is a special problem given the difficulty in distinguishing between metaphorical and polysemous usage. Comprehensiveness may be more easily managed, perhaps by means of the techniques employed in corpus linguistics, as suggested by Deignan (1999). Ultimately, though, reliability may have to be established as in other types of interpretative research – through extensive illustration and through replication.

Another question of some importance concerns the extent to which metaphorical worlds vary culturally. It is to be expected, perhaps, that researchers who belong to different 'discourse communities' (Swales, 1990) will employ different metaphors. The preceding analysis has demonstrated this (compare, for example, the metaphors of Long and Norton Peirce). As noted earlier, metaphor analysis may serve as a tool for identifying theories that are complementary and those that are conflictual. Do learners also vary in their choice of metaphor? In general, the learners investigated here shared the same metaphors, even though they came from very different cultural and learning backgrounds. The LEARNER AS TRAVELLER metaphor has also been reported in studies of Japanese learners of English (Cortazzi and Jin, 1999). It is likely, however, that differences will emerge in the metaphors used by classroom and naturalistic learners. Variation in choice of metaphor is obviously an issue in need of further study.

Irrespective of the methodological problems that applied metaphor analysts face, it is likely that metaphor analysis will figure more strongly in future research. At the very least, it serves as an important consciousness-raising tool, encouraging researchers and learners alike to examine their constructions critically and, perhaps, to modify them.

Chapter 5

'The bleached bones of a story': learners' constructions of language teachers

Rebecca L. Oxford, Teachers College, Columbia University, New York

INTRODUCTION

In her award-winning 1997 novel, *The God of Small Things*, Arundathi Roy spoke of 'Little events, ordinary things . . . imbued with new meaning. Suddenly they become the bleached bones of a story.' This chapter shares little events, ordinary things about language teachers in stories written by students. Sometimes the bones – the people and events depicted in a student's tale – show harmony of line and arrangement. Occasionally the bones lie in jarring, grating disarray, telling a story that gives us pause as we come close. In some of the narratives, the 'story-bones' form intricate patterns, while in others they are as sparse and lean as lines on a Celtic rune. In every case, the story offers us insight into the learner's understandings or constructions of the language teacher.

Why is it important to know what learners think or believe about their language teachers? Students, like all other individuals, create their own constructions of the world through social interaction (Vygotsky, 1956, 1978, 1987; Williams and Burden, 1997). One of the most intense and important forms of social interaction occurs between teacher and student. How the student perceives and constructs that interaction has a direct influence on learning (Beebe and Butland, 1994; Ehrman and Dörnyei, 1998; Oxford et al., 1998). The significant trend towards learner-centredness in language instruction (Ehrman, 1996; Magnan, 1990; Nunan, 1988; Tudor, 1996 *inter alia*) and in education in general (Hargreaves, 1996; McCombs and Whistler, 1997) supports the need to understand learners' constructions of, and engagement with, language teachers.

Beyond these abstract reasons, the best justification for exploring learners' constructions of their language teachers comes from the students themselves. In the investigation reported here, students revealed that teachers strongly influenced their lives. The comment made by Jenny, a US high school student, typified the viewpoint of many learners in this study: 'I wish that teachers could realize what an impact they have on our lives.' Many of the effects were positive, as witnessed by the remarks of Tamer and Christopher. Tamer, an Egyptian teaching candidate in English as a foreign language (EFL), wrote, 'He [the English teacher] became like water . . . and without it we will die.' 'You have made all the difference in the world to me', wrote Christopher, a master's degree student who now teaches EFL in Turkey. However, some of the influences were negative. Reflecting on harrowing experiences with a witch-like high school Spanish teacher, Jayla commented, 'Now I don't remember a single thing Ms. __ taught me. The worst part is, this woman is still allowed to cast her horrid lesson plans upon unsuspecting children.' We need to know what it is about language teachers and about teacher–student relationships – which 'little events, ordinary things' cause such powerful reactions in students.

Fascinated by questions about learners' responses to, and interactions with, their teachers and the possible effects of these upon language learning, I began to collect written narrative case studies from current and former language learners as early as 1991. As a professor of undergraduate and graduate courses in Foreign Language Teaching Methods, masters' degree courses in Teaching English to Speakers of Other Languages, and doctoral courses in Social and Psychological Factors in Teaching, I gradually gathered 162 such narratives. In subsequent years, other researchers joined me in the quest (see Acknowledgements at the end of this chapter for details), bringing the current total of narratives to 473.

The key questions of the present chapter are:

- What do learners' written narratives reveal about learners' constructions of their language teachers?
- What major themes arise in these narratives?
- How do learners emotionally respond to their language teachers?
- What theories and implications can be drawn?

THEORETICAL AND RESEARCH FRAMEWORK:
TEACHING APPROACHES

Table 5.1 identifies three major teaching approaches. The *autocratic approach* puts total power in the hands of the teacher and demonstrates large social distance. The *democratic/participatory approach* involves power shared between the teacher and the students and allows the intimacy of the 'learning alliance' to develop (Ehrman and Dörnyei, 1998; Wool, 1989). The *laissez-faire approach*, which embodies the exercise of little teacher power and enables still less student power, typically sets students adrift in confusion and shows no teacher–student intimacy. It is important not to confuse the laissez-faire approach with learner–centred teaching or autonomous learning. It is the democratic/ participatory approach, not the laissez-faire approach, that emphasizes learner-centredness and has the potential for learner autonomy (Nunan, 1988, 1999; Scarcella and Oxford, 1992; Tudor, 1996 *inter alia*). In contrast to the democratic/participatory approach, the laissez-faire approach does not centre on the learner, nor does it give the learner any real control.

Table 5.1   Three major teaching approaches*

- **Autocratic approach** – reflects strong teacher power relying on official position, coercion/punishment/threats, extrinsic rewards (manipulative, such as bribes or flattery, or non-manipulative), task-control, or some combination; can be useful for some forms of fact-learning. Might or might not involve malice on the part of the teacher. A basic belief is that students are not to be trusted. In some western studies, the autocratic approach increases time-on-task in the teacher's presence, dependency (work stops when the teacher leaves), hostility, aggression and competition. Intimacy is low.
- **Democratic/participatory approach** – reflects shared teacher–student power relying on mutual respect and expertise; allows learners to participate in decisions about curriculum and how it is taught, encourages students to take responsibility for learning and move towards autonomy, and recognizes individual differences in learning styles and interests; involves intrinsic rewards, not just extrinsic. Is sometimes called learner-centred teaching. Democratic/participatory approach often results in superior work, but this could be culture-bound. Intimacy is moderate to high.
- **Laissez-faire approach** – shows little or no direct teacher power, with none granted to learners. Teacher is psychologically or physically absent, and learners are left without mechanisms or guidance to help them assume responsibility. Despite this, some learners create their own strategies and counter-cultures for academic survival. Laissez-faire approach often results in poor learning, high stress and low group cohesion. Intimacy is low.

*There are differences in the acceptability of each learning approach in various cultures.

Source: Partly drawn from Ehrman and Dornyei (1998); Johnson et al. (1996); Lewin et al. (1939); Oxford et al. (1998); Woolfolk et al. (1990), and elaborated by the present author.

Early research in the USA – not necessarily generalizable to all cultures – demonstrated that an authoritarian teaching approach provoked hostility and aggression. Students' hostility was thirty times higher under an authoritarian teacher than under a democratic/participatory teacher, while aggression was eight times higher (Lewin et al., 1939, cited in Ehrman and Dörnyei, 1998). In the same study, an authoritarian teaching approach increased students' dedication to work while the teacher was present. This autocratic mode increased competition and dependency and did not result in excellent work by students. In contrast, the democratic/participatory approach produced superior student work. The laissez-faire approach resulted in the least learning, the least group cohesion and the most stress. (In this study, students did not directly resist any of the situations in which they were placed, but the students in the autocratic situation quit working when their teacher left the room – a form of indirect resistance.)

Research has also highlighted essential features of 'good teaching' as interpreted in the western cultural context. McCombs and Whistler (1997) reviewed educational studies going back to the 1920s. These investigators found that concern for students' specific needs is one of the most essential qualities of a good teacher. Other features of good teaching in the western context include demonstrating interest and enthusiasm about the subject, explaining it in clear and interesting ways, stimulating curiosity, being concerned and available, providing obvious structure and organization and offering useful feedback (McCombs and Whistler, 1997).

Oser, Dick and Patry (1992) conducted a tri-cultural study of expert elementary school teachers in New York, London and Vienna. Results showed that such teachers shared certain self-images. The teachers saw themselves as valuing their personal caring and moral responsibility more than their knowledge and competent presentation of the subject matter. 'It is clear that the large majority of them see themselves as *caring* individuals . . . [and show] an attitude of taking moral responsibility for their students' (Oser et al., 1992: 285, original emphasis). In addition, these expert instructors:

> [R]evealed themselves as optimistic, outreaching, loving personalities, interested in children and concerned about their needs, able and happy in relating with them and willing to put in any amount of time and effort necessary to make a success of this. Furthermore, the expert teachers had a firm picture of what they wanted the individual learners to achieve academically and in social and personality growth . . . [T]he teachers were able and eager to produce . . . a 'powerful learning environment,' fashioning the standardized curriculum to the requirements of their pupils.   (Oser et al., 1992: 288)

Despite some differences in emphasis, expert teachers in the three cultures revealed a great many similarities. The researchers were careful not to generalize beyond the western cultural tradition.

Hofstede (1986, 1991) applied a four-dimensional model of cultural differences to the teaching–learning environments in countries around the world. The dimensions included:

- *small vs large power distance,* or the extent to which less powerful people in a society accept inequality in power and consider it normal;
- *acceptance vs avoidance of uncertainty,* with greater avoidance of uncertainty being related to greater need for formal rules, consensus and structure;
- *individualism vs collectivism,* or whether one perceives one's primary responsibility to the self or to the group; and
- *assertiveness/advancement/success vs nurturance/human relations/quality of life.* (Hofstede summarized this dimension as *masculinity vs. femininity,* but that label seems unduly stereotypic.)

Hofstede assigned each of 53 countries an index score on each of the four dimensions. His correlational data (1991) showed that in large power distance countries, teachers were treated with great respect, and respect increased as teachers became older. Classrooms showed strict order and the teacher initiated all communication. In small power distance countries, teachers treated students in a more egalitarian way and younger teachers were preferred over older ones. Students from uncertainty-avoidance countries favoured structured, precise teaching assignments and teachers who were viewed as experts. Students from countries that accepted uncertainty liked open-ended learning situations and did not mind their teachers saying, 'I don't know'. In classrooms in collectivist countries, harmony and 'face' were primary values, while in classrooms in individualist countries, differing points of view were encouraged and 'face' was of minimal concern. Students in assertiveness-oriented countries focused on competition, status and instrumental motivation, while students in nurturance-oriented countries demonstrated mutual solidarity, friendliness and intrinsic motivation. Therefore, culture strongly influences the form in which teaching and learning generally occur in any given country, although individuals might differ from the general cultural patterns in a given country. The above remarks have concerned teachers and teaching in general. The next segment discusses existing constructions of language teachers.

Existing constructions concerning language teachers

Appendix 5.1 illustrates that many contrasting constructions exist concerning language teachers. These constructions are drawn from a variety of sources, such as:

- narrative case studies (e.g., Block, 1992; Cortazzi and Jin, 1996; Katz, 1996; Oxford, 1999);
- statements about various language teaching methods and approaches (e.g., Herron, 1982; Krashen and Terrell, 1983; O'Malley and Chamot, 1990; Scarcella and Oxford, 1992; Stevick, 1980, 1990);
- commentary about teachers' sometimes fetishistic responses to, and participation in, constantly changing methodological fads (e.g., Brown, 1994; Clarke, 1982; Kumaravadivelu, 1994; Maley, 1984; Pennycook, 1989); and
- descriptions of language teachers' roles in the classroom context (e.g., Breen, 1985, 1996; Breen and Candlin, 1980; Dörnyei, 1994; Dubin and Olshtain, 1986; Ehrman and Dörnyei, 1998; Kramsch, 1993; Nunan, 1992; Oxford, 1990; Rivers and Temperley, 1978 in Block, 1992).

Many constructions concerning language teachers are metaphorical in nature. Metaphors can create new understandings of a phenomenon. They are seen as so significant that writers have entitled their works *Metaphors We Live By* (Lakoff and Johnson, 1980), 'Metaphors we teach and learn by' (Block, 1992), and 'Metaphors we work by' (Thornbury, 1991). Cameron and Low (1999) have devoted an entire book to the research and application of metaphors in the field of applied linguistics. In one sense, all language is metaphorical in that 'Language works by means of transference from one kind of reality to another. It is thus essentially rather than incidentally or decoratively or even illegitimately – metaphorical' (Taylor, 1984: 8). However, this chapter uses the more constrained definition of metaphor as 'any comparison that cannot be taken literally' (Bartel, 1983: 3) or a figure of speech in which a name or quality is attributed to something to which it is not fully applicable.

Humanistic approaches to language teaching (e.g., Suggestopedia, Community Language Learning, and the Silent Way) have produced some of the most colourful metaphors about language teachers. These include therapist, loving parent, infantilizer, gardener, suggestor, liberator, facilitator, reflective listener, assistant to students in bursting cocoons and nurturer of souls (Atkinson, 1989; Stevick, 1980, 1990; Underhill, 1989). Humanistic educator

Charles Curran (1972), who strongly influenced the creation of Community Language Learning, asserted that teachers are not gods, must 'give up the god-project', and must serve the learner as knower-counsellors. In his 'insem-inational model', Curran (1972) pictured the teacher as the inseminator who passes 'living knowledge' to the learner via 'mutual "love"' (Stevick, 1980: 109). Similarly, humanistic teacher Ashton-Warner (1963) depicted herself as a spouse or lover of her students ('When I teach people I marry them. . . . All the rules of love-making apply to these spiritual and intellectual fusions').

The social context of the classroom – often neglected by researchers, as pointed out by Breen (1985) – has also spawned a number of eloquent meta-phorical constructions concerning language teachers. For instance, Breen (1985) envisioned language teachers, along with their students, as inhabitants of intric-ately complex 'coral gardens' (a metaphor for the cultural significance of the classroom), where interrelating linguistic, psychological, social and political influences exist. In a different field – science teaching – one teacher wrote: 'The teaching/learning process is like a symbiotic relationship between corals and the plants that live within them. The plants capture energy from the sun and leak out carbohydrates to nourish the corals' (Gurney, 1995: 571).

Breen (1985) portrayed language teachers, with their students, as joint conspirators in maintaining relatively predictable routines and procedures of the 'surface text' of lessons as part of the classroom culture. Similarly, Kramsch (1993) described language teachers and students as potential prisoners of social expectations in the classroom. However, Kramsch said that domination by the traditional classroom culture is not inevitable. In the classroom, many students conspire against teacher-imposed social expectations:

> The dominant culture of the classroom is constantly contested, avoided, put into question, confronted with linguistically deviant 'minority' cultures. Many learners resist the self-evident and invisible culture teachers try to impose. As observers have abundantly demonstrated . . . learners find the most ingenious ways of playing with schismatic meanings, pretending they do not understand, double-guessing the grammatical exercise, beating the system, sneaking in the forbidden native tongue, creating a counter-culture with foreign sounds and shapes.
> (Kramsch, 1993: 48–9)

As Kramsch demonstrates, descriptions of language learners are also some-times metaphorical. For instance, Ellis, in Chapter 4 of the present volume, discovers conflicting metaphors that researchers have used to describe the learner while, according to Ellis, learners' own constructions of themselves often contrasted with those of researchers.

RESEARCH PROCEDURES AND PERSPECTIVES

The study described here was composed of a series of related sub-investigations taking place in various locales. Similar research procedures and perspectives unified these efforts.

Table 5.2 Summary of participants, institution, native country, participant type, gender and data sources (total = 473)

Group	Number	Institution	Native country/participant type	Gender	Data Sources
A	36	Egyptian teacher training college at a major university in the north of Egypt	All Egyptian teaching candidates in EFL	72% F 28% M	Written essays: 'Describe a language teacher you especially liked (or disliked)'; requirement: must give essay a title, must limit essay to 1 page.
B	80	State university in southeastern US	US born (mixed ethnicities) teaching candidates in ESL, EFL, French, German, Spanish (seeking undergraduate, master's, specialist and doctoral degrees)	60% F 40% M	Written essays: 'Describe a language teacher, past or present, whom you especially liked (or disliked).' 'Describe a particular language teacher with whom you have experienced serious harmony (or conflict).' Anonymous student evaluations of the teacher Unsolicited letters to the teacher Dialogue journals
C	30	State university in southeastern US	US born (mixed ethnicities) teaching candidates in English (as a native language) (seeking undergraduate and master's degrees) and in other fields (seeking doctoral degrees)	70% F 30% M	Written essays same as for Group B
D	20	State university in southeastern US	Language teachers or teaching candidates from Chile, Germany, Egypt, Korea, Japan, Taiwan, People's Republic of China	50% F 50% M	Written essays same as for Group B

E	12	State university in central US	US born (mixed ethnicities) teaching candidates in English (as a native langauge), physical education, social studies, business and art	67% F 33% M	Written essay: 'Describe a language teacher you especially liked (or disliked).'
F	150	State university on east coast of US	Mostly US born, although some born in India, Mexico, Japan and other countries; students enrolled at the time in foreign language courses; 80% were in introductory or intermediate undergraduate courses; 10% were in more advanced undergraduate courses; 10% were graduate teaching assistants in foreign languages	50% F 50% M	Written essays: 'Describe a language teacher with whom you have had a style conflict (or with whom you had style harmony)'.
G	125	High school in southeastern US	Mostly US born (mixed ethnicities), though some foreign exchange students; all were enrolled in English classes (19 in honours English, the balance in regular English)	51% F 49% M	Written essays same as for Group B; added instruction: write another paragraph about why the teacher was the way he or she was, why the situation occurred, and what might have happened differently.
H	32	State university in southeastern US	Iceland, Finland, Bangladesh, Pakistan, India, Japan, Republic of China, People's Republic of China; international teaching assistants, mostly in science, mathematics, and technology	25% F 75% M	Written journal entries about recent US learning experiences compared to learning experiences in the home country (no emphasis on specific teachers).

Note: Approximately 120 of the narratives are presented in the current chapter. These represent well the overall tendencies of the full sample of 473 narratives.

Participants

So far the research has involved 473 participants, each of whom contributed a narrative. Information about the participants' groups, institutions, native country, gender and data sources is summarized in Table 5.2. Participants came from places as diverse as Mexico, Germany, Iceland, Finland, Egypt, Bangladesh, India, Pakistan, Chile, Korea, Japan, the People's Republic of China, Taiwan and the USA. Not all of their narratives could be included in this chapter for reasons of space. A whole volume would be required to report and interpret all the stories in a comprehensive way. However, the results presented in the current chapter represent as clearly as possible the general tendencies of the narratives from all of the participants in the study.

Participants were not chosen to be a representative sample with the aim of systematically generalizing the results to a larger population. Instead they comprised a purposive sample, selected to provide a wide range of constructions about language teachers. A number of participants were current or future teachers of second/foreign languages and wrote about their own language teachers. Participants from other subject fields (in roles such as teaching candidate, teaching assistant or ordinary university student) provided narratives about their second/foreign language teachers. High school participants who had not yet studied a second/foreign language were included if their narratives were about teachers of their native language, English.

Qualitative research using narratives

I recognized early that qualitative research was necessary to capture the richness of learners' constructions concerning their language teachers. Qualitative research is field-focused (uses the classroom rather than controlled laboratory settings), interpretative (tries to explain why), expressive (presents real 'voices' rather than depersonalized language) and detailed (attends to particulars) (Eisner, 1991). Criteria for judging the success of qualitative research include coherence, insight, practical utility, persuasive power and multiple sources (Eisner, 1991).

Narrative case studies (Kelchtermans, 1996; Schulman, 1992; Witherell and Noddings, 1991) were employed here to explore learners' constructions of their language teachers. This approach has been used in the language field to investigate the following:

- learners' perceptions of themselves, their teachers and the language learning process; and
- teachers', student teachers' and teacher developers' constructions of themselves, of students and of the language classroom.

Narrative case studies in language classrooms around the world populate the book by Bailey and Nunan (1996). A few examples of researchers who have used narrative case studies to study language learning and teaching include Bailey (1983), Block (1992, 1996), Ehrman (1996), Oxford (1996b), Oxford and Nam (1997) and Schmidt and Frota (1986).

In narrative case studies, data may come from various sources: essays, diaries, dialogue journals, letters, field observations, ordinary interviews, interviews assisted by video-recall of events, think-aloud procedures, and other forms of verbal report. In the study reported here, four sources of narrative data were used: essays written in response to general instructions, dialogue journal entries, anonymous evaluations of teachers and unsolicited letters to teachers. Table 5.2 above, shows the data sources for each group of participants. I worked collaboratively with others to elicit data from a wider range of learners in many locations than would have been possible if I were the only data gatherer. (See Acknowledgements at the end of this chapter for a list of these colleagues.)

The narratives in the current study have retained their original, sometimes idiosyncratic grammar and spelling. Only in cases where there could be some confusion for readers were any special notations made. These are clearly marked. For example, when *breath* should have been spelled *breathe*, I signified this by using *breath[e]*.

By far the greatest number of narratives were in the form of essays written in response to general instructions. The most commonly used instructions were:

• Describe a language teacher, past or present, you especially liked or disliked.
• Describe a language teacher with whom you have experienced significant harmony or conflict.

In most cases, participants were free to decide whether to focus on the positive or the negative. Researchers avoided giving instructions about using any particular form of expression (e.g., metaphor, literal description, and so forth) in the narratives. No restrictions in length were applied, except with the Egyptian EFL teaching candidates, who were limited to one page. Most participants wrote essays ranging from one to three pages, although some essays were as short as three sentences and others were as long as six single-spaced, typed pages. In all cases, confidentiality was assured. Researchers explicitly told participants that their essays would not affect course grades, teaching candidacy, or any other aspect of academic or professional progress. They encouraged participants to be as open and candid as possible. With several groups, official institutional research-participant agreements were completed and signed by respondents.

A few minor cross-group differences occurred in the essay procedures. The high school participants were given the usual essay instructions but were also asked to add an extra paragraph explaining why they thought the teacher was the way he or she was, why the situation occurred, and what could have been done differently. The Egyptian EFL teaching candidates were asked to provide titles for their essays.

Two kinds of dialogue journal were involved. In one type, US doctoral candidates kept dialogue journals in which they spontaneously commented on specific teachers and class events without any prompting or instructions. In the other type, international teaching assistants received a specific task for their dialogue journals. They were asked to write in their dialogue journals about their experiences with classrooms in the USA as compared to classrooms in their home countries. The journal entries from international teaching assistants, while not about specific teachers, were included because they offered different cultural perspectives.

Undergraduate and graduate students taking various courses at a southeastern US university were required by the university to complete anonymous evaluations of the courses and the professor. The evaluation forms contained mostly closed-ended, quantitative items, but there was space at the bottom of the forms for students to write comments about the teacher. Some students at the same institution, without prompting, wrote letters to their teacher after they had completed their undergraduate or graduate programs. These evaluations and letters offered additional narratives for the present investigation. The evaluations and letters actually concerned a language teaching methodology professor rather than a language teacher.

Analysing/interpreting the narratives

Content analysis (Huberman, 1989, 1993; Miles and Huberman, 1984; Silverman, 1993; Stempel, 1989; Strauss, 1987) was used to analyse and interpret the data. This analysis was a non-linear, highly complex process. 'It is necessary to do detailed, intensive, microscopic examination of the data in order to bring out the amazing complexity of what lies in, behind, and beyond those data' (Strauss, 1987: 10).

I began the study with a theoretical emphasis on learning styles and on 'style wars', my term for conflicts between teachers' instructional styles and students' learning styles. This emphasis was fruitful and produced some intriguing interpretations (e.g., Nam and Oxford, 1998; Oxford, 1996b; Oxford and Lavine, 1991; Oxford et al., 1991; Oxford and Nam, 1997; Wallace and Oxford, 1992). However, theories of learning styles and style conflicts were not expansive enough to explain all of the narrative data that I was continually gathering. Therefore, I moved to a grounded theory approach (Glaser and Strauss, 1967; Strauss, 1987), in which theories or hypotheses arose from the data rather than the data being interpreted in light of a preset theory. Such an approach is based on the concept that

> (T)heory at various levels of generality is indispensible for deeper knowledge of social phenomena . . . [and] that such theory ought to be developed in intimate relation with the data, with researchers fully aware of themselves as instruments for developing that grounded theory.   (Strauss, 1987: 6)

Theory is grounded when it emerges from the data through 'successively evolving interpretations made during the course of the study' (Strauss, 1987: 10). Grounded theory is conceptually dense, with lots of concepts and internal linkages, and it is filtered through researchers' own experiences and understandings as 'experiential data' (Eisner, 1991; Strauss, 1987). The interpretations made in this chapter are examples of grounded theory in action.

The grounded theory mode suggests that researchers necessarily interpret data through the lens of their own experience and values and that this needs to be stated. Therefore, I admit that I have personal and professional biases towards democratic/participatory teaching. I use versions of this approach in all of the instruction I provide, whether it occurs in courses, workshops, speeches, or my own textbooks. However, because of this strong instructional preference, I was constantly vigilant during this study not to over-interpret the data or cast an artificially glowing light on democratic/participatory teaching. I included both positive and negative comments from participants regarding this teaching approach, although in the narratives the positive remarks about this approach were much more frequent than the negative.

I benefited from early discussions with colleagues. For example, El Sayed Dadour offered certain comments about the narratives of the Egyptian EFL teaching candidates. However, all the interpretations presented below are my own, except as otherwise noted. (I take responsibility for any errors in interpretation.)

The first phases of analysis showed that the data could be understood thematically through metaphors about language teachers. The content analysis of the metaphors followed six general steps. These were: (1) choose a representative corpora of texts; (2) isolate metaphorical expressions in texts and list them; (3) decide which metaphors are worth analysing depending on the research purpose; (4) reduce the metaphorical expressions to broader metaphors; (5) sort these metaphors into coherent groups, thereby establishing the 'main metaphors'; and (6) consider possible entailments of each main metaphor and the extent to which these are or are not expressed in the corpora of texts (Koch and Deetz, 1981, cited by Ellis in Chapter 4 of the present volume).

Thus, the metaphors were not pre-established but instead arose through a long-term series of intensive interactions with the narratives. Dozens of narratives were read, re-read, and gradually organized into sets with metaphorical names, such as Teacher as Hanging Judge, Teacher as Nurturer/Inspirer/ Role Model and Teacher as Witch. Many of the metaphors were explicitly mentioned in the narratives, for example, 'the hungry monster who shouted for food'. In such cases, it was very easy to identify and label the metaphor.

However, other metaphors were inferred from the narratives. For instance, if several narratives described (in various ways) language teachers mechanistically pushing to cover all the material in the textbook in the shortest possible time, these comments were taken to imply a concern for factory-like efficiency and therefore led to metaphor of Teacher as Manufacturer. This type of labelling occurred if the students themselves did not use a specific metaphor but if they nevertheless expressed a consistent set of qualities or characteristics of the teacher that pointed towards a particular metaphor. This kind of metaphoric labelling is an interpretative practice used by Block (1992), Munby (1986) and Thornbury (1991).

The narratives and metaphors were then organized into four philosophical orientations towards language teaching: social order, cultural transmission, learner-centred growth and social reform. This early philosophical analysis of representative samples of that portion of the data is reported in Oxford et al. (1998) and is not repeated here.

INTERPRETATIVE FINDINGS

Table 5.3 summarizes the metaphors derived from the student narratives as identified within the three different teaching approaches. The data can be divided into general findings and findings according to the three different teaching approaches. We will consider some of these in more detail, but some general findings include the following:

- The vast majority of the Egyptian EFL teaching candidates employed explicit metaphors, sometimes very sensory in nature, to describe their language teachers. The metaphor of Teacher as Force of Nature (water, sun and food-provider) is a good example. Although other groups employed explicit

Table 5.3   Metaphors representing each teaching approach

AUTOCRATIC TEACHING APPROACH
Teacher as Manufacturer
Teacher as Witch
Teacher as Hanging Judge
Teacher as Tyrant
Teacher as Arrogant Animal or Person
Teacher as Preacher or Moralist
Teacher as Patron
Teacher as Gossip

DEMOCRATIC/PARTICIPATORY TEACHING APPROACH
Teacher as Challenger and Catalyst
Teacher as Force of Nature
Teacher as Entertainer
Teacher as Nurturer/Inspiration/Role Model/Counsellor
Teacher as Egalitarian or Co-learner
Teacher as Family Member
Teacher as Prophet or God's Gift
Teacher as Tool Provider

LAISSEZ-FAIRE TEACHING APPROACH
Teacher as Blind Eye
Teacher as Bad Babysitter
Teacher as Whirlwind
Teacher as Guardian of the Door
Teacher as Sleep Inducer
Teacher as Piece of Cheese
Teacher as Uninterested Footdragger
Teacher as Tool Withholder
Teacher as Absentee

metaphors to some extent, such frequencies of use could not compare to the degree to which Egyptians used these metaphors. This might well be related to the general use of language in the home cultures of the participants.

- The metaphors of Teacher as Bad Babysitter and Teacher as Gossip were found only among the US high school students. No doubt classroom culture and age played a role here.
- The metaphors of Teacher as Family Member and Teacher as Prophet or God's Gift were evident only among the Egyptian EFL teaching candidates. These reflect the general cultural values about family and religion.
- It is interesting that although the Teacher as Prophet was valued in the Egyptian environment, the Teacher as Preacher or Moralist was generally disparaged in various environments.
- International students in the USA used the metaphor of the Teacher as Egalitarian or Co-learner. Apparently the balance-of-power concept seemed remarkable to these international participants.
- Some participants presented many different explicit (or clearly implicit) metaphors in their own individual narratives, whereas other participants did not. Thus, the metaphorical richness of the narratives varied greatly.
- Narratives showed that few students were indifferent. Most participants displayed fairly strong emotional responses to the teachers they described.

The more specific findings are organized below in terms of dominant metaphors reflecting the three teaching approaches: autocratic, democratic/participatory and laissez-faire. Unfortunately, it is impossible in this chapter to explore each of the emergent metaphors in depth. Therefore, only selected metaphors are illustrated from the narratives, with the others being merely listed.

The democratic/participatory approach was by far the most popular among the participants in the study. In contrast, the autocratic and laissez-faire modes evoked responses such as disgust, fear and anger. This finding must be viewed with some caution, however, as noted later. Possibly the pure forms of these last two modes are not viewed favourably by many or most students, but when tempered with the democratic/participatory approach these two modes might have something to offer the classroom.

METAPHORS RELATED TO THE AUTOCRATIC TEACHING APPROACH

In this study, the autocratic teaching approach was much more complex and multi-faceted than is usually depicted in the literature. Although all the seemingly autocratic teachers described here maintained utmost control in the classroom, no single 'autocratic teaching approach' was identified, although there were some commonalities which will be identified at the end of the analysis of this approach.

Eight relevant metaphors arose from the narratives: Teacher as (a) Manufacturer, (b) Witch, (c) Hanging Judge, (d) Tyrant, (e) Arrogant Animal or

Person, (f) Preacher or Moralist, (g) Patron, and (h) Gossip. There is room to discuss only the first four here.

The metaphor of *Teacher as Manufacturer* was frequent. For example, David, a US graduate student preparing to teach ESL, described a university language teacher who initially claimed she would *only* speak the target language, and promised numerous chances for students to practise dialogues in 'real life' situations but who, in fact, was required to cover the entire language textbook within a given period of time. What could have been a democratic/participatory situation turned into a factory-like operation with mechanistic work quotas:

> Pages and pages of material, including dialogues, vocabulary lists, and new grammatical structures, were required for memorization each day, and nearly all of this was without being practiced or heard, and out of any context.

The 'racing syndrome' was evident in many other narratives, too, such as that of Edward, a high school student in the USA:

> The worst problem I have had has been with the teachers who rush through the material. They care more about where they are in the book by the end of the year than how much their students have learned. . . . What is the use of covering the material if no one learns anything?

Clare, a US university student, stated: 'I have difficulty in my Spanish classes when the class is rush rush rush because it doesn't give [me] anytime to think through what's being taught.' Nagla, an Egyptian EFL teaching candidate, described her worst English teacher as a mechanistic authoritarian who wanted students to act like machines 'which sew words for one day'. The perceived, non-reflective, constant propulsion described by these students generated a range of negative emotions.

A contrasting metaphor was *Witch*, reflected in the words of Seth, a US high school student who described his English teacher as a 'demon-lady who would trap us in that room, for at least 55 minutes of torture [per day]. I was helpless against such a great beast.' Salvation came by means of the counsellor, whom Seth called the 'knight, hero, angel'. Jayla, a US university student preparing to teach secondary school English, described a Teacher as Witch:

> I'm going to tell you about the worst teacher I have ever had. . . . She was my Spanish I and II teacher. Her breath smelled awful. The room was haunted by this awful stench. I was one of those kids who got bored with her very quickly and tried to liven the class a little. When I did, she would get right in my face and yell at me. . . . I hated her class. . . . Now, I don't remember a single thing Ms. ___ taught me. The worst part is, this woman is still allowed to cast her horrid lesson plans upon unsuspecting children.

A third metaphor was *Teacher as Hanging Judge*. In the pioneering days of the USA, a hanging judge was one who served as judge, jury and executioner all rolled into one. The Teacher as Hanging Judge is expected to be dictatorial and punish students, sometimes unjustifiably. This often happens when the teacher has spied the students' errors and wants to eradicate those errors. The Teacher as Hanging Judge is reflected in several of the narratives.

Carrie described a teacher who 'will single out people in the class and yell at them for half the time'. Her emotional responses were anger and a strong desire for revenge. Kay portrayed her teacher's brutal and indiscriminant response to the infraction of not appearing to be taking notes: 'I was taking notes, but he didn't know. He came to me and started yelling at me. It hurt my feelings so bad that I started crying.' Mindy described the Teacher as Hanging Judge in terms of using several particularly harsh forms of evaluation and punishment, such as being forced to sit on 'The Block', where social ostracism and physical discomfort were combined. Similarly, Sonia, a Chilean EFL teacher, described the teacher-induced terror that for her has reverberated through the years:

> Whenever each of us made a mistake she screamed at us, saying, 'You are potato sacks,' and . . . 'No mistake is allowed here.' . . . I turned little by little to become shy and astonishingly introverted, sweating each time I had classes with her. . . . That professor wondered how I could be so shy. Years after, I gave her the answer, 'I was so afraid of you that something in my mind didn't work and got stuck in there, becoming a blank space, unable to think.' . . . I am marked by this experience.

The *Teacher as Tyrant* was the metaphor arising from several narratives. For instance, Mohamed, an EFL teaching candidate in Egypt, talked about a teacher who was a warlike tyrant who 'wanted to make us feel ultimate inferiority in order to practice a kind of sadistic invasion on our minds and souls'. Larissa, a US high school student, described her English teacher as a bellicose tyrant who was 'still in a war'. Susie, a US master's student and experienced teacher, wrote about her tyrannical English professor in these words: 'When he came to class he was ready for war!' Elham, an EFL teaching candidate in Egypt, believed her tyrannical teacher failed at getting students interested in the English language because of being filled with hate: 'It was not easy for me even to look at my teacher's face; she was always giving us the impression that she does not like English, hates herself, and hates us.'

In sum, the participants' accounts of their autocratic teachers revealed lack of concern or empathy for the student, belief that the students were basically stupid or inferior, a focus on errors and single interpretations, the use of threats and insults, and an external reward structure. With such teachers the students expressed feelings of disgust, repulsion, fear, embarrassment, anger and helplessness.

METAPHORS RELATED TO THE DEMOCRATIC/PARTICIPATORY TEACHING APPROACH

The next teaching mode, democratic/participatory, aroused much more positive responses, although not in all cases. In the democratic/participatory teaching approach, teachers were seen to treat the students as if they had well functioning, intelligent minds. Teachers and learners worked together. The eight metaphors deduced in relation to this teaching approach included: Teacher as (a) Challenger and Catalyst, (b) Force of Nature, (b) Entertainer, (c) Nurturer/Inspiration/Role Model/Counsellor, (e) Egalitarian or Co-learner, (f) Family Member, (g) Prophet or God's Gift and (h) Tool Provider. The first five of these are explained below.

Some students, such as Sharon, a US university student, suggested the metaphor of *Teacher as Challenger or Catalyst*. She described her university German teacher:

> He was an excellent teacher, very fluent in the language, he also challenged us everyday in class. Since he had spent sometime living and teaching in Germany, he was very knowledgeable about the German language, culture, and people. Painting out maps on the classroom, Dr. D would show us where he had visited. . . . The teaching and learning did not stop in the classroom. We ate [together on campus and at Dr. D's house], speaking German. The German language was so fascinating and Dr. D was such an excellent instructor that I continued on and took a total of twenty-four hours in German studies.

A second metaphor was *Teacher as Force of Nature*, appearing in three narratives from Egyptian EFL teaching candidates, Tamer, Amal, and Dina. In Tamer's words:

> He [the English professor] treated us as human beings or as friends. He know the psychology of his students. . . . He became like water everyone like to drink it and without it we will die . . .

Amal described her English professor in exuberant, sensory, nature-oriented terms: 'This teacher looks like the sun . . . when she enters the class the light, the warm, the beauty, the flower enter with her.' Dina described her English teacher as teaching her to 'taste language as I taste food'. She admired the teacher for putting the English language in her mouth and giving her the opportunity to really taste it. She declared his influence on her, saying, 'He created a good person out of me.'

The *Teacher as Entertainer*, as described in the narratives, offered entertaining language activities in an effort to put more fun into the classroom. There seemed to be an implicit distinction between 'tasks' (work) and 'activities' (fun). The entertaining teacher often used surprise and cultural experiences as part of instruction. Usually the entertaining teacher reduced social distance and warmly invited students to participate. As US high school student Gay stated: 'I enjoyed every minute of [this class] because of the teacher. He made learning fun and easy with jokes and sayings.' Brant, a future physical education teacher studying at a US university, described a high school Spanish teacher as:

> A big, jolly man who loved to tell stories. He would always come into class everyday with his guitar around his back and a big grin. He would make us practice songs in Spanish. . . . He was always in a good mood and seemed to always make everyone laugh.

However, for some students, classroom entertainment became excessive. Young, a Korean doctoral candidate earning her US doctorate in teaching EFL, expressed misgivings about one of her university professors, who 'liked to act, dance, mime, and move around in the classroom' but rarely wrote anything on the chalkboard. 'Personally, I had difficulties adapting to such activities because I am an introvert.' Mickey, an adult student studying Spanish at a US university, commented: 'I learned very little in the class. It was more of an atmosphere of fun and games. She was the star performer. The students were an audience. We often felt it was time to get down to work, but it never quite came.'

The *Teacher as Nurturer/Inspiration/Role Model/Counsellor* motif appeared numerous times. For example, US graduate student Al commented on his former Latin teacher:

> I had a very patient instructor who taught step-by-step and helped me extensively. I wanted personal attention, and he gave it in abundance. He was a Jesuit priest from Mexico who had taught for 30 years. He could be very strict, so some students thought he was an asshole, but I didn't. He called on us in class and wanted us to have our homework done on time. He guided me very well, told lots of stories of the old country, was very nostalgic, and showed tremendous patience, following the pace of every student. He made sure I understood everything. I got a B in the course and was happy, not anxious at all.

Journal entries from graduate students developing into teachers reflected an appreciation of the Teacher as Nurturer/Inspiration/Role Model. For instance, Joe's journal stated:

> Very inspiring! . . . Wow! Another amazing class! . . . The dedication you model as an educator has really made an impact on me. . . . You are a model for teachers and professors, always looking at the good side of everyone and building them up from their good points.

A different metaphor was *Teacher as Egalitarian or Co-learner*. Paulo Freire (1970) suggested the role reflected in this metaphor. Richard-Amato described Freire's concept in the following way: 'Sometimes the teacher is a student and the students are teachers in a dialogue through which all individuals can benefit' (Richard-Amato, 1988: 33). This metaphor emerged in the essays of Sanchao, who said:

> I am from China, a country with very old and deep-rooted culture. . . . American teachers seem to be more democratic and have more two-way communication with students. In America, students can talk with the teacher and dress more casually, but not without respect to the teacher. Meanwhile, teachers can also be more relaxed in a class.

The even-handed nature of the instructor as a co-learner was obvious in the narrative of Hitoshi, a Japanese high school exchange student in the USA:

> I do believe that the teacher is also one of the students. There is no end in learning. And if the teacher . . . stopped listening to students' ideas and opinions, and ignored what students what to learn, there would be no interest in the class.

Those narratives that exemplified the democratic/participatory approach generally portrayed teachers who were compassionate, loving, interesting, warm, sustaining, empowering and accepting. Most responses to the democratic/participatory approach were positive (e.g., confidence, 'learning pleasure' and appreciation), although some students expressed discomfort, seemingly due to personality or cultural differences between teacher and student.

METAPHORS RELATED TO THE LAISSEZ-FAIRE TEACHING APPROACH

Nine metaphors clustered together to reflect the laissez-faire teaching approach: Teacher as (a) Blind Eye, (b) Bad Babysitter, (c) Whirlwind, (d) Guardian of the Door, (e) Sleep Inducer, (f) Piece of Cheese, (g) Uninterested Footdragger, (h) Tool Withholder and (i) Absentee. Here we will explore only the first five of these metaphors.

According to Wright (1987), laissez-faire teachers can be viewed as simply not doing their jobs. Certainly this teaching mode raises questions about the degree of caring and interest possessed by the teachers who adopt it. Some laissez-faire teachers closed their eyes to what was going on in the classroom, thus leading to the metaphor *Teacher as Blind Eye*. Donna, a US university teaching candidate who planned to teach high school social science, described the behaviour of her high school teacher of Spanish: 'I remember one test day, the guy that sat in front of me had his book open on the floor beside him and the teacher went to the back of the room for something and she came back up our row and she just stepped over his book and never said a word.' According to several narratives, teachers who turned a blind eye to this kind of cheating demonstrated that they did not care about the students.

Some teachers treated adolescent or adult students like children or infants without exerting proper control. Such an instructor could be called the *Teacher as Bad Babysitter*. US high school student Craig stated: 'Oh, and she treats us like elementary students, [saying] "super-duper!", "hot-dog!"' According to Mitch, another US high school student, 'A teacher should not baby-sit' because:

> There is no order in her classroom. The students carry on like immature preschoolers.... Because she does not administer any form of punishment, they continue their exploits without concern for rules.

A third metaphor unifying many narratives was the *Teacher as Whirlwind*. In a whirlwind, everything becomes confused, mixed up and out of order. The following narratives demonstrated the out-of-control feeling students experienced in encounters with this kind of teacher. Pauline, a US doctoral student in education, depicted a university language teacher as being confusing because of disorganization:

My teacher never gave precise directions for any assignment. She was very unorganized, unprepared for daily lessons. She might announce a certain topic we might cover during the next class. Students would prepare for that topic and then she would cover something entirely different.

The fourth metaphor, *Teacher as Guardian of the Door*, emerged once. Angie, an Egyptian EFL teaching candidate in Egypt, wanted help from her English teacher in secondary school, but the teacher did not give it. 'All I wanted is someone to open the door for me to enter. . . . I wanted him to respect my efforts. He never took notice of who we really are, we were vessels, we were faces or may be names.'

Teacher as Sleep Inducer, the fifth metaphor, was popular with many students. For example, Maysa, a female EFL teaching candidate from Egypt, complained that her worst secondary school English teacher made students want to sleep in the teacher's dark atmosphere.

[W]e were always yawning through his lesson, and by the end of the period we felt that we are about to sleep. He was lazy and his laziness was creeping upon our minds till we felt it is dark and we wanted to say, 'good night.' I hated his class to the extent that I hoped his class to be the last class in the schedual to go home directly and sleep.

A US high school student, Hanna, said, 'One clue that a teacher should notice is if more than one half of a class is in a deep coma, maybe it's time to take a look at her style of teaching.'

In short, in the eyes of the learners, laissez-faire teachers did not appear to *care* about students or teaching. The laissez-faire teaching approach eliminated the possibility of classroom closeness between teacher and student. Some laissez-faire teachers were perceived as unhelpful or indifferent to the needs of their students. Many appeared to be so disorganized that they did not provide the structure that many students craved, while others did not impose any classroom discipline. Still others were interpreted as boring, uninterested in the subject, unwilling to provide the necessary tools for learning or unenthusiastic about everything they did in the classroom. None of the students were happy with the false freedom that the laissez-faire classroom offered.

SYNTHESIS AND CONCLUSIONS

This chapter has illustrated some of the plethora of constructions of the language teacher derived from a study of student narratives. Through a long period of assessing, sorting and weighing, the themes of these narratives were captured in particular metaphors about language teachers. The narratives and their explicit or framing metaphors were eventually interpreted in terms of three general teaching approaches: autocratic, democratic/participatory and laissez-faire. The autocratic teaching approach emerged quite distinctly in many of the narratives. The highly autocratic teacher maintains a large distance from the students and offers sharp, sometimes harsh discipline. With the autocratic teachers described in this investigation, various participants felt powerless, unhappy, disgusted, angry or rebellious.

Generally speaking, teachers described as using the democratic/participatory approach appeared to form personal bonds with students; bonds which helped motivate and activate students to learn. The democratic/participatory teaching approach did not obviate the need for discipline, structure or order. In fact, teachers who worked in a democratic/participatory mode appeared to pay attention to their students' needs and provided the structures that were seen by the students as necessary for their learning. At the same time, such teachers often allowed students to take an increased part in classroom decision-making. Most participants expressed positive feelings towards the teachers who appeared to use the democratic/participatory mode.

The laissez-faire teaching approach was evident in a number of metaphors although this approach has not been extensively researched with regard to language instruction. However, as shown by the students' vivid descriptions in the current study, this teaching approach might occur more often than is generally realized. Descriptions of this ultimately dysfunctional approach arose in stories about both high school and university teaching. In each case, the participant's response was negative and participants were especially condemnatory of the lack of concern, caring or interest shown by the laissez-faire teacher.

Implications for language teaching

What features relate to satisfying, motivating instruction? Crookes and Schmidt (1991) and Dörnyei (1994) agreed upon some essential elements that stimulate motivation for language learning: interest, relevance and expectancy of success. Crookes and Schmidt (1991) added: intrinsic or extrinsic rewards, decision to learn, persistence and high behavioural involvement. Dörnyei also identified some aspects of student motivation particularly influenced by the language teacher: affiliation, power or authority, modelling, task presentation and feedback.

The features of good teaching identified by McCombs and Whistler (1997) are comparable to Dörnyei's list:

- interest, enthusiasm, clarity and stimulation of curiosity (related to Dörnyei's task presentation and modelling);
- concern and availability (relevant to Dörnyei's affiliation);
- provision of obvious structure (part of Dörnyei's power or authority, in the good sense);
- provision of useful feedback (identical to Dörnyei's feedback).

Findings in this study suggested that, when the attributes listed above were identified and positively interpreted by students, they saw themselves as motivated, buoyed, eager, energized and happy. They felt connected to the teacher, the language, and each other. When negativity crept in by means of teachers' behaviours or attitudes (e.g., sarcasm, frenetic pace, preaching or punitiveness, disinterest, inattention to students' needs, lack of organization or imagination, and so on), learners clearly became negative themselves. Under such circumstances, various students appeared to be demotivated, deflated, frustrated, bored, unhappy, isolated and/or resistant. Self-efficacy was low (Bandura, 1982), and the locus of control (Weiner, 1986) was outside the helpless, powerless learner. According to the narratives, reactions such as these occurred when there was either too much control or too little control by the teacher.

The findings from this study therefore suggest many implications for the classroom. A few of these are:

- Teachers should recognize the major role they play in many language students' lives and the responsibility that this entails. Above all, teachers need to be alert to the strong links between their own behaviours and attitudes and the motivation and performance of their students.
- Learners need opportunities to give voice to the importance of the teacher–student relationship. They also need chances to express their specific needs and interests. To create such opportunities, teachers could use classroom discussions, interviews, one-to-one informal conversations, journals, letters, formative evaluation sheets, or other means.
- Whenever possible, teachers should consciously create a bond with each student. This is difficult in very large language classes, but it is nonetheless possible via personally directed comments and through certain assignments, such as dialogue journals, which increase the communication between teacher and student.
- Teachers should consider their exercise of power and intimacy in the language classroom and should ask themselves whether how they exercise these constitute a message that teachers want to perpetuate.
- Teachers should reflect on which general teaching approach – autocratic, democratic/participatory, or laissez-faire – is their prevalent mode in the eyes of their students and query themselves about whether this is what they intend and whether it is the most effective mode.
- Perhaps a combination of teaching approaches might be useful in certain circumstances. For instance, selected characteristics of the autocratic teaching approach, which appears as a whole to be largely dysfunctional in its purest form, might be effectively combined with a more democratic approach in a back-and-forth movement as dictated by the occasion, the language task and the characteristics of the students. Such characteristics might include a concern for structure, systematization and precision.
- Teacher education and in-service faculty development should provide a forum for current and future teachers to discuss the issues raised in this chapter. Perhaps teachers might study the data presented here and come up with their own different interpretations, possibly to reflect on their own teaching styles.

This chapter has focused on what occurs in classrooms, especially the creative constructions by students of their language teachers. The study reported here has shown the great significance of the classroom teacher in the life and learning of students. As Christopher wrote to his professor, 'You made all the difference in the world to me.' As the present study revealed, such strong responses – both positive and negative – are very common and the teachers appeared to have a huge influence upon their students.

Going beyond just the regular classroom or the tutorial setting, it is fair to say that the teacher is important in virtually every formalized language learning situation that can be imagined. Even in environments that rely on autonomous work by students, such as certain self-access centres and particular kinds of individualized, technology-assisted distance education, the language teacher often plays a significant role in terms of e-mail, teleconferencing and the shaping of materials, procedures, and technology.

Future research

Looking broadly at the classroom situation, it will be important in the future to consider two-way or multi-way influences among students and their teachers. The mutual effects of peer on peer, as well as the mutual influence of students and teachers on each other, are still to be more fully explored in language classrooms and especially in terms of the effects of these upon the process of language learning.

In addition, future research should consider which characteristics of language teaching are the most honoured in different cultures. Some cultures might differ from other cultures in terms of educational values and the roles of the teacher and the learner (Hofstede, 1986, 1991). Even when two different cultures seemingly share certain values and roles, these cultures might give different weights to them. For instance, an instructional aspect that appears primary in one culture, for example, affiliation or closeness between teacher and student, might be less important in another culture emphasizing the teacher's provision of organization and structure. However, the whole concept of culture is problematic from a postmodern view in that what we often know as a culture is not a homogeneous entity but rather a dynamic amalgam of factors, often analysed in terms of privilege and oppression. Differences also exist in the receptivity of individual students to certain teaching approaches. Cultural trends are a fascinating and potent variable, but future researchers must not forget to look for individual attitudes, beliefs and thoughts. The narrative case study presents and preserves the voice of the *person* within the social context. In making this point, the chapter has now come full circle. The 'bleached bones' of the narratives have been displayed, poked and studied from various angles to discern their inner meanings concerning learners' constructions of language teachers. Although commonalities were found, each story was unique in its forms of expression and in its special twists and turns. As Aundathi Roy stated, 'Never again will a single story be told as if it were the only one.'

APPENDIX 5.1   CONSTRUCTIONS OF LANGUAGE TEACHERS
(a partial list only)

contracted professional	Block (1992)
devoted professional	Block (1992)
parent	Block (1992), Ehrman & Dörnyei (1998), Oxford (1999)
enforcer	Block (1992)
orchestra director, musical director	Block (1992)
play director	Oxford (1990)
choreographer	Katz (1986)
entertainer	Katz (1986)
researcher	Block (1992), Breen & Candlin (1980)
all-seeking, omniscient god	Block (1992)
not a god	Curran (1972)
member of a priesthood	Maley (1984)
grail seekers	Maley (1984)
salvation seekers	Maley (1984)
treasure hunters	Cortazzi & Jin (1996)
obscuritanists	Maley (1984)
friend	Block (1992), Scarcella & Oxford (1992)
comrade	Block (1992)
co-learner	Freire (1970, referring to any teacher, not just a language teacher), Breen & Candlin (1980)
earth mother	Katz (1996)
professor (content-focused)	Katz (1996)
vessel-filler	Willing (1991)
journeyer	Cortazzi & Jin (1996)
cook	Cortazzi & Jin (1996)
plant cultivator, gardener	Cortazzi & Jin (1996), Oxford (1999)
puppeteer	Oxford (1999)
doctor	Oxford (1999)
parrot-trainer (for Audiolingual)	Oxford (1999)
factory manager	Oxford (1999)
zookeeper	Oxford (1999)
input provider	Krashen & Terrell (1983), O'Malley & Chamot (1990), Scarcella & Oxford (1992)
strategy instructor	O'Malley & Chamot (1990), Oxford (1990), Scarcella & Oxford (1992)
scaffolder	Scarcella & Oxford (1992)
tapestry weaver	Scarcella & Oxford (1992)
guide	Scarcella & Oxford (1992)

decision-maker	Nunan (1992), Scarcella & Oxford (1992)
motivator	Dörnyei (1994), Oxford & Shearin (1994)
multiculturalist	Scarcella & Oxford (1992)
aid in bursting the cocoon	Stevick (1980)
inseminator	Curran (1972)
spouse or lover	Ashton-Warner (1963, referring to any teacher, not just a language teacher)
mental-gymnastics teacher	Herron (1982)
nurturer of souls	Gadd (1998)
infantilizer	Lozanov in Stevick (1980, 1990)
organizer, co-ordinator	Breen & Candlin (1980), Oxford (1990)
facilitator	Breen & Candlin (1980), Oxford (1990), Scarcella & Oxford (1992)
negotiator	Breen & Candlin (1980)
seer of potential	Breen & Candlin (1980)
monitor	Breen & Candlin (1980)
coach	Rivers & Temperley in Block (1992)
resource person, idea person	Dubin & Olshtain (1986), Oxford (1990)
needs analyst	Richards & Rodgers (1986)
group process leader/manager	Ehrman & Dörnyei (1998), Richards & Rodgers (1986)
consultant	Oxford (1990)
diagnostician	Oxford (1990)
member of classroom culture with students	Breen (1985)
joint conspirer for maintaining routines	Breen (1996)
potential prisoners of social expectations	Kramsch (1993)
recipient of resistance	Kramsch (1993)
person caught in a web of method	Kumaravadivelu (1994)
person watching an endless cycle of life, death, rebirth of method	Kumaravadivelu (1994)
consumer buying repackaged methods	Kumaravadivelu (1994)
toiler in trenches	Clarke (1982)
sailor in tempestuous sea	Clarke (1982)
tyrant-follower	Clarke (1982)
individual vulnerable to the pendulum of method	Clarke (1982)
investor	Maley (1984)

fortress defender	Maley (1984)
manoeuverer	Maley (1984)
acceptor of prescriptions from educational imperialists	Pennycook (1989)
member of learning alliance with student	Ehrman & Dörnyei (1998), Wool (1989, referring to any teacher, not just a language teacher)

ACKNOWLEDGEMENTS

I deeply appreciate the help of my colleague Rebecca Massey in the final editing stages of this chapter. I also give great thanks to those colleagues who provided narratives. In addition to my own 162 learner narratives, Roberta Lavine, Cassandra Harrington, Amany Saleh, and El Sayed Dadour gathered an additional 311 additional stories from their students. In alphabetical order, all of the colleagues to whom I address my gratitude are: Barcelos, Universidade Federal de Viçosa, Brazil; Dadour, Mansoura University, Damietta, Egypt; Harrington, Athens High School, Alabama, USA; Lavine, University of Maryland, College Park, Maryland, USA; Longhini, University of Rio Cuarto, Argentina; Massey, North Carolina State University, Raleigh, NC, USA; Saleh, University of Arkansas, Jonesboro, Arkansas, USA; and Tomlinson, University of Alabama, Tuscaloosa, Alabama, USA. In addition, great thanks go to the students who provided the narratives. Finally, thanks to novelist Arundathi Roy for her wonderful, thought-provoking images.

Chapter 6

Overt participation and covert acquisition in the language classroom

Michael P. Breen, University of Stirling

Language learning evolves *out of* learning how to carry on conversations.
(Hatch, 1978: 404)

The focus (in SLA) should be . . . on observing the construction of co-knowledge and how this co-construction process results in linguistic change among and within individuals during joint activity.   (Donato, 1994: 39)

INTRODUCTION

In the twenty-two years since Hatch introduced to second language acquisition research the potential contributions to the process of learners' participation in discourse there has been continued investigation of learner interaction with teachers and other learners, with native speakers and non-native speakers. Several researchers have identified such interaction as the crucible wherein the linguistic and communicative environment made available to the learners will shape the process and outcomes of language development. As with first language acquisition research, this reliance, even in part, upon the significance for learning of the language made available to learners during interaction is challenged by those who give primacy to the learners' internal cognitive processes (Durkin, 1987). This latter stance is exemplified by the theory that learners are biologically endowed with a Universal Grammar, the principles and some of the parameters of which remain accessible to L2 learners through their first language (Chomsky, 1981, 1986; White 1989). Such a theoretical starting point is taken by Braidi in identifying what she sees as the failure of interaction research to reveal its affect upon grammatical development in particular. She suggests that such research needs to focus more specifically upon the actual grammatical structures within interaction with the primary purpose of uncovering Universal Grammar 'triggers' (Braidi, 1995). Researchers who have asserted particular contributions of the learners' 'linguistic environment' to acquisition certainly recognize that it is the interface between such contributions and the learners' internal capacity for language that is pivotal in the acquisition process (Krashen, 1985; Long, 1996). However, the identification of the particular observable features of the linguistic and communicative environment which may best tune into these capacities, thereby enabling a developmental change in learner competence, is a project yet to be completed in second language acquisition (SLA) research.

The issue is clearly an urgent one for language pedagogy and particularly in any examination of the contributions of the language classroom. Virtually coinciding with Hatch's identification of the potential role of learner participation in discourse and Long's influential specification of this in terms of overt interaction (Long, 1981), the theoretical and pedagogic rationales for communicative language teaching (CLT) placed a premium upon overt learner participation in the interaction afforded by the classroom and its activities. Since that time, despite an ongoing diversity of interpretations and its later fragmentation into approaches such as 'task-based', 'learner-centred' or 'autonomous language learning', many language teachers would assert that the teacher's engagement of learners in overt participation is a defining characteristic of CLT. This is not to say that overt participation in the language class is a characteristic unique to CLT, before its introduction or since. Previous approaches or methods advocated learner output – constrained, perhaps, by the rigours of imitation and repetitive practice of teacher or textbook models. One of CLT's innovations was to advocate spontaneous learner communication through talk about topics and issues that were immediately meaningful to them. The pedagogic emphasis shifted from the verbalizing of de-contextualized language items or forms to the purposes language serves in the interpretation and expression of meaning in social contexts (Widdowson, 1978).

Therefore, in addition to seeking clear justifications for what has become a relatively widespread pedagogic practice, there are two contributory motivations for examining learners' overt participation in the language classroom. The first is to identify its actual characteristics and the second is to trace its impact upon language acquisition. These two motivations are the concerns of the present chapter. Its particular focus will be upon overt participation in terms of learner talk, specifically in the context of the classroom. The chapter begins with a review of some of the key arguments in SLA research which either support or question the contributory role of learner talk. This provides a context for an evaluation, in the second part of the chapter, of research evidence on the relationship between overt contributions of learners in classroom interaction and the outcomes for their learning. From this evaluation, it is deduced that the evidence for the impact upon acquisition of learner participation in classroom interaction may be constrained by the particular perspectives of the research. The chapter concludes by identifying potential avenues for future studies of learners' participation that may better reveal the actual relationships between the external communicative environment and learners' developing competence.

DOES OVERT PARTICIPATION CONTRIBUTE TO
SECOND LANGUAGE ACQUISITION?

Particular contributions of the learners' overt production or output to language development have been identified in terms of two influential hypotheses and the research that has informed them. Both hypotheses assert the insufficiency of input from the linguistic environment as a condition for language acquisition. Both identify as exemplary evidence for this assertion the relative under-achievement in speech production as compared with remarkable progress in listening and reading of students who have participated for several years in content-based French immersion programmes (Lapkin et al., 1991; Swain, 1985, 1991; Wesche, 1994). Each hypothesis therefore identifies additional necessary conditions for acquisition to occur. The interaction hypothesis proposes that learners need to participate overtly in interaction of a certain quality and the output hypothesis proposes that learners can benefit in particular ways from their own language output.

The interaction hypothesis argues that, during communication, learners and more competent speakers are likely to adjust their language production, conversational structure, message content, or all of these when they recognize a lack of comprehension on the part of their interlocutor (Long, 1981, 1996). This 'negotiation for meaning' is overtly revealed in the ways that interlocutors either avoid or repair communication breakdowns through such devices as repeating, reformulating, requesting clarification, checking on comprehension, or confirming understanding, etc. (comprehensive reviews of research on negotiation for meaning are provided by Long (1996) and Pica (1994)). Long argues that: 'The semantic transparancy achieved by interactional modifications as speakers negotiate for meaning is important . . . not just because it makes input comprehensible, but because it makes *complex* input comprehensible' (Long, 1996: 451, original emphasis). Therefore, overt negotiation for meaning during interaction renders input accessible to a learner which would not usually be comprehensible, either because of meaning content or relative complexity of form or both. Such accessibility, according to this hypothesis, can engage the learners' internal capacities for language development. A crucial function claimed for overt interaction of this kind is that, because learners may intend to share meaning that is, at the time, transparent to them, they have the attentional space to focus on the form of both their own production and an interlocutor's response and are thereby enabled to compare the two – to 'notice the gap' between their own production and a more target-like version of it. It is at such moments that potential for a refinement in an aspect of the learners' own language system can occur (Doughty and Williams, 1998; Long, 1991). Researchers who regard negotiation during interaction as having these characteristics claim that such negotiation can reveal the developmental relationship between learners' overt participation in communication and their innate capacity for acquisition.

In sum, on the basis of a growing foundation of evidence, the interaction hypothesis proposes that learner participation in interaction that entails negotiation for meaning has the potential to alert learners to failures in making themselves understood and, from this, to adopt devices both in how they converse and in the form of their utterances. The very failure to understand or make oneself understood immediately may therefore 'push' learners to reformulate and refine what they say. Through this, they may analyse input and refine their own output in more conscious ways and, thereby, attain greater awareness and control of the new language.

The output hypothesis echoes some of these proposals. In addition to the possible contribution of learners' regular language production to emerging fluency, Swain identifies three major functions of learner output (Swain, 1995). Referring to studies of even relatively young learners, she argues that they can notice and become alert to particular deficiencies in their own language output even without feedback (Swain and Lapkin, 1994). Secondly, when obtaining even implicit corrective feedback of various kinds to their output during negotiation for meaning, it appears that learners will modify about one-third of their output in reaction to it – will produce 'comprehensible output' – and that there is some evidence that these modifications become part of the learners' productive system (Nobuyoshi and Ellis, 1993; Pica et al., 1989). Swain therefore attributes to learner output an hypothesis-testing potential. She regards learners' modification of only a proportion of their output in response to feedback as evidence of a *selective* focusing which itself suggests that learners test very particular hypotheses about the target language at different times. The third potential of learner output is that it can serve a metalinguistic purpose in the sense that learners, given the appropriate conditions, are capable of negotiating with each other about form. During such negotiation, particularly within collaborative tasks requiring the planning and construction of written texts in the target language, learners can articulate their emerging control over aspects of language through conscious analysis and reflection. Referring to studies of this kind of collaborative activity by Donato (1994) and LaPierre (1994), Swain suggests that they provide good evidence that a significant proportion of the specific aspects of the target language, which are identified by the learners as problematic and about which they overtly negotiate a solution, are actually acquired and retained. For instance, in the case of the LaPierre study of grade eight early immersion learners, over 70 per cent of both correct *and* incorrect target language solutions earlier negotiated by them were recalled in post-tests a week later. However, the episodes in which the beginner learners negotiated a *correct* solution outnumbered episodes in which incorrect solutions were negotiated by almost seven to one. A crucial observation here is that such overt metalinguistic work, like hypothesis-testing through output, is selective. Both are spontaneous within interaction and we cannot predict what aspect of language may warrant, for the learners, a negotiated resolution. Similarly, we cannot be sure from our analysis of an interaction whether learners are actually focusing upon form or upon meaning or, indeed, devoting most effort to maintaining face or social solidarity with their interlocutors by merely appearing to keep the conversation going. We can be more confident in assuming that different learners are very likely to learn different things through their output and even from the same interaction.

While the interaction hypothesis does not question the primacy of comprehension of input from the linguistic environment but articulates certain conditions under which input is rendered comprehensible through conversational work, the output hypothesis makes a pivotal distinction between the processes of learner comprehension and production of speech. Swain (1995) reminds us of the characteristic redundancy of speech to a listener and the other non-linguistic clues that face-to-face interaction can provide, and quotes Lightbown and Halter as concluding from their study of a comprehension-based ESL programme:

> [T]hat the kind of processing which is necessary for comprehension is different from the kind of processing which is required for production and, ultimately, for acquisition . . . the ability to *decode* language, that is, the ability to understand the meaning conveyed by a particular sentence, is not the same as *code breaking*, that is, discovering the linguistic systems which carry the meaning.
>
> (Lightbown and Halter, 1993: 23, original emphasis)

In specifying the development of syntax and morphology as the foundations of accurate production which is, for her, evidence of genuine acquisition, Swain gives primacy to output as a code-breaking process which demands greater analytic control over the language on the part of the learners in contrast to what she sees as the more open-ended, meaning-focused and selective processing that typifies comprehension.

In sum, on the basis of both the evidence that is taken to support the interaction hypothesis and additional evidence of learners' negotiations about form, the output hypothesis proposes that learner talk can facilitate fluency, generate feedback which enables noticing gaps in current language production as compared with target forms, test the learners' hypotheses, and focus upon metalinguistic features when planning written production. Like the interaction hypothesis, those learner modifications of output during interaction that appear to seek to avoid or repair failures in understanding are here interpreted as evidence of learner awareness and, thereby, greater analytic control over the form of the new language. In addition, the output hypothesis highlights the unpredictable selectivity of learners' hypothesis-testing, noticing and attention to form and/or meaning during the flow of interaction. Perhaps more so than the interaction hypothesis, it gives significant weight to language production in the acquisition process alongside that of comprehension, not only as the accessible evidence of genuine acquisition, but also as *the* process that transforms input into the acquired system through more effortful learner analysis and control.

Both of these influential hypotheses are not, of course, immune from problems. For instance, both propose two particular phenomena as pivotal:

first, a level of analytical attention that enables learners to notice the gap between their own outputs and well-formed and appropriate feedback and, secondly, that the immediate modifications learners may make in their own talk carry a strong likelihood of being retained over time as part of the acquired system. On the issue of noticing, Pica concluded her review of the research on negotiation during interaction with the following caution:

> [T]hese data show how learners' attention *can* be brought to differences between their own production and a target model. However, we must emphasize *can*, because negotiation data seldom obviously show whether or not learners perceive these differences. Overall, we can safely say that negotiation provides the *opportunities* to attend to L2 form and to the relationships of form and meaning. Whether they indeed do cannot be observed, or even inferred, most of the time. This may not reflect a fault of negotiation, but rather the current state of research instruments. (Pica, 1994: 520, original emphasis)

On the issue of the retention of modifications in the learners' output subsequent to negotiation, Pica concluded in an earlier paper that we currently lack sufficient and appropriate longitudinal data of the accommodation of such changes in the learners' interlanguage (Pica, 1992). It is this current lack of data on the impact of learners' modified talk upon longer-term acquisition which Krashen also identifies as undermining the output hypothesis in particular. It is, perhaps, not surprising that the SLA theorist who has asserted that it is *only* comprehensible input which is consistently effective in increasing language proficiency should fail to appreciate the significance of Swain's emphasis upon the differences between the processes of comprehension and production and the specific contribution of the latter to acquisition. Krashen (1994, 1998) acknowledges that interaction may have a contributory function in language acquisition; essentially as a good source of comprehensible input. However, he offers two further challenges to the output hypothesis. First, he cites evidence suggesting that acquisition can occur without learner output. Perhaps a limitation of the evidence he offers is that it is mainly derived from studies of vocabulary acquisition through written input or literacy development through reading. Nevertheless, his second challenge appears to be more strongly supported by available research. He asserts that learner output and, particularly, modified learner output occurs very rarely during interaction, citing evidence from studies of learner–native speaker interviews, and from learner–learner and learner–teacher interactions in classroom situations. This seeming scarcity of opportunity for learners to modify their own production implies, for Krashen, that it is not a necessary contribution to acquisition. There is a problem with the scarcity argument, of course. Some plants need very little rain in order to grow, but they do need rain if they are to grow at all. Just as we require confirmatory evidence that learner output facilitates later acquisition, we also need evidence from those learners who have rare opportunities to modify their talk while participating in interaction to discover whether or not their language development is consequently delayed. Indeed, this is precisely

Swain's conclusion from the disparity between immersion students' high levels of understanding compared to their relative under-achievement in production. Krashen concludes his argument against the output hypothesis by urging an increase in learner access to comprehensible input. An alternative conclusion might be to urge an increase in learner opportunities to produce language, not least to enable us to confirm, through longitudinal research, whether or not it actually has an impact upon the rate and quality of acquisition.

There is one component of Krashen's theory of language acquisition which is strangely lacking from both the interaction hypothesis and the output hypothesis. He identified this as the 'affective filter hypothesis' (Krashen, 1994). The lack of an affective dimension in interaction and learner output is all the more incongruous given the primacy attributed to the sharing of *meaning* as the catalyst for everything else that the hypotheses identify as significant for acquisition. The effort towards meaningful communication and the process of learning to achieve it engages deeper levels of interactants' socio-cognitive identity than may be transparent on the surface of talk. Similarly, the hypotheses attach crucial significance to cognitive processes such as attention and awareness, even straying into the notoriously complex phenomenon of learner consciousness. There is a long-established literature on human cognition wherein processes such as attention, memory and the construction of knowledge are rarely discussed without reference to the fact that such processes are permeated with emotion or affect. Anxiety, fear, arousal, avoidance, empathy, motivation, self-esteem, etc., will be present to varying degrees in any interaction, and such affects certainly characterize learning (Bransford, 1979; Claxton, 1984; Eysenck, 1986; Neisser, 1976; Stevick, 1976 *inter alia*). Krashen's affective filter may be interpreted as narrowly mechanistic as some SLA researchers' reliance on the metaphorical discourse of 'inputs' and 'outputs', but it enables him to make a crucial observation in relation to the scarcity of the latter. He cites evidence to suggest that classroom activities or techniques that 'force output' from learners, which is beyond their acquired competence, generate levels of anxiety that appear to distract them from genuine language use and its development (Krashen, 1994: 67). There is some sleight of hand here, of course, for the proponents of both the interaction hypothesis and the output hypothesis make a clear distinction between requiring learners to mimic de-contextualized chunks of language which are beyond their current competence, which are seen to be typical of pedagogy that focuses on language *forms*, and the kinds of classroom tasks that 'push' learners to modify their output through negotiation for meaning (Long, 1996: 448). However, the omission of the socio-affective dimension of language learning, particularly in the analysis of talk that occurs in the public space of the classroom or the interpersonal space of task work, remains as a hindrance to both hypotheses in fully explaining *how* language may be acquired specifically through classroom interaction in context. This issue will be returned to later, while our attention now turns to examining more closely the evidence relating to learner participation within language classrooms.

DOES OVERT PARTICIPATION IN THE CLASSROOM FACILITATE LANGUAGE ACQUISITION?

If we look at the linguistic and communicative environment provided by many language classrooms with a view to seeking evidence of learners' overt participation through their interaction and output, both Swain's and Krashen's observations on its scarcity appear to be justified. However, even the seeming scarcity of such opportunities has to be explained, not least for pedagogic reasons. A brief evaluation of the evidence may help to reveal, as with Pica's recognition of the limitations of the 'current state of research instruments' as applied to negotiation, whether or not the scarcity of learner participation is a function of how classroom data is currently obtained and examined. In this evaluation, we will first focus upon classroom talk more broadly, and then follow by focusing upon the evidence from classroom-based task work.

Classroom talk

As Chaudron (1988) and van Lier (1988) make clear in their earlier reviews of the research in second language classrooms, interaction in the language class appears on the surface very much like lessons in other subjects. They confirmed a dominant pattern of the interaction in which teachers initiate, learners respond, and teachers follow-up their responses by repetition, reformulation or other forms of more explicit evaluation. Occasionally, in certain language classes in particular, a teacher's reformulation is often repeated verbatim by a learner or the whole class because they have learned to interpret its illocutionary force as being as a model to be overtly imitated. Van Lier pointed out that such interactions are located within a kind of communal monologue directed by the teacher at the whole class wherein learner contributions are woven into the teacher's text. Although our focus here is less upon a teacher's participation in the interaction than that of the learners, how teachers communicate in the classroom provides the frame within which learner overt participation is attributed particular significance or value. For instance, research suggests that some teachers exercise the right to two-thirds more fluency practice in the classroom than all the learners put together, although, perhaps not surprisingly, teacher talk is often characterized by modifications found in native-speaker speech to non-native speakers outside classrooms. Of direct relevance, however, such modifications appear to be more emphatic when teachers address learners whom they regard as having lower proficiency (Dahl, 1981; R. Ellis, 1985; Griffiths, 1991; Hamayan and Tucker, 1980; Henzel, 1979; Kliefgen, 1985; Wong-Filmore 1982). It seems, therefore, that the degree of modification in a teacher's direct interaction with an individual learner conveys other messages beneath what is actually said; in this case a judgement of a learner's perceived capabilities. This layered meaning of many teacher utterances also resides in the prevailing pattern of error correction subsequent to certain learners' utterances. The apparent inconsistency of error correction is only partly explained by the real-time pressure of classroom interaction. Many teachers selectively correct errors depending upon who makes them and on the basis of their judgement of a learner's ability, resilience and emotional state. There are likely to be two outcomes at least from this very common aspect of teacher talk. First, different learners may attach different values to teacher reactions to what they say and may either fail to distinguish a teacher's correction from other kinds of teacher utterance or assume that almost all teacher responses to what they say are an evaluation of their language abilities (Lyster, 1998; Nystrom, 1983; van Lier, 1996). Secondly, and more significantly, how teachers respond to their participation may superimpose a degree of risk for many learners and the possibility of threat to their self-esteem in a public situation.

However, classroom communication reveals further complications not usually identified in the analysis of momentary interactions. Van Lier (1988) suggests that the observable talk of the language class constantly shifts due to its being characterized by four types of interaction that serve different purposes: teacher instructions, teacher's elicitations of student responses, and procedurally structured learner activities such as small group or dyadic tasks, all of which are occasionally punctuated by small talk or student asides. Van Lier indicates that these different types of talk reflect different degrees of teacher control over topics or activities. We may also deduce that each of the four types of interaction will facilitate or delimit types of participation on the part of learners. This inter-textual nature of classroom communication has been identified at a deeper level by Allwright as a 'discoursal dilemma' wherein a teacher and students are engaged in a constant balancing of conflictual pressures between the social and the pedagogical (Allwright, 1989, 1996). The social pressure pushes the interaction towards an event which is socially acceptable and even socially productive to everyone in the classroom so that any face-threatening act is likely to be avoided. On the other hand, the assumed purpose of a language class generates pedagogic pressure that pushes the interaction towards an event which is pedagogically acceptable and, preferably, pedagogically productive so that it is likely to become face-threatening and cognitively demanding because it will reveal the limits of knowledge of at least some of the participants. This dilemma results in an almost constant ambiguity inherent in the interaction with the likely result of different understandings or interpretations of the functions of certain utterances. Allwright's identification of the social significance of classroom interaction is confirmed by Senior's recent detailed study of teachers' views on what they regarded as a 'good language class' (Senior, 1999). On the basis of a study involving initial questionnaires and classroom observation, and a series of interviews over almost a year, Senior discovered that the teachers almost unanimously defined a good language class as one that exhibited 'social cohesion' in the sense of a collaborative and supportive classroom milieu and that teachers adopted a range of social strategies and ways of communicating that they believed facilitated its maintenance. Although Senior focused mainly upon the teachers' perceptions of their classes for adult learners, she also obtained evidence that the students also gave a high priority to the social atmosphere in their classes.

It seems, therefore, that the opportunities for participation made available to the learners occur within at least four interweaving types of text: communication through the target language, metacommunication about the target language, communication about the teaching–learning process (its procedures and classroom routines), and spontaneous asides about any of these things, all of which may be more or less orchestrated directly or indirectly by the teacher. And learners have to navigate through this inter-textuality, identifying the textual cues which signal a transition from one kind of talk to another and, crucially, the particular significance and potential meanings of each type of talk. It is very likely that different learners, as a group and individually, will be more or less skilled in such navigation. Further, however, this inter-textuality is framed within what Allwright has identified as 'discoursal dilemmas' within the interaction, which is an ongoing tension between social and pedagogic purposes that render the text of lessons potentially ambiguous for those who overtly engage in it and for those who choose to interpret it more covertly. Adopting Allwright's distinction, any moment in the interaction, regardless of teacher intention, may be interpreted by one learner as serving pedagogic purposes while, for another learner, it may be seen as serving social purposes and both are likely act upon their interpretations in different ways.

We might conclude from observable patterns of the interactive text of language classes that learners are not actually required to participate very much, not least because of the pressure to devote much attention to keeping track of the teacher's text and being alert to the moments when they have to contribute to it and, occasionally, to the teacher's reactions to their contributions. In essence, learners seem to be most often positioned in a responsive role within the frame of classroom communication (Politzer et al., 1981). However, what can we glean from the research on the outcomes for learning, even from their overt participation in this responsive role? Strong (1983, 1984), for example, discovered that a high response rate from certain learners to teacher questions and elicitations correlated with their higher achievement in tests largely based upon the grammar, pronunciation and vocabulary of classroom talk. Seliger (1977) suggested that those learners which he identified as 'high input generators' performed better on an aural comprehension task than did less participating learners. In their study of 'the good language learner', Naiman, Fröhlich, Stern and Todesco (1978) found that learners who raised their hands more and more often responded to teacher elicitations did better on tests than other learners.

Studies by Lightbown (1980, 1991), Snow and Hoefnagel-Hohle (1982), and Spada and Lightbown (1993), while confirming the finding in earlier studies that learners were often able to produce accurately those linguistic forms that occurred frequently in classroom communication, particularly showed high retention rates of interrogatives. Given the prevalence of teacher questions in the text of lessons, this may not be surprising. However, frequency of occurrence of aspects of language may not be the only explanation. Learners are obliged to be particularly alert to questions in case they are directed to them individually. These studies also found that not only questions but other kinds of utterance directed specifically to individual learners correlated with higher gain scores in tests of the forms of these utterances taken by the same individuals. It appears that, while it may not be surprising that frequency of certain forms of language in the text of lessons render them more accessible, teachers' requests for overt responses from learners, such as questioning or nominated turns or even personal observations, may, in turn, influence the learning outcomes of individuals.

In general, therefore, overt learner participation in the classroom is most often orchestrated by the teacher and is occasionally spontaneously offered by certain students. Its possible effects upon acquisition remain ambiguous, however. Day's (1984) replication of Seliger's study of 'high input generators' (Seliger, 1977) and Ely's (1986) investigation of learner-initiated utterances found no relationship between overt learner participation and later test attainment. In tracing learners' 'uptake' from lessons of previously unknown vocabulary, studies by Slimani (1989, 1992) and Dobinson (1996) confirmed Allwright's hypothesis that, while overt interaction in a class may provide learning opportunities, different learners are likely to learn different things from it (Allwright, 1984). Both researchers discovered that low participating and even non-participating students often recalled as much or more from lessons as did high-participating learners. Slimani found that students recalled more previously unknown linguistic items from lessons if they were topicalized or introduced into the text of the lesson by *students* rather than those topicalized by the teacher. She deduced that low-participating learners were directly benefiting from their high-participating colleagues. This suggests that the more proficient students in a class, who appeared to be those more willing to participate, were taking on the burden of interactive work but without gaining from it. In other words, proficiency in the language may enable greater participation rather than participation leading to gains in proficiency. Slimani's study also cast some doubt on the claim that conversational modifications lead to greater comprehensibility and, thereby, increased likelihood of acquisition. In fact, she found no relationship between the number of conversational adjustments occurring in the text of lessons around specific linguistic items and the 'uptake' of these items by learners.

Dobinson traced the 'uptake' immediately after lessons of particular vocabulary which 24 students recalled as previously unknown to them. She further tested students to find out whether the vocabulary, embedded within a Vocabulary Levels Test (Nation, 1982), was retained by them after two and six weeks and she found very high retention rates across the sample. (She softened the likelihood of test-effect by testing half her sample only after six weeks.) As in Slimani's study, she discovered that different learners mostly recalled and retained different new vocabulary from the same lessons with 152 words recalled as new across all 24 students. Of the 61 words recalled by over half the students, only 17 were identical. This may not be surprising, of course, because different learners enter a class with different gaps in their knowledge. Interestingly, 92 per cent of vocabulary items recalled as new by three-quarters of the students were overtly mentioned during classroom interaction by the teacher, the students, or through a taped audio input, and 75 per cent of recalled vocabulary had been repeated more than once at some point in the lesson. Although Dobinson did not trace recalled items in conversational modifications by the students, she discovered a different pattern from Slimani regarding the topicalization of items. For instance, of the 17 identical words identified as new by more than half the students, these were topicalized a remarkable number of 257 times during interaction – an average of just over 15 topicalizations for each word – of which 163 were teacher topicalizations and 94 student topicalizations. In addition, Dobinson found that these words had involved an average of 14.7 turns per word, of which 7.5 were teacher turns and 7.2 were student turns. It therefore seems that, if the students took about the same number of turns as the teacher in mentioning a particular vocabulary item that was seen to be new by more than half of the students, it was likely to be recalled and retained by them. However, there appeared to be an optimum amount of both topicalization and turn-taking around new words associated with recall, where some words occurring in well over the average number of topicalizations or turns were recalled by few students, while other words rarely topicalized or occurring in few turns were recalled as new by over three-quarters of the sample.

Dobinson also confirmed Slimani's finding that it was not necessary for some learners to participate overtly in the interaction at all in order for them to recall and successfully retain vocabulary. For instance, the five students who did not contribute a single turn in their lessons recalled a total of 27 previously unknown words, while the five students who contributed the most turns in their lessons – an average of 37.2 turns a lesson – only recalled a total of 30. More startling, perhaps, was the finding that the 12 students who took least turns in lessons (only 25 overall) recalled exactly the same number of new words (76) as the twelve students who took most turns in lessons (224 turns overall). In essence, some students who rarely participated recalled as many new words as those who participated a great deal. In both studies, therefore, some learners appeared to gain from teacher–student interaction in which they themselves never overtly participated. It therefore seems, at least from these two studies of vocabulary retention, that overt participation is not necessary for acquisition. It also appears that the overt interaction of a class will not clearly predict what is uptaken and acquired by individual learners. Perhaps it is not the salience given to an aspect of language through interactive work that makes a difference for its 'uptake' but its relative *significance* for those who work on it in covert ways. When Dobinson asked the students in her study why they thought they had recalled the particular new vocabulary that they did, they mostly replied that it was those items which were initially *incomprehensible* to them and to which they therefore had to devote focused individual work during the class to find out their meanings through the dictionary, through association with familiar words, or whatever.

Task interaction

A high proportion of recent classroom-based research has become focused on learner–learner interactions during tasks, thereby building upon earlier quasi-experimental studies of native–non-native speaker interaction. The kinds of classroom task that may facilitate interaction among learners confirms the significance of the kind of 'pushed output' (Long, 1996: 448) which we find in learner responses to teacher elicitations. A task that entails an information gap between interlocutors that is unfamiliar to them, that engages learners in social exchanges about shared goals and problems, that is undertaken by learners of different levels of proficiency, and that demands a single, closed solution for successful completion appears to encourage learners to have longer turns, produce more complex language and devote more time to explicit negotiation for meaning than any other kinds of task (Berwick, 1990; Long, 1989, 1996; Mackey, 1996; Pica, 1992; Plough and Gass, 1993).

However, research on interaction during task work within the classroom context reveals a similar ambiguity in terms of its effects upon leaning as we have seen in teacher-fronted interaction. For instance, echoing Musumeci's (1996) discovery that, when incomprehension occurs during teacher–student interaction in content-based lessons, the problem is often by-passed rather than leading to further negotiation, Foster (1998) found the similar avoidance in classroom-located tasks. Students were simply not predisposed to negotiate for meaning when they confronted moments of incomprehension. Some studies have also revealed that the quality of learner language during task work may be less what they are actually capable of producing (Higgs and Clifford, 1982; Seedhouse, 1999). Seedhouse's analysis of a large number of learner interactions during task work in a range of classroom situations revealed that student talk appeared to be constrained both by the nature of the turn-taking and the linguistic forms that seemed to be required to complete the task. He found a high proportion of indexical or single-word interactions in which meanings were not negotiated overtly because students relied more upon the often unspoken, implicit content and procedure of the task. Seedhouse deduced that much task work might actually encourage learners to communicate in a particular variety of language beneath their productive capability. That is, learner interaction is embedded within the text of the specific task rather than facilitative of learners' development of the language beyond the immediate context. This is an important observation to which we will return in the next section of this chapter.

Of course, the characteristics of the tasks undertaken by students in these studies may not have had the design features of those tasks which have been identified as facilitating 'pushed output'. Tasks that encourage somewhat open-ended conversations are more likely to enable learners to avoid problems in understanding rather than modify their talk (Long, 1996). Skehan suggests that certain tasks may facilitate fluency in learner language at the resultant cost to accuracy and complexity (Skehan, 1996). The particular demands of a task, as with the demands of classroom talk between teacher and students, will certainly frame its potential interactivity and, therefore, what may be learned from it. This recognition that some tasks may encourage learners to focus too much on what may be meaningful *for them* at the cost of the form of their utterances is one of the motivations for the current interest in tasks that encourage a more explicit focus on form.

But it is not only the design of tasks that shape how learners interact while undertaking them. Block (1994) and Kumaravadivelu (1991) discovered that learners may interpret the purposes and procedures of task work differently from what teachers had intended. Similarly, Kasanga (1996) and Newton and Kennedy (1996) found that students learned different things from task work depending on how they defined the task. Student perceptions of task requirements strongly influenced how they actually worked upon it through their interaction. Students' definitions of a task are, of course, framed by their definitions of the context in which they are working (Breen, 1985). The classroom, for the learner, is not a neutral environment made up of 'inputs' and 'outputs' that carry only literal meaning and immediate value. Indeed, even the quasi-experimental situation in which native speakers are requested to interact with non-native speakers is embedded within its own social pragmatics, perhaps including the requirement willingly to suspend disbelief for the researcher's sake. Such context-appropriate pragmatics are likely to frame and select the *specific* meanings that attract the negotiative effort of the particular interlocutors. In addition, as Aston pointed out when evaluating interaction data from learner dyads, a significant amount of negotiation may, in fact, be a function of the incomprehensibility of the task or a lack of clarity to the interlocutors concerning its procedures rather than expressing their effort to render each others' input more comprehensible (Aston, 1986). Applying conversational analysis to interaction data, he indicated that learners were just as likely to modify their talk in order to establish and maintain rapport and to signal interpersonal acceptance of what one another was saying regardless of whether they understood. Aston deduced that a social perspective on learner conversational adjustments during interaction would reveal that they are likely to serve more functions than making a potential meaning clearer. He concluded that too much negotiation for meaning might actually undermine mutual comprehensibility, not least because of its impact upon the socio-affective relationship between interlocutors. Even Dobinson's (1996) findings on repetition and turn-taking in relation to 'uptake' suggested that there was not a clear relationship and that too much of either appeared to be dysfunctional.

There is growing evidence that a broader socio-affective perspective on task work in the classroom situation can reveal much that is missed in a focus upon the interaction alone. Coughlan and Duff (1994) discovered that learners' willingness to go beyond merely getting the task over and done with as quickly as possible was highly context dependent. How they interacted was influenced by their mutual familiarity, the time they saw as being allocated to the task and, crucially, the location of the task itself within other classroom activities. Tasks, like momentary interactions in lessons, are also embedded within the wider lesson-by-lesson narrative of classroom work, and their significance for the learners is never merely immediate but related in various ways to the larger narrative of thinking and acting in the particular situation. This implies that any task, however well designed to 'push output', may be redefined and worked upon by students in ways that might actually constrain and hide their spoken language potential. Platt and Brooks (1994) seem to confirm this in finding that students' own purposes are critical in influencing both their experience of a task and how they perform within it. They found students adopting strategies such as merely going through the motions of interaction, using the first language where they could to clarify task procedures, relying on single-word exchanges and other paralinguistic clues to solve the problem, and slipping out of the interaction to indulge in private speech to sort things out individually. Not all of these strategies may be nonproductive, of course. For instance, Ohta (1999), building on the ideas of Vygotsky (1987), argues that private speech during classroom work provides evidence of students formulating their own responses even though the teacher may not directly seek these through elicitation. In task work, such reformulations may be available to partners in the task rather like the interactive efforts of the higher participating students in the Slimani and Dobinson studies. However, Platt and Brooks suggest that students within a particular classroom culture may give such high priority to task completion and solving its inherent problem that, in doing so, they avoid or hurry past comprehensibility troubles which require them to modify their speech.

This recent evidence from studies of interaction in tasks appears to support Liddicoat's observation regarding earlier studies of 'negotiation for meaning' that there is:

> [T]he need for a more sophisticated understanding of what is meant by interaction and of the relationship between interaction and social context. In particular, there needs to be a more careful discussion of the identities available for participants in a particular interaction.   (Liddicoat, 1997: 316)

He goes on to question SLA researchers' reliance on the mere quantification of those features of interaction that are taken as typifying participants' efforts to modify their input as failing to capture what actually occurs during interaction. Focusing only upon the presence or absence of conversational adjustments in data might therefore distract us from other aspects of interaction that are highly significant to learners and which, in turn, have an impact upon language development – be it positive or negative. The different interpretation attributed by Firth and Wagner (1997: 295) to the same short stretches of interaction originally provided by Gass and Varonis (1985) suggest that any meanings that are salient for learners during interaction (the 'insider' perspective) may be different from those that are salient to different researchers ('outsiders'' perspectives). In fact, as Firth and Wagner suggest, some overt conversational modifications taken as evidence for negotiation of meaning may have less to do with comprehensibility of input and more to do with the social pragmatics of the task situation. Conversely, as we have seen from evidence of classroom interaction, meanings that become salient to one or other participant during task work and that *do* have a positive impact upon that person's language development might never be overtly negotiated. That these points may be obvious does not undermine the key issue that, if interaction during task work is to be taken as a source of evidence for what may contribute to language acquisition, the actual *significance in context* of both the task and the interaction for the participating learners needs to be further explored.

Conclusions from classroom research

What can be concluded from the studies here reviewed on teacher-orchestrated interaction and learner–learner interaction during classroom-based tasks regarding the benefits to language acquisition through learners' overt participation? This is an urgent question for language teachers because, unlike the priority of the researcher to discover which particular aspects of learner talk might correlate with later acquisition, the teacher needs to know how to create those conditions in the classroom where overt learner participation will maximize the likelihood of language development. Some of the main conclusions from these studies can be summarized as follows:

- It remains to be proved that overt participation by learners in classroom or task interaction can lead to the acquisition of previously unacquired aspects of the language which are generated by that interaction. To date, evidence for this is ambiguous, even regarding very specific aspects of language such as vocabulary or particular forms of language chosen by a teacher as a deliberate focus within interactive work.
- Overt classroom and task interaction is inter-textual and multi-functional in being made up of, at least, communication about content, language and classroom procedures and spontaneous asides both in teacher-orchestrated talk and in learner–learner talk. Learners have to navigate through this inter-textuality identifying and adopting textual cues which may signal a transition from one kind of talk to another and, thereby, the potential meanings of each kind of talk. It is probable that different learners, both as a group and as individuals, will be more or less skilled in such navigation. Their task is further complicated by the extended text of lessons being continuously ambiguous in serving both a social and pedagogic purpose. Therefore any moment of interaction may be interpreted differently by different students depending upon the purpose they superimpose upon it.
- Teacher communication that 'pushes' learner output by demanding overt responses from learners, such as questioning or nominated turns or even personal observations, may, in turn, influence their individual learning outcomes.
- How teachers respond to their participation may superimpose a degree of risk for many learners and the possibility of threat to their self-esteem in a public situation.

- Perhaps more proficient students in a class are those more willing to participate, thereby taking on the burden of interactive work but not necessarily gaining from it. Therefore, proficiency in the language may enable greater participation rather than participation leading to gains in proficiency.
- It is possible that non-participating learners, who may be less proficient, are gaining from others' participation in class.
- The overt interaction of a class will not clearly predict what is uptaken and acquired by individual learners. It may not be the salience given to an aspect of language through interactive work – such as topicalisation and repetition, extended turn-taking, or conversational modifications – that makes a difference for its 'uptake' but its relative significance or incomprehensibility for those who work on it in covert ways.
- Certain task work in the classroom situation might encourage learners to communicate in a particular variety of language or forms of language beneath their productive capability. Interaction is embedded within the discourse of the specific task and may not enable the development of the language beyond the immediate interactive requirements of the task.
- Even in a task which exemplifies design features that entail negotiation for meaning learners may give such high priority to the task's completion, or solving its inherent problem, or maintaining face that, in doing so, they avoid or by-pass comprehensibility troubles which might require them to modify their speech.
- Student definitions of a task are framed within their definitions of the classroom context in which they are working. These definitions in turn encourage learners to interact on the basis of what they deduce as a context-appropriate pragmatics, which are likely to frame and select the *specific* meanings that attract the negotiative effort of learners.
- Conversational adjustments during interaction are likely to serve other social functions in addition to, or instead of, making clearer a potential meaning. Too much negotiation for meaning might actually undermine mutual comprehensibility, not least because of its impact upon the socio-affective relationship between interlocutors.
- As with Pica's deduction from her review of the research on whether or not learners notice the gap between target forms and their own interlanguage production (Pica, 1994: 520, op. cit.), what learners actually *acquire* from overt participation in the classroom cannot be observed nor confidently predicted or inferred from the interaction. Echoing Pica's conclusion, this may not reflect a fault within learners' participation in the classroom, but rather the current state of research perspectives upon it.

Allwright's identification of the 'discoursal dilemmas' in classroom communication for teacher and learners and recent studies, such as those of Coughlan and Duff (1994) and Platt and Brooks (1994), suggest that we need to look beyond the surface of the teacher–learner and learner–learner talk to at least uncover its diverse meanings and significance in terms of what participants intend by it and how they interpret it. Both the interactive hypo-thesis and the output hypothesis tend to encourage the attribution of a *particular* force to conversational modifications: that they primarily manifest negoti-ation for those meanings which are seemingly unclear to the interlocutors. Further, such meanings are at risk of being interpreted by the researcher in a paradoxically decontextualized way in the sense that their transparency is taken to reside in the *immediate* topic or content about which teacher and learners or learner and learner are *assumed to be* interacting. An analysis only of the surface text of exchanges in classroom or task work can result in decontextualization in two ways. First, the interactions are often extracted from the more extended text of a lesson or task work and, indeed, from the extended text which teacher and students have created over the series of lessons in their work together. A more extensive analysis of even the text of lessons or of dyads working together on a series of tasks over time is more likely to reveal the specific functions of a momentary interaction that is embedded within them. And, crucially, such extended texts are more likely to reveal the layered and changing nature of the functions of talk as the culture of the particular classroom or the relationship between dyads of learners develop. Secondly, and more important, the surface texts provided as evidence to support the two hypotheses are most often analysed in literal terms, devoid of even their potential social and affective significance or value for those who actually generated them. Such a partial view of the meaning potential within teacher–learner and learner–learner interactions in context seriously dilutes what is claimed to be a crucial variable in the research and, therefore, weakens its explanatory power. Classroom and task interaction has meaning potential that is layered in being both superficially immediate and traceable to an explicit topic or content yet also always framed *intrapersonally* within both the conscious and unconscious learning agenda of the individual learners and framed *interpersonally* within the discourse of the language classroom. The former is, of course, less accessible to the researcher. The latter, however, may be more accessible and, therefore, a medium through which we may better understand both the process and outcomes of learner participation.

BEYOND INTERACTION TO DISCOURSE

If we seek to trace the possible impact upon acquisition of the linguistic and communicative environment of a classroom and, more particularly, the learners' overt participation in it, we have to move beyond perceiving it as seemingly 'non-negotiable' (Long, 1996: 453), wherein rarity in learner out-put seems to be the norm (Krashen, 1998; Swain, 1995). We also have to explain such things and, more significantly, how it is that some learners are nevertheless successful acquirers *and* producers of language as a result of having access to it primarily through a classroom. Krashen would argue that they had the good fortune to enter a class that was particularly input-rich. Proponents of Universal Grammar might well dismiss classrooms as merely sources of degenerate performance data wherein the learners' inherent acquisition device does virtually all of the work in any case. If we try to trace aspects of the observable surface talk of the classroom or a task in the subsequent output of learners with a view to proposing a causal relationship, this may be seen as an impoverished perspective on the learning process that reduces language development to an input stimulus and output or uptake response mechanism. It was precisely this view of learning that Chomsky (1959) dismissed as an inadequate account of language acquisition. The ambiguity of findings from current classroom-based research might encourage us to deduce that, if a learner develops aspects of language as a result of overt participation in classroom interaction, this development is little more than chance or mere coincidence. We still need to try to explain why learners learn different things from the interaction and why some learners learn from classroom interaction while some do not. And the answers are not likely to be available in the observable text alone.

The research perspective

I suggested earlier that both the interaction and output hypotheses overlook the socio-affective significance of the data on which they rely and of the contexts from which they obtain such data. I have argued elsewhere that research on language acquisition in the classroom is constrained by an asocial perspective on the interaction that occurs within it (Breen, 1985, 1996). Recently, Firth and Wagner (1997) urged a reconceptualization of SLA research by locating the study of acquisition within discourse as a broader frame for the analysis of learner interaction, especially in settings other than experimental settings, that would more accurately uncover the constraints upon, and actual achievements of, communication for learning. Such a reconceptualization, they argued, would enable researchers to 'understand and explicate how language is used *as it is being acquired through interaction*' (Firth and Wagner, 1997: 296, original emphasis). In reply to Firth and Wagner, Long expressed scepticism 'as to whether greater insights into SL *use* will *necessarily* have much to say about SL *acquisition*' (Long, 1997: 322, original emphasis). Gass (1998) replied to Firth and Wagner in essentially the same terms:

> [T]he emphasis in input and interaction studies is on the *language* used and not on the act of communication. . . . The research question central to SLA that I and others ask is: How do people *learn* a L2? – The question is not: How do people *use* a L2, unless the latter question is a means of getting at the former.
>
> (Gass, 1998: 84 and 85, original emphasis)

Gass's reference to 'use' as the window on to 'acquisition' is precisely the matter at issue. Long's assertion that SLA researchers who have studied interaction have 'often explicitly focused on at least some dimensions (of context) in their work' (1997: 318) also begs the questions as to *which* dimensions of context and *how* these dimensions have been analysed and interpreted. These recent interchanges within SLA research have been little more than the rehearsal of rather misleading dichotomies between language 'use' versus 'acquisition' and 'language' versus 'communication' that merely constrain the research enterprise. Gass appears to reflect a commonly held view in much SLA research that 'language' is synonymous with 'grammar' and acquisition is, therefore, acquisition of the rules of grammar (1998: 83–4) and not, seemingly, the development of communicative competence in a new language (Canale and Swain, 1980). We shall return to this issue later. But the blunt distinction between 'use' and 'acquisition' merely blinds us to much finer distinctions than exist between using language in everyday communication in a range of contexts and using language in order to acquire it or refine one's control over it in, for example, the context of a language class or learning task.

If we learn a language in the company of others in a classroom, then we cannot avoid participating, even silently, in social activity that is not just a superficial frame for our work on language data. Social relationships in the classroom orchestrate what is made available for learning, how learning is done and what we achieve. These relationships and the purposeful social action of teaching and learning are realized through the jointly constructed discourse of lessons. The data in terms of both the form and meaning of language made available to learners are socially filtered through this discourse and, thereby, rendered subtly distinctive from what research has described as 'naturally occurring' language data in a different context. Furthermore, because the forms and meanings made available to learners in a classroom are a collective product with which teacher and learners interact actively as both creators and interpreters, and because what learners actually learn from the classroom is discursively constructed, any explanation of how language is acquired in a classroom must locate the process *within* the discourse of that class. Outcomes from task work, if undertaken in a classroom context, also have to be explained with reference to the discursive context which generated them. In essence, language 'use' in a classroom is woven within the discourse of that classroom. From the perspectives of teacher and learners, the opportunities for, and processes of, its 'acquisition' are simultaneously woven within the discourse. In replying to Firth and Wagner's (1997) criticism of SLA research in its seeming construction of the learner or non-native speaker as deficient, both Gass (1998) and Long (1997) justifiably point out that the stance of a learner in relation to language use is, by definition, different from that of a proficient user of the language. However, within the discourse of a classroom, the learners' stance renders 'use' and 'acquisition' as not clearly separable; there is a constant interrelationship. One of the defining features of a classroom context is that 'use' and 'acquisition' co-occur within discourse in a mutually informing or dialectical process.

How, therefore, might we characterize classroom discourse in ways that may better reveal this dialectic and its socio-affective significance for those participating in it? Fairclough (1989, 1992) has provided a particular framework for the analysis of discourse which is made up of three related levels or components. For him, any instance of discourse can be seen as being simultaneously a piece of text, an instance of discursive practice and an instance or realization of social practice(s). Applying this framework to the language classroom, the *text* of lessons is all the observable language or communicative data, be they spoken, written or in other visual media from pictures and diagrams to facial expressions. It is this dimension of discourse upon which both the interaction and output hypotheses and much classroom research have tended to focus. *Discursive practices* are how such text is produced and interpreted and how the different types of text are combined or entwined in a particular context. Teachers and learners in the classroom produce, interpret and combine texts just as teaching materials, in whatever medium, are also produced and combined by people not present in the classroom but for teacher and learners to incorporate and interpret in ways that serve their immediate purposes. Finally, *social practices* refer to the organizational and institutional circumstances that generate and delimit both the specific text and discursive practices of lessons. Social practices include not only those broader cultural and situational factors which locate classrooms as having a particular function and identity, but also those taken-for-granted but significant practices such as how the furniture is organized, or how long a lesson should last, or whether learners will be tested on the completion of their studies. More crucially, perhaps, both teacher and learners are actually positioned and constructed *as teachers* and *as learners* by the discursive and social practices of the classroom group. The daily routines and procedures which teachers and learners jointly establish in order to work together in a relatively harmonious way are also significant social practices constructed through the discourse of lessons that further realize the underlying culture of the language class (Breen, 1985). This three-dimensional nature of classroom discourse, therefore, is made up of the social practices of the classroom group that shape the discursive practices of teacher and learners and these discursive practices generate the text of classroom interaction. However, the process is also reflexive in the sense that the text of lessons may, as it unfolds, express or limit alternative discursive practices and these, in turn, may facilitate or constrain alternative social practices. Negotiation for meaning during interaction and task work is therefore the surface text embedded within, and generated by, the discursive and social practices of any classroom.

To date there are no studies of the possible relationships between language classroom discourse defined in this way and language acquisition. In considering how SLA research appears to construct the learners, I suggested in an earlier paper that an important learner contribution that remains to be investigated is that of the learner as a discursive practitioner within the classroom (Breen, 1996). The main conclusions from research on learners' overt participation in the classroom offered in the previous section of this chapter suggest a more detailed elaboration of the likely *discursive* contributions of learners. From the research we may deduce that learners appear obliged to adopt, to varying degrees and at various times, at least the following discursive practices during classroom work:

- Adopt a responsive role to the teacher's management of the text of the lesson, being particularly alert to nominated turns, questions and other procedural requirements seemingly addressed to you and be ready to act appropriately.
- Look out for those cues in the text that reveal its different and changing purposes so that you can appropriately interpret the function or functions of a particular moment so that, if you are called upon to participate or you choose to participate, your contribution will be appropriate and acceptable.
- With the teacher and other learners observe routines and procedures which have been gradually established in the class so that lessons unfold as manageable social events as well as being useful to your own learning agenda.
- Manage self-presentation by trying to contribute overtly only at times when the risk to your image, as you see it in the eyes of the teacher or fellow students, seems to you to be low.
- If you understand what is being asked of the class and you are confident you know how to respond, volunteer the information appropriately. If you don't understand, avoid saying anything and, if you wish to avoid being nominated, perhaps indicate that you understand.
- If the teacher asks something of you directly which you understand, respond appropriately. If you don't understand, wait in silence for a moment until someone else is nominated or indicate in some way that you don't know the answer or, if you are more confident, say that you don't understand.
- Look out for things in the interaction that are familiar to you and use these as cues to interpret what is incomprehensible. If something is incomprehensible that seems to you important to know, do your own work on this either immediately or when you have the chance.
- Listen particularly to what fellow learners say in the class in case their communication with the teacher may make some things clearer that serve your own purposes and learning agenda.
- Depending on your estimate of the difficulty of a task, your fellow students' ability in the language and their self-confidence in the situation, adapt your own overt contributions accordingly. If you don't understand what a fellow student is saying during task work, either indicate that you don't, if you can, or indicate that the student should continue so that things might become clearer. If you find the task particularly difficult, rely as much as you can on what your interlocutor says. If both of you seem to be finding it difficult, seek ways around it that make it easier to complete or agree to abandon it.

Learners' capacity to manage their intrapersonal and interpersonal activity within the context of a language class may therefore be summarized as the successful navigation of its discourse through discursive practices that may maximize personal benefit and minimize personal cost. Research in language classrooms to date suggests that learners overtly participate in language lessons through pragmatic reliance on such practices. It is also on the basis of such practices that learners jointly construct lessons with a teacher. However, being pragmatically appropriate in the language class may or may not facilitate language acquisition. If we accept Hatch's claim that language learning evolves out of learning how to participate in conversations (Hatch, 1978: 404, op. cit.) and Donato's proposal that language development arises from the co-construction of knowledge in joint activity (Donato, 1994: 39), a crucial issue that warrants investigation is: *In what ways might learners' seemingly appropriate navigation of classroom discourse and the tasks within it relate to success in language development?*

The pedagogic perspective

Clearly, different learners may be more or less successful at such navigation not least because, from their personal perspectives, the text and discursive practices of the discourse are potentially dynamic. However, both teacher and students as a group are likely to work at making the discourse more predictable and, therefore, manageable. Hence, the underlying social practice of gradual and joint establishment of routines, procedures and taken-for-granted values and meanings that will characterize the emerging culture of the particular classroom group. As a contributory factor, learners are likely to have prior experience in applying many of the discursive practices I have so far tried to articulate. If they are older than the early grades of elementary school, they will have had a good deal of practice in navigating classroom discourse before entering the language class. It is likely that the requirement to exercise such practices defines for them what a classroom *is*. Learners will superimpose upon any language class the expectation of exercising such practices regardless of what they may be encouraged to do that might be different. If learning a language is embedded in the discourse of the language class, a key pedagogic question is whether or not this discourse enables learners to participate in other contexts wherein the discourse may be different. The pedagogic challenge may be to build upon and extend in particular ways the discursive practices that learners assume they must exercise in many classrooms so that the distinctions between classroom discourse and other realms of discourse become eroded. This appears to be the significant matter of enabling opportunities for discursive practices that transform classroom discourse into a *means of access* rather than something that is folded in upon itself (Breen, 1998; Duff, 1996; van Lier, 1996).

It is on the issue of a specific discourse embedded in the classroom context that a research agenda and a pedagogic agenda may be seen to overlap. The discursive practices I have identified may appear, at first sight, to place limits upon learners' overt participation which is proposed as beneficial for language acquisition by both the interaction and output hypotheses. For example, building upon Long's identification of the characteristics of tasks that 'push output' (Long, 1996: 448), we could envisage classroom interaction as a kind of macro-task within which learners' work on specific tasks may occur. Seeing classroom communication in this way, we can ask *which* of learners' discursive practices are likely to constrain or create the kind of interaction in which they may:

- Identify shared goals in their learning and within classroom work;
- Undertake unfamiliar ways of working and deal with unfamiliar content as part of classroom work;
- Work together in mixed proficiency dyads wherein the more proficient interlocutor and the less proficient interlocutor have equal opportunity to take on the sending and the receiving roles;
- Undertake the kind of cooperation that is required when they have to share different information in order to complete classroom work;
- Seek and achieve specific predetermined or pre-planned purposes and solutions within tasks and other activities in the classroom;
- Communicate in the classroom in ways in which topics and sub-topics are recycled in seeking to solve particular problems or issues.

If these conditions have been identified as facilitative of negotiation for meaning in tasks, their implementation in the macro-task of classroom interaction is an important pedagogic issue. And the related research issue is: *what interpersonal meanings and significance* actually generate and sustain the interaction for the participants although these may not be observable directly in its surface text? This question leads to more specific research questions such as:

- How is a shared goal identified and to what extent may it be shared?
- Do learners render seemingly unfamiliar content and tasks more familiar in how they define and work on them?
- How do learners of different proficiency levels actually define and exercise their role in a dyadic interaction?
- How do learners compensate for information that is lacking or is not shared during classroom interaction or within a task?
- Is what appears to be a single purpose or solution the same purpose or solution that an individual learner seeks or derives from a task within classroom work?
- What do learners define as the contextually appropriate extent of negotiation on a particular topic or problem? And so on.

In essence, we need to be alert to the fact that the conditions that we have so far identified as enabling negotiation for meaning and the evidence we cite for this are very much a particular interpretation of both the conditions and the evidence. Learners may or may not attach similar significance to them and it is likely to be the conditions to which *they* attach significance for their own learning agendas that have an impact upon their language development.

In general, therefore, how learners exercise their discursive practices in a learning context will relate to the value they attribute to some conditions rather than others and this may change over time depending upon the socio-affective and psycholinguistic characteristics of the learners, such as relative

proficiency, confidence, self-image, motivation, and so on. The text of negotiation for meaning in task work, for example, can therefore be seen as the
surface realization of a complex of individual learner contributions within
joint activity. Crucially, what *mediates* between the surface text of interaction
and such deeper contributions is how learners act discursively in context and
why they act in the ways they do. Hence the need to investigate the text of
interaction *in the context of* the discourse of both the classroom and the task
work within it. The investigation of discursive practices in the language classroom therefore allows us greater access to the learning process as social
action and affective engagement in an ongoing relation to psycholinguistic
development.

BEYOND OVERT PARTICIPATION AND LANGUAGE ACQUISITION

So far this chapter has focused upon the learners' overt participation in the
classroom, the arguments and evidence relating to its contribution to language acquisition, and the limits of a research focus upon only the text of
teacher–learner or learner–learner interaction. I have proposed that, if we
perceive negotiation for meaning as the catalyst for language development,
we need to explore deeper than the surface interpretations of an interaction
by investigating the discursive practices of learners that both generate and
sustain the interaction and imbue it with situated significance and meaning.
I have also suggested that an explanation of how language is learned in a
classroom that rests upon meaningful interaction has to take account of the
socio-affective dimensions of the process in relation to the psycholinguistic
and that a focus upon learner discursive practices within classroom discourse
provides a means for doing so. In the light of this foregoing discussion, I wish
to conclude by offering some key implications for future research on learner
participation in the classroom in relation to language acquisition.

Redefining the variable of learner participation

One conclusion from reflecting on the research on learner participation is
that a significant proportion of it is not likely to be overt much of the time.
Overt participation may appear relatively scarce or constrained in many
teacher-fronted classrooms and it may need certain kinds of interaction to
'push' it to the surface, but most learners in these circumstances *are* continually participating. Consciously and unconsciously they are engaging certain
discursive practices framed within and, in turn, shaping the social practices
they regard as appropriate to the situation. An even broader research agenda
would be to analyse language classroom discourse to trace further those
socio-political influences upon the discourse that may facilitate or constrain
certain kinds of teacher and learner participation (Chouliaraki and Fairclough,
1999; see also Norton, Chapter 8 in the present volume). Overt participation
may sometimes provide us with clues as to the discursive significance and

meaning – in addition to the immediate surface meanings – which learners give to, and derive from, classroom and task interactions. We may also be able to trace particular discursive practices through an examination of how learners participate, both explicitly in what they do or say and implicitly in their seeming inaction or silence. And we may trawl through these kinds of data in order to seek relationships between them and particular language learning outcomes. However, at least three conditions would be required of the research if we seek valid evidence for relationships between participation – as more broadly defined – and acquisition. First, interaction from the same classroom must be studied over time. Subtle shifts in interaction and its underlying meanings are not revealed by extracted samples of talk in lessons or tasks that manifest instances of conversational adjustment. Even the surface text of classroom talk has a dynamic that entails longitudinal study for this to be revealed. From the day a class meets for the first time through to when a degree of equilibrium is reached in routines and procedures, there are likely to be critical moments at which underlying social and discursive practices become more explicit. Access to the layers of meaning in interaction becomes possible through close study of the evolution of the culture of the class because teacher–learner and learner–learner interaction are framed within this evolution.

Secondly, because the actual significance and meaning of moments of the text may not be transparent much of the time, the researcher must get as close as possible to the participating learner's interpretation of that text. Any text carries potential meanings arising out of its discursive significance in context, and the researcher's imposition of a particular meaning or function of an utterance is always at risk of being either partial or flawed. The actual meaning about which negotiation appears to occur or the actual meaning or significance which learners attribute to the different moments of interaction reside with the learners and not in the text, except in a superficial sense. What will be salient to a learner during interaction – what will be 'noticed' – may be unpredictable from moment to moment. However, adopting a discoursal perspective on the classroom enables us to study the interaction as arising out of particular social positions, actions and perspectives that learners – and teachers – attribute specifically to classroom work. We are necessarily involved in an investigation of a complex of variables, but the study of the meaning and significance given to, and derived from, classroom interaction by its participants does not entail a relativist stance on the part of the researcher. The search is for *particular* discursive practices, and the texts that both realize and generate them, that may facilitate or inhibit language development.

A third condition for obtaining valid evidence on the relationship between participation and acquisition is that the research must break out from the current risk of circularity. This risk resides in the prediction that certain conversational adjustments in interaction will lead to acquisition because evidence of acquisition from some previous study suggested that *the same* conversational adjustments were responsible. We need to discover what learners *actually* acquire from having participated in interaction. There is some evidence to suggest that learners do retain different things from even the same shared interaction. Therefore, it may be more beneficial to start from evidence of whatever learners acquire from interaction and, from these, trace back to the discursive features of the interaction to uncover their possible influence upon what has been acquired. It may appear to save time focusing upon learners' interactive work that stimulates the use of a *particular* aspect of language to discover whether or not it is produced in a post-test or within spontaneous talk at some later date. However, it is almost a truism to suggest that other intervening circumstances may have just as likely enabled the later production of the particular aspect of language as did the original inter-action. More important, a focus on a selected aspect of language that occurs in the text of lessons may distract the researcher from unexpected, diverse and even more resilient learning outcomes. The uncovering of outcomes leads us to reconsider how a good proportion of SLA research defines what is acquired.

Redefining outcomes

The debate about possible distinctions between acquisition and learning and the relationship between them has occupied a number of SLA researchers in past years and this is not the place to rehearse the arguments (for a recent discussion, see Zobl, 1995). However, the issue has become muddied of late with the appearance of the term 'uptake' in a number of research studies (Lyster and Ranta, 1997; Slimani, 1989 *inter alia*). The term is generally applied to aspects of language which learners appear to have retained from explicit data, usually during interaction, and which can be traced through immediate post-tests or recall at some later time. However, its operational definition across studies is ambiguous and its relationship to the more generic concept of acquisition remains unclear. For instance, *immediate* uptake from interaction during a lesson or task is not reliable evidence of acquisition. We cannot be sure if such uptake is either evidence of something previously acquired, merely imitated rather than acquired, or actually acquired. The appearance of the notion of uptake may be symptomatic of some uncertainty in SLA research about what constitutes adequate evidence for genuine longer-term acquisition from classroom or task interaction. There is little doubt that such evidence remains sparse and the intervention of variables other than the interaction itself complicates the issue. A common rationale offered in those instances where learners apparently fail later to produce forms of language, despite previous interactive work that either implicitly or explicitly focuses upon them, is the appeal to learner readiness, or failures on the part of the learners to 'notice', or the learnability of the particular forms in relation to the current state of the learners' interlanguage. Of course, such explanations may be correct in certain circumstances. If we believe that interaction does make a difference, however, a clear distinction needs to be made between interaction that merely enables learners to pro-duce what they have already acquired or merely imitated and interaction that genuinely 'pushes' their language developmentally. This, of course, entails pre-testing and longitudinal investigation to avoid the risk of assuming a prior lack on the part of a learner for which interaction may compensate. Nevertheless, a question arises here with regard to pre- and post-testing. Should testing comprise as closely as possible the kinds of interaction which we identify as revealing negotiation for meaning? (This particular issue is discussed from a testing perspective by McNamara (1997)). If this is not seen to be necessary, then we are displacing the influence of context upon language production and, thereby, assuming that the capacity for meaningful and appropriate interaction is not a component of the language being learned.

A major implication, therefore, of adopting a discoursal perspective on the relationship between learner participation and language acquisition relates to how we may define the dependent variable in the whole process; the language that the learner acquires. In seemingly preserving its own territory, SLA research in the main has pursued its endeavours as if over twenty years of sociolinguistic, pragmatic and discoursal perspectives on the nature of language had hardly existed. There are exceptions, of course, as in the studies of second language pragmatics and sociolinguistic influences upon second language use as exemplified in Beebe and Takahashi (1989), Blum-Kulka, House and Kasper (1989), Kasper (1996a), Kasper and Kellerman (1997), Tollefson (1995), Wolfson (1989) and Wolfson and Judd (1983). We saw earlier how Gass asserted that SLA research was primarily concerned with the acquisition of language – as contrasted with 'communication' – and that, for her at least, 'language' is synonymous with the rules of grammar. Gregg has similarly argued that, in contrast to the domain of grammar, 'any attempt to construct a theory of language acquisition in the domain of pragmatics or communication is going to be handicapped by the lack of a well-articulated formal characterization of the domain' (Gregg, 1989: 24). However, it is questionable whether all grammarians would agree with his premise. Some sociolinguists and discourse analysts would certainly challenge his conclusion. We cannot deny the complexity of the task of investigating language acquisition that defines language as characteristically framed *within* its social use and the learning of it as being therefore dependent, as Donato expresses it, upon joint activity that co-constructs 'linguistic change among and within individuals' (Donato, 1994: 39). The interaction and output hypotheses hinge upon evidence grounded in contexts of use yet they appear not to follow through the implications of doing so. The kind of discoursal view of language acquisition explored in this chapter locates language as the text of social activity that is imbued with potential meanings and, thereby, potential learning opportunities constantly generated by the discursive and social practices of the creators of that text. Language development through interaction is inseparable from these practices enacted in particular contexts. A discoursal perspective on language development identifies such development as the capacity to communicate in particular contexts wherein the rules of grammar are a contributory part of such a capacity. Grammatical knowledge is located as a means for the production and interpretation of text through discursive practices in social contexts. While contributing to a more precise characterization of the kind of classroom discourse that can be directly beneficial to acquisition, the kind of discoursal perspective on language development that is offered here may also extend our understanding of the acquisition process itself *and* what we define as the outcomes of the process.

If the proposals offered here appear to render the study of the relationship between learner participation in interaction and language acquisition more complex than the interaction and output hypotheses allow, then, to adapt Pica's conclusion on studies of negotiation (Pica, 1994: 520, op. cit.), the limitations may reside more in the hypotheses and the research processes upon which they currently rely rather than in the actual nature of interaction. The study of discourse has progressed markedly since Hatch recognized the learning of how to undertake conversations as the crucible for acquisition. It is time, perhaps, to reconsider what this actually implies if we seek to relate context and acquisition and, thereby, realign learners' social and affective contributions to language development in mutual relationship with their psycholinguistic contribution.

Chapter 7

(S)econd (L)anguage (A)ctivity theory: understanding second language learners as people

James P. Lantolf, The Pennsylvania State University and Aneta Pavlenko, Temple University

INTRODUCTION

In her interesting and reasoned response to the controversial paper by Firth and Wagner (1997), Kasper (1997) discusses one of the core assumptions of Anglo-Saxon scientific tradition: that the object of study of any (social) scientific enterprise is constructed by distilling out features considered to be irrelevant to the specific goal of the given scientific enterprise. In the case of second language acquisition (SLA), according to Kasper, researchers need to peel away the multiple and complex layers that constitute real individuals in order to focus attention on one or two features of interest to us – specifically people's identities of a 'learner' and/or a 'non-native speaker' of a given language. Kasper admits that this is a 'highly reductionist', though apparently necessary, move, for without it we would not be able to determine clearly 'the aspect that is common to the studied agents, and relevant in the global research context (or discourse universe) of L2 study generally and L2 acquisition (SLA) specifically' (Kasper, 1997: 309).

We do not want to dispute the legitimacy of the scientific method and its extensions into the social sciences; nor do we wish to argue that progress has not been made in explaining aspects of SLA through the implementation of the scientific method in our field. However, we believe there is also much to be gained by considering the relevance of an alternative approach to research – an approach sometimes referred to as the hermeneutic tradition, or romantic science (see Luria, 1979). The foundation for this tradition was laid in the writings of the eighteenth-century Italian scholar, Giambatista Vico, especially in his monumental work *Scienza Nuova*, which appeared in English for the first time in 1948. In his *New Science*, Vico challenged the validity of the Cartesian approach to scientific research in general, but most specifically with regard to the study of human culture, society, history and mind. This is not the place to go into the details of Vico's arguments against Cartesian science. We will simply borrow the words of Isaiah Berlin, who in his superb presentation of Vico's complex, and at times confusing, statements on the human sciences, remarks that for Vico the study of the non-physical features of human beings clearly required moving beyond the search 'for and from generalizations and idealized models derived from the uniformities of the co-presences and successions of phenomena' and to a concern over describing 'human experience as concretely as possible, and therefore to emphasize variety, differences, change, motives and goals, individuality rather than uniformity or indifference to time or unaltering repetitive patterns' (Berlin, 1976: 89).

Vico has had a rather remarkable degree of direct and indirect influence on such important thinkers as Dilthey, Herder, von Humboldt, Hegel and Marx (see Berlin, 1976; Taylor, 1985), and probably through Hegel and Marx on the great Russian psycholinguist, L.S. Vygotsky (1987), whose theory we adopt to carry out our project. During an approximately ten-year period following the Russian Revolution, Vygotsky addressed himself to the problem of constructing a unified psychology. In his view, the discipline had become fractured as a consequence of the jockeying for dominance that arose among the various schools in their quest to claim the mantle as the only legitimate 'scientific' approach to the study of psychological processes (Vygotsky, 1997). Briefly, Vygotsky perceived that the various currents within psychology could be divided according to two postulates: *surface* psychology and *depth* psychology. The former was represented by Gestalt theories, and other phenomenologically based theories, such as those of Wilhelm Wundt, which assumed that 'mental phenomena are immediately given to the subject who experiences them' (Yaroshevsky and Gurgenidze, 1997: 351). The latter, represented primarily by Freudian psychoanalysis, attempted to explain mental behaviour on the basis of unconscious forces that were vaguely rooted in biological drives. Vygotsky rejected surface psychology because it simply could not 'discover the regularities behind the surface of the phenomena that determine them' (Yaroshevsky and Gurgenidze, 1997: 352). Indeed, if everything were on the surface, science would be a tautological exercise, at best. While Vygotsky acknowledged, in agreement with depth psychology, that biological factors clearly played an important function in psychology activity, they were insufficient to account for uniquely human ways of thinking.

Vygotsky argued that to understand the specifically human mind it was essential to bring meaning, sense, emotion, expressiveness and with these, culture and history, which Wundt had exiled to disciplines such as anthropology and history, back into the picture in a central way (see Cole, 1996; Danziger, 1990, 1997). He referred to this new unified approach as *height psychology* – a psychology which not only took account of our natural biological endowments, but at the same time recognized the importance of 'the supra-individual world of developing human culture' (Yaroshevsky and Gurgenidze, 1997: 353). Some modern scholars, such as Wertsch (1985), have criticized Vygotsky for failing to explore fully the role of biological factors in human psychological processes. While we do not wish to quarrel with Wertsch on this point, we would like to point out that in a previously unpublished paper by Vygotsky, which appears as a separate chapter entitled 'The historical meaning of the crisis in psychology: a methodological investigation', in Vygotsky (1997), he strongly underscores the importance of biology in the formation of human consciousness. Nevertheless, a cornerstone of sociocultural theory is that it is our cultural history and not our biology that endows us with uniquely human ways of thinking. Eventually, Vygotsky, along with his colleagues, A.N. Leont'ev and A.R. Luria, succeeded in laying the foundation for what was to become the sociocultural theory of mind – a theory of real individuals rather than idealized abstractions that approaches its objects of study much more from the hermeneutic (interpretative) and historical standpoint than it does from the traditional experimental approach to research.

Perhaps one of the most lucid characterizations of romantic science was offered by A.R. Luria in his intellectual biography written near the end of his life:

> Romantics in science want neither to split living reality into its elementary components nor to represent the wealth of life's concrete events in abstract models that lose the properties of the phenomena themselves. It is of the utmost importance to romantics to preserve the wealth of living reality, and they aspire to a science that retains this richness.   (Luria, 1979: 174)

The task we set for ourselves here is to explore the implications of Vygotsky's theory in its contemporary formulation, activity theory, for understanding the nature of the relationships between real individuals and languages other than their first. It is, to cite Berlin again, about looking for what is unique and different rather than distilling 'the common kernel of dissimilar cases' (1976: 89).

A theory which considers humans from a more holistic, concrete and less idealized perspective can generate significant insights, as is becoming apparent from research in discursive psychology, general education and even certain areas of cognitive science. Consequently, we believe that space must be opened up within our field for a historical-interpretative approach to scientific research. We would, however, also like to remind everyone, ourselves included, that just as with other theories and models, we are constructing a particular view of people through what Burke (1966: 45) calls a *terministic screen*, or particular type of lens which directs our attention in certain directions and deflect it from others. The observations we make, or indeed anyone makes, are but implications of the particular terminology in terms of which the observations are made.

ACTIVITY THEORY

Several scholars, building on the original work of Vygotsky, have contributed to current thinking on activity theory. Among these are Davydov (1999), Engeström (1987, 1999), A.N. Leont'ev (1978, 1981), Wertsch (1998), and

Zinchenko (1995, 1996). Our summary of activity theory relies heavily on the work of these scholars, if not explicitly, then certainly implicitly. There is a fundamental difference between activity theory and other theories of mind that is important to consider. Activity theory differs from the Piagetian view in arguing that the social environment is not the context in which mind is formed, but the very source out of which specifically human kinds of mind develop. It differs from the neo-nativist position in that while it acknowledges the important role of our biologically endowed mental architecture, it assigns precedence to the content of mind (see Frawley, 1997). Hence, higher forms of mental functioning, including voluntary attention and memory, planning, logical thinking and learning, arise as a consequence of the appropriation of culture – earlier human experience as accumulated through time in a society. The task of scientific investigation is to determine how general mental concepts develop out of specific activities, and this task is accomplished through the investigation of the history of human beings, either as individuals, societies, cultures, or as a species, and of the activities through which they transform their worlds and are in turn transformed by their worlds.

Activity theory insists that any analysis of human mental activity must be carried out in its natural environment, which encompasses natural and culturally constructed objects or artifacts, abstract objects or ideas, as well as the world of other human beings, that is, the sociocultural world. In this, it is in agreement with contemporary poststructuralist approaches to language learning which examine discursive practices in their local contexts, demonstrating that different meanings may be assigned to the 'same' practices in different contexts (McKay and Wong, 1996; Norton Peirce, 1995; Pavlenko, forthcoming). The fundamental insight of the theory is the inseparability of thinking and activity (Zinchenko, 1996). Thinking and doing are not construed as polarities, since thinking is always motivated by some need and directed at some object designed to fulfil that need. Thus, while traditional approaches to the study of mind and mental behaviour focus on the study of the individual and what the individual is doing, sociocultural theory incorporates three additional dimensions to this enterprise: *how* the person is acting (i.e., in consort with artifacts or other individuals), *where* the person is acting (e.g., the experimental laboratory, the classroom, the public domain, etc.), and why the person is acting (i.e., the motives and goals underlying the activity) (Wertsch, 1998). Although Wertsch, following Burke's (1966) *pentad*, or five questions necessary to understand human social and psychological behaviour, does not include *when* the activity occurs, we believe that there is some merit in including this as a sixth question. We base this on the work of Coughlan and Duff (1994), who show how the same person carries out the same task in a markedly different way at two different points in time. The dimensions above are incorporated in the six fundamental principles of activity theory:

1. The human mind is formed and functions as a consequence of human interaction with the culturally constructed environment.

2. The cultural environment is as objective as physical, chemical and biological properties.

3. Activities are oriented to objects (concrete or ideal) and impelled by motives or needs (physical, social and psychological). Actions are directed at specific goals and are socioculturally designed means of fulfilling motives. Operations are the specific processes through which actions are carried out and are determined by the actual conditions in which the activity unfolds.

4. Mental processes are derived from external actions through the course of appropriation of the artifacts made available by a particular culture, both physical and semiotic (signs, words, metaphors, narratives). Internalization is not simply a matter of a verbatim copy of what was carried out, but a transformation of this activity as the mediation becomes private.

5. Mediation through the use of culturally constructed tools and others' voices (or discourses) shape the way people act and think as a result of internalization. The mechanism underlying mediation is a functional organ or system (Luria, 1973, 1979) formed through the intertwining of biologically endowed human abilities and the capacities passed on to us by our predecessors in the form of culturally constructed artifacts of a physical and symbolic nature. For example, we can think of a native or expert user of a language as forming a functional system in which the language ceases to be a tool separable from the person but is so tightly intertwined with who the person is that to interfere in some way with their language is to interfere with the person. On the other hand, second language learners can be viewed as individuals attempting to learn how to use a second semiotic tool and thus it is much easier to distinguish the person from the tool. Becoming a proficient user of the language from this perspective is about forming a composite functional organ of person–artifact in which one can no longer determine where the person ends and the tool begins or vice versa.

6. To understand human activity, including mental activity, means to know how it developed into its existing form.

ACTIVITY THEORY AND SLA AGENCY

We would now like to consider some implications of activity theory for second language learning, which from this perspective is about much more than the acquisition of forms: it is about developing, or failing to develop, new ways of mediating ourselves and our relationships to others and to ourselves.

We believe that learners have to be seen as more than processing devices that convert linguistic input into well-formed (or not so well-formed) outputs. They need to be understood as people, which in turn means we need to appreciate their human agency. As agents, learners actively engage in constructing the terms and conditions of their own learning. Recently, McGroarty (1998) and McKay and Wong (1996) have made similar arguments, although from a slightly different theoretical stance than we espouse here. McKay and Wong, in particular, have argued for a more contextualist and poststructuralist perspective on agency, whereby 'the learners' historically specific needs, desires, and negotiations are not simply distractions from the proper task of language learning or accidental deviations from a 'pure'. or 'ideal' language learning situation, rather, 'they must be regarded as constituting the very fabric of students' lives and as determining their investment in learning the target language' (McKay and Wong, 1996: 603). Our view of agency is based on Taylor's (1985) proposal that human agency is about more than performance, or doing; it is intimately linked to significance. That is, things and events matter to people – their actions have meanings and interpretations. It is agency that links motivation, more recently conceptualized as investment by Norton Peirce (1995), to action and defines a myriad of paths taken by learners. Agency, in turn, is socially and historically constructed and is part of a person's *habitus* (Taylor, 1985), or dispositions appropriated in childhood that incline us to act and react in specific ways (Thompson, 1991: 12). Thus, the views of any given individual with regard to language learning would be influenced by language ideologies available to them (Lippi-Green, 1997; McKay and Wong, 1996; Schieffelin et al., 1998). Change in one's habitus is possible because 'human agents are capable (given the right circumstances) of critically analyzing the discourses which frame their lives, and of claiming or resisting them according to the effects they wish to bring about' (Burr, 1995: 90).

Our first illustration of the importance of agency in conceptualizing language learning outcomes comes from Gillette (1994), who considers the relevance of an individual's history in the formation of their motives and goals for studying a second language. One of her central arguments is that the kinds of learning strategy people deploy in learning another language are heavily influenced by their histories, in which the motives or reasons for studying a second language and their related goals are rooted. From our perspective on agency, we would argue that the motives are about the significance languages and language study have for the individuals in their lives as humans. Without such a perspective, the actions of all of those involved in the behaviour we call language learning in a given classroom are frequently assumed to be directed at the same goal – learning the language. This is why virtually all of the studies, experimental or otherwise, carried out on SLA, generally refer to the participants as language 'learners'. We contend that in many cases this may well be a misnomer.

Consider the comments from two of Gillette's students, one, R, deemed to be a successful learner, and the other, J, judged to be unsuccessful. R, whose parents are from a Francophone region of Canada, makes the following comment on the significance of languages in her life: 'My earliest impression of another language goes back to about when I was seven or so. I was enrolled in Hebrew School . . . I remember doing well, learning and retaining the language, and used the language a bit when I went to Israel with my family in 1980' (Gillette, 1994: 199). Gillette points out that R consistently attempts to use what she learns and this in turn stimulates her to progress further in her language ability. And even though R reports enrolling in a French class to fulfil a university language requirement, she sees clear relevance of language study for her major interest which is to be a writer: 'Although I am taking this class as a requirement, I appreciate the exposure to another language because I am a writer, and the more I learn about different languages, the better I can be as a writer' (ibid.). In fact, languages seem to matter so much for R that she persists in her study of French, despite an apparently negative experience in her previous semester's class: 'Unfortunately, I didn't like the instructors I had for 102, and they didn't teach much (the lab instructor treated us like two-year olds!)' (ibid.).

J, on the other hand, projects a very different history – a history in which language study, and perhaps even university study, do not have the same significance for him as they seem to have for R. J comments: 'I am not a big fan of learning French, or other foreign languages. The reason why I am in this class is to fulfil the language requirement for Arts and Science majors' (Gillette, 1994: 198). Notice that J ostensibly gives the same reason as R for enrolling in the class. And similarly to R he seems to have had a bad earlier experience with language study. In speaking of the terror he experiences at coming to French class each day, he remarks: 'I got this way from taking FR 101 last year. The teacher I had was very tough and demanding. The way she taught the class turned me off from day one, and I have struggled with the language ever since' (ibid.).

R and J both had prior negative experience, and while they were apparently not identical experiences, J claims that his turned him off studying French, while R did not let her experience deter her from pursuing her interest in languages. We believe this is because languages *matter* for R (i.e., they have significance in her life), while for J they do not. Consequently, while both learners claim they are in the class because of a language requirement, R has the goal of learning the language, but J does not. For instance, J's diary contains the following entry with regard to a class assignment:

> It's 1:30 a.m. I just finished our homework that is due 9:05 Monday morning. Like usual, I put off all my homework all weekend until now.... Despite my late start I feel I did all right on the homework. I realize these study habits are wrong, but when it comes down to French or watching the NCAA Basketball Tournament, basketball wins outright.   (Gillette, 1994: 201)

One of J's final comments in his diary makes quite clear that language study has little meaning in his life, even though he is required to learn, or should we say, 'study', one in order to exit from the university:

> Tonight I tried to do the prestory so I can attempt to participate in class tomorrow. I got part of it done, but two things are preventing me from caring whether or not I finish it. One, I'm still dejected about my exam, and two, it's baseball season. The Phillies open their season tonight against the Pirates. My life has purpose again. Each spring I get excited about baseball season, and I tend to let my school work slip.   (Gillette, 1994: 204)

Similarly, McKay and Wong (1996) discuss the relationship between agency and language development of four adolescent Chinese immigrants in a Californian high school. They demonstrate that the students' previous histories, socioeconomic backgrounds and discourses of power surrounding them contribute to development of very different agencies and learning paths for the four students in superficially similar circumstances. For instance, one of the students, Michael, derived satisfaction and agency from being positioned as an athlete and a popular friend (to both Chinese and non-Chinese) and thus did not feel the need to develop his academic English skills any further. Norton, in the following chapter, reveals how adult students' community identities in particular have a significant influence upon how they exercise agency as learners of language.

In sum, from the perspective of activity theory, it is not necessarily the case that all of the people in language classes have the goal of learning the language and the reason for this is because they have different motives for being in the class, because in turn they have different histories. It doesn't matter that in the operational domain they are all engaged in the same overt behaviours, for example, listening and repeating, reading and writing, communicative/task-based group work. Cognitively, they are not all engaged in the same activity. And this is ultimately what matters, because it is the activity and significance that shape the individual's orientation to learn or not. This orientation, it turn, is perceived by us as dynamic and flexible and subject to possible change once the individual's circumstances change.

Mediation and peripheral participation

While above we emphasized the individual and socio-historically shaped nature of agency, in what follows we argue that agency is never a 'property' of a particular individual; rather, it is a relationship that is constantly co-constructed and renegotiated with those around the individual and with the society at large. This view of agency as both unique to individuals and co-constructed allows us to ponder upon the nature of mediated relationship between learners and communities of practice and its two possible stages: peripheral and full participation in a particular community of practice.

According to Engeström's (1987) formulation of activity theory, the relation between the subject and the object is not only mediated by the immediate tools (materials as well as ideas) that are employed by the individual, but also by the community in which the individual is embedded and ultimately formed as a person. Similarly, Lave and Wenger (1991) argue that learning is fundamentally a situated activity and that as such 'learners inevitably participate in communities of practitioners and that the mastery of knowledge and skill requires newcomers to move toward full participation in the sociocultural practices of a community' (1991: 29). In essence, learning is about mediated participation. The community can be an entity as broad as a society or culture, or as narrow as a particular language classroom. From the sociocultural stance, an isolated human mind functioning with complete autonomy from other minds is an impossibility. This is not to deny that people think when they are alone, but this activity already carries with it the historical consequences of other mediation.

The key concept that captures the mediated relationship between newcomers and old-timers in a given community of practice is that of 'legitimate peripheral participation', conceptualized by Lave and Wenger as 'a set of relations among persons, activity and worlds, over time and in relation with other tangential and overlapping communities of practice' (1991: 98). By allowing others to participate legitimately from the periphery and from their move towards full participation, communities of practice, including cultures, ensure their own reproduction. That is, from the perspective of Engeström's model, individuals do not simply position themselves in a community; rather, there is a dialectic struggle between the learner and the community out of which emerges the learner's position and identity. From Lave and Wenger's perspective, much rides on the nature and extent of access offered to the individual by the community of practice. That is, is full and legitimate participation made available or not?

A recent study of ESL students' transitions to mainstream classrooms in Australia (Miller, 1999) illustrates the problems encountered in the move from the periphery to the full membership, and different attitudes that may be espoused by different communities of practice with regard to newcomers. Miller (1999) traces the pathways of three students, new arrivals from Bosnia, Salvador and Vietnam, who first study English at the intensive English reception centre and then are transferred to the mainstream high school. She demonstrates that while Newnham, the intensive ESL centre, is perceived by the students as a very supportive and positive environment, their faith in the newly acquired linguistic skills is immediately shattered upon transition to the Yarra high school:

> But when you come to high school, it's really difficult, it's . . . you think you know English when you're at Newnham, or if you're getting really good, but when you come to high school, you just, you're just lost . . .
>
> (From the interview with Neta, a Bosnian student, in Miller, 1999: 156)

The interactions with Australian students who are not making the same efforts as the ESL instructors to understand and support the learning efforts of the new students may prove shocking and result in a long, difficult and isolated transition phase:

> We came to school and like, I didn't have, I didn't have many friends, or most of the time I just stayed up here, up in ESL, because there was no people who spoke my language then. It was only me. So all these Australian people, they are nice but like, now they really won't, you know, talk to you.
>
> (From the interview with Neta, a Bosnian student, in Miller, 1999: 156)

As both McKay and Wong (1996) and Miller (1999) point out, what is at stake in these linguistic, social and cultural transitions is the learners' multiple identities which become sites of contestation and renegotiation. This complexity of 'a multitude of fluctuating, at times conflicting, needs and desires' (McKay and Wong, 1996: 603) cannot be adequately captured by the view that assigns a single 'learner' identity to all learners, since, as pointed out recently by Rampton, 'social, cultural, and ethnic border fences transect the zone of proximal development' (1999: 335).

The importance of considering learners' multiple identities in discussing language learning outcomes is underscored in a number of recent studies which discuss the role of gender as a system of social relations in second language learning (Ehrlich, 1997; Pavlenko, forthcoming; Polanyi, 1995; Siegal, 1996). These studies demonstrate that differences in gender relations between different communities of practice result in gendered agency and, in turn, in gendered language learning outcomes (for an in-depth discussion, see Pavlenko, forthcoming). To begin with, cross-cultural differences in gender ideologies and practices may propel some learners to change communities of practice, while discourage others from doing so. This gendered agency is expressed in an interview conducted by one of the authors of the present study with Christina, a 27-year-old Polish woman who arrived in the USA as a graduate student and stayed on, earning a doctoral degree from an Ivy League institution. While discussing the reasons for which she left Poland and chose the USA and English as her everyday medium of communication, Christina suddenly turned to gender, indicating that her disassociation from Poland may have been 'gender-based':

> I have no natural desire to go back, no natural desire at all . . . uhm . . . to be Polish and to live in Poland, no connection to the land. . . . I have connections to my family but they are of a completely different nature, they seem to be unconnected to . . . to the country . . . uhm . . . the sense of what a woman is supposed to do with her life . . . and even though my mother is pretty independent and has an intellectual job, still, I have a sense that I wouldn't be . . . uhm . . . gender-free. Even here I am not really gender-free, to any extent, I am probably much less independent than most American women . . . uhm . . . but still . . . I am . . . more in control, I suppose, of what I do with my life than I would in Poland . . . uhm . . . I really would be an old maid in Poland by now, whereas here my choice to . . . uhm . . . choice, it's again a . . . a problematic word . . . but the fact that I am, I don't know, not married or don't have a family . . . uhm . . . at my age is not a problem . . .

(Interview in English by A. Pavlenko, June 1998)

An opposite situation is described in a study by Siegal (1996) who argues that western women studying Japanese in Japan perceive certain gendered linguistic behaviours (e.g., use of honorific morphology to indicate speakers' relative status) as unacceptable and engage in resistance strategies. In terms of a more traditional view of proficiency and its assessment, one might be obliged to evaluate the performance of these women as erroneous and unsuccessful, since at times their behaviour was neither culturally nor linguistically appropriate. However, these traditional views fall short when it comes to the explanation of why these women chose the particular positions *vis-à-vis* a particular community of practice.

A co-constructed nature of agency, as influenced by gender as a system of social relations, is also visible in Polanyi's (1995) description of the study abroad experience. The researcher reanalysed the findings of Brecht and Davidson (1995), who reported that despite no significant differences in speaking and listening skills between American university men and women before departing for a study abroad experience, upon returning from Russia, the men outscored the women on the same tests. On the basis of close study of the students' written and tape-recorded journals, Polanyi concluded that the sexual harassment continually experienced by the women in their inter-action with Russian men severely restricted their movements within the com-munity and thus prevented their full participation, which was not the case for the men in the program. Kline (1993) reached a similar conclusion in her study of American study abroad students in France. However, in this case, it was found that the women improved in their literacy skills to a greater extent than did the men, because as a defence against the sexist and hostile atti-tudes they encountered within the French-speaking community, the women sought refuge in books and other reading materials. Both studies report a situation in which women were denied full access to the respective commun-ity of practice and instead were kept on the periphery of the community as a result of the activities of the male representatives of the host community. In our view, this hardly qualifies as legitimate peripheral participation. In the Russian case, the kind of language abilities and verbal defence skills that the women were able to develop while marginalized, and thus left on the peri-phery, are not the kinds of abilities generally tested in most proficiency tests, since most such tests are interested in assessing exchange value (display) rather than use value of knowledge and abilities.

Another study which explored an American experience in Russia is the research conducted by Blender (1997), who attempted to help American university students overcome 'culture shock' in a study abroad program in Russia. Blender's goal was to help students avoid culture shock through a pre-study session on group dynamics and by integrating several Russians into the students' travel group once the group reached Russia. His motivation for taking such action arose out of an experience in which a group of students, after an initial period of euphoria upon arriving in Russia, settled into a period of considerable hostility towards Russians and their culture. The stu-dents formed their own support group in which several, though not all, of the students expressed extremely negative and abusive attitudes towards Russia. They criticized everything Russian from the metro to food to behavi-our of Russians in an openly hostile and aggressive manner. Above all, they resisted attempts of those accompanying the group to establish interaction with Russians (e.g., they insisted on eating their meals together in isolation from Russians). One of the findings of the study is that the majority of students failed to show any gains in scores on reading and speaking tests as a result of their stay abroad. From our perspective, the circumstances described by Blender represent a case of people resisting access to a community of practice by intentionally and aggressively remaining on the periphery. They managed collaboratively to construct a barrier that blocked all attempts at mediation. It is very important to underscore that these were American university students who were planning to return home as soon as possible; clearly, immigrants and refugees in the majority of the cases do not have this freedom of choice, and have to make attempts to become integrated in the society.

It is instructive to compare the Russian study abroad situation with the Siegal's (1996) account considered earlier. Both cases are similar to the extent that they are about resistance to access to a community of practice; but they are also crucially different in the ways the resistance was constructed. Western women in Siegal's study actively sought access to the community but without mediation by the rules and norms of gendered behaviour. Blender's Russian students, on the other hand, actively sought to avoid any access to the community – rules and norms for access were not even an issue. Thus, Siegal's study is about resistance with participation, while Blender's is about resistance without participation. Polanyi's (1995) study, in turn, demonstrates how bids for participation may be differentially accepted by the host society based on the gender identities of the participants – American men were more welcome than women and thus participated in a greater number of positive and helpful interactions.

Based on the evidence discussed above, we argue that agency is a co-constructed phenomenon. If learners' histories do not justify an investment in a particular language, the learners may remain on the margins of a particular community of practice as unwilling temporary visitors (Blender, 1997; Gillette, 1994). Similarly, the learners may position themselves on the periphery if they choose marginal participation in the target community (McKay and Wong, 1996; Siegal, 1996). The learners may also remain on the periphery, if their attempts to participate are rejected by the host community (Miller, 1999). On a larger, societal level the latter case is particularly well described by Lippi-Green (1997) who discusses how US ideologies of monolingualism and monoculturalism lead to discrimination against, and marginalization of, non-native speakers in contemporary American society. Finally, as will be discussed below, if learners' bids for participation are positively viewed by the members of the target community, L2 learners and users may become full participants in their second language community.

Full participation

In what follows, we would like to explore the relationship between agency (or rather agencies involved) and full participation in the host community. An excellent description of what negotiation of such access may involve is presented in the celebrated language learning account by Eva Hoffman, *Lost In Translation: A Life in a New Language* (1989). Briefly, at the age of thirteen, Hoffman and her family emigrated from their native Poland to Vancouver. Her narrative documents the struggle she experienced to reconstruct her identity as a North American intellectual woman, which, as theoretically analysed in Pavlenko (1998) and Pavlenko and Lantolf (2000), entailed the necessity of constructing a new inner voice through the appropriation of other voices in the new community. As in Siegal's case, this process for Hoffman was quite conscious. The differences between her original and new communities were stunningly transparent for her. Again, as in Siegal's experience, it is the transparency – and the support from the communities of practice along the way – that enabled Hoffman to make choices throughout her reconstruction. One critical realization that she needed to overcome was the fact that her history up to the age of thirteen, a history of a Polish girl, no longer served her in her new community, and she was forced to begin to build a new North American narrative. This necessitated her actively seeking out old-timers, artifacts and resources to mediate her integration into the community and of the community into her. Sadly, her mother seemed unable to do this and as a consequence lost her capacity to deal with her children, especially Eva's younger sister, as a parent. Eventually, Hoffman, following a good deal of struggle and psychological pain, was successful in gaining full access to her new community which meant that she was able to construct new ways of meaning and a new inner voice. Here again, as in Siegal's case, success is a matter for the individual (interacting with others) to determine. In other words, it is non-observer dependent.

The co-constructed nature of agency is always present in the successful cases of second language learning and discursive assimilation. Some understanding of what these transitions entail comes from a series of life-story interviews with late, post-puberty bilinguals conducted by one of the authors for this project. The story of one of the participants, a previously mentioned Polish female, almost mirrors Hoffman's story, except that Christina started learning English as a teenager in Poland and then came to England as an adult out of her own volition:

> I think I've always had a lot of ambition, a lot of drive, and ... um ... (laughs) and the Western world was, was *it*, I mean, that's where you got a good education, that's where you got a life, and, of course, I grabbed the first opportunity that came around, and, and somehow that became a big project, I, I ... a project, I think, that's what I would call it ... I sort of remember my first year, um ... in London, that was when I just went to, to work on the black market, and worked in all, in all these, you know, pizza places, and I was standing close to the Westminster Abbey, on the Thames, and looking at the Thames, and kind of making silent promises to myself, that, you know ... I am coming back! (laughs) ... you know, I am coming back, I am gonna, I am gonna live here, work here, learn here, and, and I came back the following year to Sussex to study ... um ... um ... it was like 'I'll make it' and it was like *the* most difficult thing to do, and it seemed that that's what I, what I had to do, and, of course, from, from then on it was also a question of ... never giving up and ... kind of doing the impossible (smiles), never going back ...
>
> (Interviewed in English by A. Pavlenko, June 1998)

Clearly, the success of a transition from one linguistic identity to another will depend on the interaction between one's own intentions and those of the people in one's environment. What happens in a case when there is no resistance to linguistic assimilation from a particular environment is illustrated by the story of the well-known French writer, historian and literary scholar, Tzvetan Todorov, who did not begin learning French, except for some half-hearted attempts at the university, until he arrived in France at the age of twenty-four:

> So, um . . . so, then I arrived in France, I was twenty-four years old at that time, and . . . I . . . started, um . . . well, I continued studying French for a little while, I went to the Alliance Française for four months, and soon I felt that I wasn't learning anything anymore, so I continued just using the language, I didn't know many Bulgarians, I knew a few, but . . . only saw them rarely and very soon all my friends . . . were non-Bulgarian so I couldn't speak any other language with them or at least it, it couldn't, couldn't occur to me, um . . . and we spoke French. And so French became, little by little, my . . . my first language . . .
>
> (Interviewed in English by A. Pavlenko, March 1997)

Similarly, Christina, once she came to England, chose to interact with English-speaking people only, attempting to renounce all her connections to Poland:

> I remember being put off by the idea of meeting Polish people in Britain and it seemed like, well, that's not *the reason* why I am there, I am there *not* to meet Polish people, and the idea that I should get along with Poles, just because they are Poles seemed kind of off putting, to say the least . . . and . . . So, I don't seek out friendships with Polish people, I know very few around here, in fact . . . I have no natural desire to go back, no natural desire at all . . . uhm . . . to be Polish and to live in Poland, no connection to the land . . . I have connections to my family but they are of a completely different nature, they seem to be unconnected to . . . to the country . . .
>
> (Interviewed in English by A. Pavlenko, July 1998)

As seen in the excerpts above, the two informants did not experience much resistance to their linguistic assimilation from the host communities. A different situation is presented in an interview with a twenty-year-old Russian–English bilingual majoring in industrial and labour relations at a North American university, and whose family had emigrated to the USA when he was thirteen years of age. His story is a poignant example of some-one who encountered resistance from the community but was nevertheless still able to find ways to participate in its life:

> I mean, if I had any other way, if I had to do it all over again, I'd probably pick the same experience, because just the whole emigration experience, it taught me a lot . . . so, I'd pick the same way . . . I guess it taught me to be persistent, go through a lot before I came here, and then, once you come here, you don't really – the obstacles never stop, you keep meeting people that might not like you, and don't wanna talk to you . . . One thing, I mean, they never let you forget, because they treat you like a Russian person, the fact that you may have that little accent, you know, they keep bringing it up, so it is really hard for you to forget that you are Russian, that you are not from over here . . . they remind you that you are Russian and you can't get away from that . . .
>
> (Interviewed in English by A. Pavlenko, March 1997)

When asked whom 'they' refers to, the speaker responded:

Well, one thing is, just the American people in general . . . you know, the way you talk to them, they kind of let you know that you are different, whether it's your language, whether it's the way you dress, whether it's the kind of music you listen to . . .   (Interviewed in English by A. Pavlenko, March 1997)

In this brief narrative we observe a clash of agencies. One is an agency of resistance from the community of practice and the other an agency of engagement on the part of the Russian. Unlike Blender's American university students, who in a sense were not risking a great deal in the long run as a consequence of their resistance to Russian culture, the Russian student here was risking his entire life if he could not find a way of accessing the new community. Clearly, the resistance he encountered was and is memorable. Despite the persistent resistance, the student nevertheless appears to have found ways of negotiating access, while at the same time preserving his Russian identity, which was also important to him.

CONCLUSION

While we could discuss in more detail these and other examples, we believe that the evidence presented above is important enough to encourage future researchers to develop robust and detailed case studies documenting the activities of people on the periphery of linguistic communities of practice and how they gain or are denied (full) participation in these communities. We also hope that the evidence provided by us and by others working in a similar direction (McKay and Wong, 1996; Miller, 1999; Norton, 1997; Norton Peirce, 1995; Polanyi, 1995; Siegal, 1996) warrants a more complex view of second language learners as agents, whose actions are situated in particular contexts and are influenced by their dynamic ethnic, national, gender, class and social identities.

We have considered how sociocultural theory in general and activity theory in particular construes second language learners. The general theory conceives learners first and foremost as individuals whose formation as thinking and learning beings depends crucially on the concrete circumstances of their specific histories as language learners and as members of the communities of practice to which they belong and to which they aspire. The general theory maintains that human beings develop specifically human ways of behaving (socially, physically and psychologically) as a consequence of the mediational means (artifacts and social relations) made accessible to them or by them. The specific theory of activity consists of a set of principles that accounts for the dynamic formation of the functional organs (systems) of the human mind(s). These functional organs comprise the integration of biologically specified capacities (e.g., natural, unmediated memory, involuntary attention) with the artifacts constructed and the discursive relations specified by communities of practice through history. An essential element in all of this is humans as agents; that is, as beings for whom things have meaning and make sense and who have the potential to alter the physical as well as symbolic conditions under which we live. In this way, we can also potentially change how we make sense of ourselves as agents that participate in concrete communities of practice.

We have attempted to show how the theory can be extended to people struggling to learn languages other than their first. One of the important claims of the sociocultural perspective, and this point emerges clearly in activity theory, is that since cognition is situated and distributed, we should not expect any two individuals to learn and develop in precisely the same way even if the material circumstances, or conditions, of their learning appear similar. Activity theory tells us that we also need to take into consideration the individual's goals and motives for engaging in any particular activity, be it cognitive, emotive or physical. The interaction among these features influences the course that learning/development will ultimately take. Thus, our first contention is that agency is not an 'anything goes proposition', but is instead shaped and reshaped by a learner's unique concrete history. This point is exemplified by Norton's account, in the chapter that follows, of adult students' experience of transitions between different communities.

Our second contention is that activity is a distributed process and hence we must take account not only of the individual agent, but we must also recognize that other agencies are involved in the mental life of humans as well. The relations among agencies are variable – at times they can be conflictive and at times collaborative. The co-constructed nature of agency clearly has profound consequences for how we understand the outcomes of learning and development, and ultimately identity. To begin with, it allows us to reconceptualize and to foreground in more detail different motives and goals that learners may have as they undertake to learn a foreign or a second language and to appreciate fully the ways in which learners seek to exercise their agency, sometimes unsuccessfully, to shape their own learning experiences (see Lantolf and Genung, 2000). Next, it also allows us to see their motivations, goals and actions as dynamic and subject to change, predicated on the attitudes espoused by those around the learners. Thus, while we may see that one's initial desire to learn a language may become extinguished in the process, whereby a learner settles for an intermediate level of proficiency (Siegal, 1996), we can also postulate that learners' agencies can be positively reshaped in the process of agency-enhancement (McKay and Wong, 1996). Thus, the second part of Blender's (1997) study demonstrates that as a result of his efforts at pre-training, the second group of American students in Russia did indeed seek access to the community and were apparently successful given the improvement in their test scores upon return.

This outcome illustrates our third contention, that activity theory and, in particular, the notion of agency have implications for the pedagogical enterprise. In fact, because the theory is derived from principles of historical-dialectic materialism, it refuses to privilege one site over any other as a testing ground for its theoretical statements. Thus, activity theoretic research is carried out in such normal settings as government offices, milk packing plants, airplane cockpits, banks, computer companies and classrooms (see Engeström and Middleton, 1996). The experimental laboratory has no special status and is seen as just another site where things happen. In fact, some have even argued that the laboratory may be a place where less than normal human activity unfolds (see Danziger, 1990).

Because the theory insists on unifying theory and practice, and because the theory is fundamentally dialectic (not in the Hegleian idealistic sense but in the Marxist materialistic sense), it is committed to the proposition that by changing the material circumstances (artifacts and social relations) under which individuals operate, it is possible to help people move their learning and development forward. Hence, to test this claim, it is not sufficient only to observe what transpires in those places, such as language classrooms, where learning happens, but the theory compels the researcher to intervene in communities of practice in order to help find ways of ensuring that all individuals have access to full participation and with it the opportunity to develop to their fullest potential.

A.A. Leont'ev, in specifically addressing second language pedagogy, argues that any normal learner should be able to learn and freely communicate in the language and asserts that if the learner fails, 'the fault would most probably be with us – textbooks, authors, methodologists, teachers' (1981: 81). The task of pedagogy, for Leont'ev, is to organize and reorganize the material circumstances that allow for maximal development in each individual. Leont'ev is not arguing for a universal magic bullet that works always and everywhere and for every learner, nor is he taking a stance that denies agency. This would be antithetical to the principles of the theory. On the contrary, he is advocating a pedagogy that not only recognizes but builds upon the uniqueness of the concrete individuals that come together to form the community of practice known as the language classroom. He writes: 'if all are reduced to the same common pedagogical denominator, the successful outcome of the learning process will be put in jeopardy and, what is more, the development of the pupil's personality may be handicapped' (ibid.). This is not merely an acknowledgement of learner variables. Indeed, focusing on variables is, if nothing else, misguided, since it is not the variables that should be our concern, but the concrete individuals who come to the learning site with specific histories, personalities and agencies. It is our task to discover these through observation and interaction with the learners and to build upon what we find in ways that enhance the likelihood that any given person will have the opportunity to learn and develop. Leont'ev poignantly reflects this perspective in his remark that language aptitude, or as he puts it 'gift for language' (ibid.), is an ability that emerges in the course of the activity of learning and is not a prerequisite for it. Education, second language, or otherwise, has the responsibility of organizing the classroom community in ways that allow students to become aware of this and then to be actively engaged in co-constructing their own learning with others in the community.

Finally, the view of L2 learners and users as agents interacting with other agents allows us to argue that the learning process will necessarily result in different outcomes for different people. Thus, standardization is anathema to the theory and its pedagogy. In making the preceding statement, we are in no way intending to argue that sociocultural theory is the only way to construe learners and the learning process. Nevertheless, we believe that the theory allow us to explore the processes and consequences of learning languages both in the natural as well as classroom settings that might otherwise remain hidden.

Chapter 8

Non-participation, imagined communities and the language classroom

Bonny Norton, University of British Columbia

INTRODUCTION

A practice that has begun to receive some attention in the language education literature is that of resistance and non-participation in second and foreign language classrooms. Canagarajah (1993), for example, reports on the non-participation of students in a Sri Lankan classroom in which he was teaching English as a second language (ESL). By the third month in the year-long course, participation had fallen to 50 per cent, while comments and drawings in textbooks provided convincing evidence of the students' ambivalence towards learning English. Giltrow and Calhoun report that most of their forty Guatemalan refugee informants had 'retired from the ESL classroom, either by physically removing themselves and no longer attending regularly, or by adopting an aloof, unengaged way of attending' (1992: 63). Norton Peirce, Harper and Burnaby (1993) note the complex reasons why workers resisted participation in a workplace ESL program, linking non-participation to larger socioeconomic issues. Language learners in other contexts, such as a South African university, have resented being labelled as 'disadvantaged' (Thesen, 1997), while others have used code-switching as forms of resistance (Lin, 1997; Rampton, 1995b). In this chapter, I examine the relationship between non-participation and what I call the 'imagined communities' of two ESL learners in Canada, linking the discussion to the learners' changing expectations of ESL courses, their shifting identities and their unique investments in the target language.

My use of the term 'non-participation' is drawn from the work of Wenger (1998: 164), who, working within a community of practice framework (Lave and Wenger, 1991), argues as follows:

> We not only produce our identities through the practices we engage in, but we also define ourselves through the practices we do not engage in. Our identities are constituted not only by what we are but also by what we are not. To the extent that we can come in contact with other ways of being, what we are not can even become a large part of how we define ourselves. (Wenger, 1998: 164)

159

This perspective on non-participation, and in particular its relationship to questions of identity, has theoretical promise in the analysis of non-participation of learners in the language classrooms. It offers explanatory potential to aspects of overt and covert participation identified by Breen in Chapter 6 and it exemplifies learner agency in action as discussed by Lantolf and Pavlenko in Chapter 7. Indeed, as Faltis (1997) has argued, the work of Lave and Wenger offers interesting theoretical perspectives for future research in language and education, a trend that has already achieved some momentum (see, for example, Toohey, 1998, 2000). In this chapter, I take the opportunity to draw on the work of Lave and Wenger (1991) and Wenger (1998), in particular, to analyse data from a study I conducted with immigrant language learners in Canada (Norton Peirce, 1995; Norton, 2000) which addresses the conditions under which two learners, on two separate occasions, withdrew entirely from participation in their ESL classrooms. In drawing on a community of practice perspective, I do not propose a definitive analysis of the data, however. My purpose is to examine the data through a new theoretical lens, with a view to enhancing my understanding of the learners' stories of non-participation. Such stories, which are seldom heard and rarely analysed, offer an important contribution to research on second language learning and teaching, focusing as they do what works – and does not work – in classrooms.

I begin the chapter with a more detailed examination of Wenger's theories of non-participation, linking this theory to his conception of identity and modes of belonging. Thereafter, I turn my attention to the stories of Katarina and Felicia, whose experiences of marginality led to the most extreme form of non-participation: withdrawal from the language class. I discuss and analyse the data with reference to the notion of imagined communities, which helps to explain the learners' acts of resistance. After examining the relationship between imagined communities, investment and language learning, I conclude with some reflections on the pedagogical implications of my research.

THEORIZING NON-PARTICIPATION

Lave and Wenger (1991), working within an anthropological framework, are centrally concerned with the relationship between learning and the social situation in which it occurs, a relationship they refer to as situated learning. Through a process of *legitimate peripheral participation* newcomers interact with old-timers in a given community setting, become increasingly experienced in the practices that characterize that community, and gradually move towards fuller participation in that community. Lave and Wenger recognize, however, that particular social arrangements in any community may constrain or facilitate movement towards fuller participation, noting as follows:

> The key to legitimate peripheral participation is access by newcomers to the community of practice and all that membership entails. But though this is essential to the reproduction of the community, it is always problematic at the

same time. To become a full member of a community of practice requires access to a wide range of ongoing activity, old-timers, and other members of the community; and to information, resources and opportunities for participation.

(Lave and Wenger, 1991: 100)

They present data from a variety of communities of practice, illustrating variability in the access each provides to activities, other people and resources for participation. In more recent work, Wenger (1998) has developed more fully the notions of participation and non-participation, focusing in particular on their relationship to the construction of a learner's identity. He argues that our relation to communities of practice involves both participation and non-participation, and that our identities are shaped by combinations of the two. Non-participation in some communities is inevitable because our experiences include coming into contact with communities to which we do not belong, in Wenger's graphic words, 'catching, as we peek into foreign chambers, glimpses of other realities and meanings' (1998: 165). This kind of non-participation differs from that when we are non-participatory in the practices of communities to which we *do* belong. In the latter case, his distinction between *peripherality* and *marginality* is a useful one. By 'peripherality', he refers to the fact that some degree of non-participation can be an enabling factor of participation, while 'marginality' is a form of non-participation that prevents full participation.

STORIES OF NON-PARTICIPATION

The two stories of non-participation are drawn from a study of immigrant language learners in Canada, conducted in the early 1990s (Norton, 2000; Norton Peirce, 1995). The purpose of the study was to investigate the relationship between identity and language learning, focusing on language learning practices in the home, workplace and school. The five participants in the study included Mai from Vietnam, Katarina and Eva from Poland, Felicia from Peru, and Martina from Czechoslovakia, all of whom were recent immigrants to the country. Data was collected over a twelve-month period through interviews, a diary study and participant observation. Katarina and Felicia's stories of non-participation, which receive more elaborate treatment in Norton (2000), follow.

Katarina's story

Shortly after their arrival in Canada, all of the five learners participated in the same six-month ESL course. After the course was complete, two of the learners, Katarina and Martina, were given the opportunity to take an additional nine-month subsidized English skills upgrading course. Katarina and Martina were in the same class and had the same teacher. After four months in this course, Katarina dropped out of the course in anger and indignation. At a diary study meeting, Katarina explained why she no longer wished to participate in the class. She said that she had come into conflict with her teacher because her teacher had said that Katarina's English was not 'good enough' to take a computer course, intimating that Katarina spoke 'immigrant English'. Katarina was angry and never returned to the class.

At the diary study meeting, Katarina indicated that she felt her instructor did not take her teaching job seriously because the students were immigrants, and Katarina said she was made to feel 'stupid' in class. Katarina had liked her first ESL class, where she learnt new vocabulary, read the newspaper and learnt grammar. But with the second ESL teacher, she felt like a student in first grade, objecting to having to learn '72 definitions for test' and listen to the teacher all day. At the meeting she asked Martina how she felt about the teacher, saying, ' "Immigrants, immigrants" – Martina, maybe you think this is normal?' In addressing Martina this way, Katarina imitated the teacher's voice, saying 'immigrants, immigrants' in a dismissive tone of voice. She then sought affirmation from Martina that her interpretation of her teacher's attitude was a valid one. Receiving no satisfaction from Martina, she positioned Martina as someone who had limited expectations of her teachers, acquiescing to the identity 'immigrant' without struggle. Martina, indeed, had other investments at stake and remained in the course until she was awarded a certificate. Katarina, having left the ESL class, entered the computer course and successfully completed the 18-month program.

Felicia's story

At another diary study meeting, Felicia described her unhappy experiences in a Grade 12 ESL course that she was taking with a group of adult immigrants in a local school. The teacher had asked each of the students to bring in information about their home country to share with the class. After the session, the teacher summarized the main points that had been raised, but neglected to mention the points that Felicia had made about Peru. Felicia was angry, and asked the teacher why she had not included Peru in her summary. The teacher explained that Peru was not a major country under consideration. Felicia never returned to the class.

NON-PARTICIPATION AND IMAGINED COMMUNITIES

In developing their theories of situated learning and communities of practice, Lave and Wenger (1991) draw on research in which newcomers to a community, such as a community of midwives, tailors or insurance claim agents, participate in attenuated ways with old-timers in the performance of community practices. The purpose of such joint participation is for the less experienced participants to increase their expertise in the performance of community activities. Thus communities are composed of participants who engage in differential ways with the practices of their communities, engagement which constitutes learning.

In conceptualizing the language classroom, such theories seem particularly apt in situations in which second language learners (newcomers) enter a classroom in which speakers of the target language (old-timers) constitute the more experienced members of the community. It is important to note, however, that school classrooms are characterized by many kinds of expertise, and that native English speakers – like language learners – would be newcomers to a variety of school practices and agendas. Toohey's (1998, 2000) research with ESL children in a public school, who attend classrooms in which the majority of children are native English speakers, shows a community which includes many 'mentors' who are experienced English speakers. In my research, however, the classrooms in which Katarina and Felicia participated were not communities in this sense. All of the members of their classroom communities, apart from the teacher, were newcomers; the only old-timer was the teacher. The question that arises then is what community practices did Katarina and Felicia seek to learn? What, indeed, constituted 'the community' for them?

In this regard, Wenger's discussion on identity and modes of belonging is a useful one. Drawing on his research with insurance claims processors, Wenger notes that the claims processors' experience of both participation and non-participation reached beyond the walls of their office:

> They see themselves as participants in social processes and configurations that extend beyond their direct engagement in their own practice. They have to make some sense of the many artifacts they encounter coming from practices they do not have access to. They may have to use their imagination to get a picture of these broader connections.   (Wenger, 1998: 173)

Wenger develops this point by hypothesizing that there are three modes of belonging, referred to as engagement, imagination and alignment, respectively. By 'engagement' he refers to active involvement in mutual processes of negotiation and meaning; 'imagination' addresses the extent to which we create images of the world and see connections through time and space by extrapolating from our experience; 'alignment' addresses the extent to which we coordinate our energies and activities in order to fit within broader structures and contribute to broader enterprises.

It is the second mode, that of 'imagination', that I believe is central to an understanding of the non-participation of Katarina and Felicia. As Wenger notes:

> My use of the concept of imagination refers to a process of expanding our self by transcending our time and space and creating new images of the world and ourselves. Imagination in this sense is looking at an apple seed and seeing a tree.   (Wenger, 1998: 176)

As Wenger notes, imagination should not be confused with misleading fantasy or withdrawal from reality. This mode of belonging, he argues, is a creative process of producing new images of possibility and new ways of understanding one's relation to the world that transcend more immediate acts of engagement. At the same time, however, imagination does not necessarily result in the coordination of action. It is here that the notion of alignment becomes central, because it is through alignment that learners do what they have to do to take part in a larger community.

It is possible to argue that the communities of practice that characterized Katarina and Felicia's learning trajectories were communities of the imagination – what could be called imagined communities. When Katarina and Felicia entered their language classrooms, they not only saw a classroom with four walls, but envisioned a community that transcended time and space. Thus although these learners were engaged in classroom practices, the realm of their community extended to the imagined world outside the classroom – their imagined community. It is important to note further that while Katarina and Felicia has similar investments in their imagined communities, they each had differential access to these communities. Katarina had almost no connection with her imagined community of professionals in Canada, while Felicia's connection to Peruvian expatriates, although tenuous at times, held greater promise for access.

Katarina and Felicia's imagined communities

More specifically, then, what exactly were Katarina and Felicia's imagined communities, and how does this notion help to explain these learners' non-participation in the ESL classroom? In order to address these questions, it is necessary to consider Katarina and Felicia's particular histories and changing identities. In her native country, Katarina had been a teacher who had taught for seventeen years. In this position, she was a highly respected professional. When she came to Canada, she could not find employment as a teacher, and enjoyed little status or respect as a part-time homemaker for the Community Service, a job that was only good 'for now'. She eagerly sought recognition from people who were fellow professionals, and wished to have a profession in Canada in which she could meet like-minded people. Her imagined community, then, was a community of professionals. In essence, Katarina's imagined community was as much a reconstruction of her past as it was an imaginative construction of the future; as in Poland, it was only members of her imagined community (the teacher, the doctor) who could validate her history and her identity as a professional. Thus Katarina's ESL teacher was not only a language teacher, active in practices of engagement, but an old-timer in an imagined community, a community in which Katarina believed she had already achieved old-timer status. When Katarina felt that her ESL teacher failed to acknowledge her professional history, positioning her as a newcomer, she was angry. When, indeed, the teacher appeared to discourage Katarina from taking a computer course that would give her greater access to her imagined community, she refused to continue participating in the course. It is significant that Martina, on the other hand, whose imagined community, history and investments were distinct from those of Katarina, successfully completed the upgrading course.

With reference to Felicia's response to her ESL teacher's omission of Peru in a summing-up exercise, I thought at the time that Felicia had overreacted to this event. However, when I understand the event within the context of Peru and Peruvians as central to Felicia's imagined community, the teacher's marginalization of Peru takes on added significance. Felicia had been very reluctant to leave Peru. She had led a privileged life in her native country and had left only because of the increasing turmoil in the country. As she wrote,

> We downed our standard of living in Canada. We used to have a relaxed life in our country. My husband had a very good job. Canada doesn't give my husband the opportunity to work. I never will understand why the government gave him the professional visa.

Felicia vehemently resisted the immigrant label, summing up her feelings as follows, 'I've never felt an immigrant in Canada, just as a foreigner person who lives here by accident.' Felicia's friends at work validated her Peruvian identity, but it appeared that her ESL teacher did not appreciate the significance of Peru to her. Indeed, the very reason why Felicia may have been accepted by her friends at work was because she positioned herself as a 'wealthy Peruvian' rather than a recent immigrant in the workplace.

> I was talking with the ladies who work with me, about a land that I'm selling in Peru. Last month there was a person interested to buy it. My sister in law was talking with her for many days, and called me by telephone collect, receiving my instructions to sell, but at last the lady didn't buy the land. And I have to pay about $600 for calls.

In sum, for both Felicia and for Katarina, their extreme acts of non-participation were acts of alignment on their part to preserve the integrity of their imagined communties. Non-participation was not an opportunity for learning from a position of peripherality, but an act of resistance from a position of marginality.

IMAGINED COMMUNITIES, INVESTMENT AND LANGUAGE LEARNING

I have argued thus far that while Katarina and Felicia were actively engaged in classroom practices, the realm of their community extended beyond the four walls of the classroom. This imagined community was not accessible to the teacher, who, in each case, focused her energy on practices of engagement, rather than on practices of the imagination. It was for this reason that Katarina and Felicia ultimately withdrew from their ESL classes. The second argument I wish to make, however, is that different learners have different imagined communities, and that these imagined communities are best understood in the context of a learner's unique investment in the target language and the conditions under which he or she speaks and practises it.

The concept of investment, which I have introduced in Norton Peirce (1995), signals the socially and historically constructed relationship of learners to the target language, and their often ambivalent desire to learn and practise it. The notion presupposes that when language learners speak, they are not only exchanging information with target language speakers, but they are constantly organizing and reorganizing a sense of who they are and how they relate to the social world. Drawing on Bourdieu (1977), I have taken the position that if learners invest in a second language, they do so with the understanding that they will acquire a wider range of symbolic and material resources, which will increase their value in the social world. Learners will expect or hope to have a good return on their investment in the target language – a return that will give them access to the privileges of target language speakers. Thus an investment in the target language is also an investment in a learner's own identity, an identity which is constantly changing across time and space.

It is interesting to note, by way of example, that for all the participants in the study, their motivation to speak was mediated by investments that conflicted with the desire to speak. Although all the participants took extra courses to learn English, participated in the diary study, and wished to have more social contact with anglophone Canadians, all the learners felt uncomfortable talking to people *in whom they had a particular symbolic or material investment.* By symbolic investment, I refer to the desire and need learners had for friends, education and religion, while material investment references the desire for capital goods, real estate and money. I wish to argue that the very people to whom the learners were most uncomfortable speaking English were the very people who were members of – or gatekeepers to – the learners' imagined communities. Data to support this position was obtained in response to the question: 'In general, when do you feel comfortable speaking English and when do you feel uncomfortable using English?' In response to this question, the data from Katarina and Felicia is compelling. It is significant that Katarina, who had a great affective investment in her status as a professional, said that she felt most uncomfortable talking to anglophone professionals: 'I feel comfortable using English when I speak with my school friends. I feel uncomfortable using English when I speak with my teacher, with the doctor', she said. Felicia, on the other hand, who had great affective investment in her Peruvian identity, felt most uncomfortable speaking English in front of Peruvians who speak English fluently. As she said:

> I feel comfortable using English with people I know and have confidence with them, specially with the ladies who I meet each week to practice English and Spanish conversation. I feel uncomfortable with new people and never can speak English in front of Peruvian people who speak English correctly.

The central point here is that a learner's imagined community invited an imagined identity, and a learner's investment in the target language must be understood within this context. Both Katarina and Felicia were highly invested in the target language, but for different historical reasons and with different consequences for their engagement with speakers of the target language. Both learners believed that they had a legitimate claim to old-timer status in their imagined communities, but had learnt, at the same time, that they could not take this status for granted. It was this ambivalence that led to their discomfort in the company of experienced participants in their imagined communities. While both learners could speak English in the company of friends, they were both silenced in different ways by different kinds of old-timer.

In this regard, the study provides convincing evidence that language learning is a social practice that engages the identities of learners in complex and sometimes contradictory ways. By 'social practice' I refer in particular to its formulation by Lave and Wenger:

> In contrast with learning as internalization, learning as increasing participation in communities of practice concerns the whole person acting in the world. Conceiving of learning in terms of participation focuses attention on ways in which it is an evolving, continuously renewed set of relations. . . . Insistence on the historical nature of motivation, desire and the very relations by which social and culturally mediated experience is available to persons-in-practice is one key to the goals to be met in developing a theory of practice.
>
> (Lave and Wenger, 1991: 49–50)

In this view, the anxiety Katarina and Felicia experienced when they attempted to speak to members of their imagined communities must not be seen as an invariant characteristic of their ability in the target language. Their difficulty was differently constructed in diverse encounters with target language speakers and must be understood with reference to their investment in particular kinds of social relationship.

CHANGING EXPECTATIONS OF LANGUAGE COURSES

If learners' imagined communities are best understood in the context of their investments in the target language, what are the implications for classroom teaching? How can teachers address the imagined communities of learners in classrooms in which there may be over thirty learners, each with her or his own investments, histories and desires for the future? This question is a subset of a larger question concerning the expecations that learners have of their language classes and the kind of curriculum they might find most useful in seeking old-timer status in a given community. In order to address this issue, at least for adult immigrants, I draw once again on the contributions of the language learners in my study. In a questionnaire, administered in December 1990, I asked the following question:

> Please examine the course descriptions for three different English language courses for new adult immigrants in Canada. Please rank the courses from 1 to 3, starting with the one you think would be most useful to new adult immigrants who do not speak English as a mother tongue.

> *COURSE A. In this course, most of the time will be spent learning English grammar, pronunciation, and vocabulary. There will be some free conversation and newspaper*

work. Students will work mostly from language textbooks and grammar exercise books.

COURSE B. In this course, most of the time will be spent learning English by learning about Canadian society: the health care system, schooling, housing, transportation, work. Students will work mainly from material designed for new immigrants to Canada.

COURSE C. In this course, most of the time will be spent learning about job opportunities in Canada: how to read advertisements, how to fill out job applications, how to interview for jobs. Students will work from community newspapers and classified advertisements, and take part in role plays.

Course A can be broadly identified as a traditional ESL course, in which the focus of instruction is on the linguistic code of the target language; Course B is characteristic of a more communicative approach to language teaching; while Course C could be defined as a course in English for Specific Purposes. Clearly there are important overlaps between the courses, but for the purposes of the research, I wished to make them prototypically distinct.

It is interesting that in December 1990, four of the learners indicated a preference for Course A, while Felicia preferred Course C, saying that 'Course C is one of the ways a person can learn English and at the same time to learn something important'. The reason why most of the learners preferred Course A is best summed up by Katarina:

> If somebody want to live for good in Canada, should be spoken the English language. In this course, people will spend most of the time learning English grammar, pronunciation, and vocabulary because it is base English.

At that time (December 1990) all the learners, including Felicia, drew sharp distinctions between language as a linguistic system and language as a social practice. The learners hoped that the linguistic code could be mastered with little reference to the conditions of its use, and they assumed that interaction with other Canadians would give them the information they needed about the way of life in Canada, job opportunities in Canada, and access to resources in Canadian society. It is significant that by December 1991, however, only twelve months later, the participants had begun to question the usefulness of a more traditional second language course. By that time, all the learners indicated that they wanted more practice using English in the classroom so that they could transfer their skills to learning contexts outside the classroom. In an interview on 23 January 1991, Eva said that the lack of opportunity to practise English in the classroom meant that she felt 'scared' when she had to use the language outside the classroom:

> Practice is the best thing to learn. When we were by the school we were in a lot of contact with English, but when I had to go out to work and speak the language, I was so scared. You don't have the practice, just the structures.

Although all the learners agreed they needed the opportunity to practise English in the classroom, they did not agree on what kind of curriculum the language teacher should develop. The learners had different expectations of formal language classes because of their unique experiences of natural language learning outside the classroom. They looked to the formal language classroom to *complement* the kind of learning that took place in other sites. Thus Mai, for example, who had the opportunity to speak English in the workplace, wanted the opportunity to *write* in the ESL class: 'Speaking I can learn every way – outside, in the bus, on the bus, or on the train. Everywhere. But for reading and writing I have to go to school.' Martina, on the other hand, who had a great deal of writing practice in her upgrading courses, wanted the opportunity to talk in the ESL class: 'If I wrote, I can correct by myself and I can think about it. The problem with speaking – I don't have time to think about it. But if I write something, it's not big problem.'

As a result of experiences in their communities, the learners also indicated that they would like an ESL course to familiarize them with the cultural practices of Canadian society. The learners suggested that the ESL course had given them a rather idealized picture of the kinds of communicative contexts in which they would be required to use English outside the classroom. Martina wrote the following in her diary entry of 17 February 1991: 'After the ESL course when I had the interview, they asked me very different questions, the ones that we didn't study in school and I was very surprised.' Such a comment was an echo of a previous statement she had made in an interview on 17 January 1991:

> Ya, I was there. I had interview about two hours long. They want to know everything about me. They asked different questions. I never heard these question. Some question was 'What I will do if the boss was shouting at me'. And I was very surprised. I thought 'My boss never, never shouted at me'.
>
> And I don't know, I said 'If I do something bad, I try to do better. And I will apologize'. But I don't know because never, never, I don't think about it.

Of particular concern is that all of the learners had come to the realization that their access to anglophone Canadians was compromised by their position as immigrants in Canadian society. Martina said that Canadians are 'fed up' with people who don't speak English. Eva said that a co-worker had indicated that he didn't like working with people who 'aren't Canadian'. Felicia said that Canadians 'look down' on immigrants. Indeed, all the learners noted that whenever a breakdown in communication occurred, it was they who felt ashamed, while the target language speaker expressed impatience. Like the learners in the European Science Foundation Project (Bremer et al., 1996; Perdue, 1993), the learners in my study had found that the onus is on the *learner* to understand and be understood, and not on the native speaker to ensure that the learner understands.

In sum, despite their initial enthusiasm for Course A, the learners found that intensive instruction in grammar, pronunciation and vocabulary was of limited value when they had little opportunity to interact with the wider community. Even when opportunities did arise, as I have indicated above, they found that there were particular social conditions under which they were most uncomfortable and unlikely to speak. (On this issue see also

Auerbach and McGrail, 1991; Cumming and Gill, 1992; Goldstein, 1996; Rockhill and Tomic, 1995.) It is important to note, further, that Katarina and Felicia's acts of resistance took place *after* their initial exposure to a course similar to Course A. As Katarina said, she liked her first ESL class, where she learnt grammar and vocabulary and occasionally read the newspaper, but in the second ESL class, in which she resisted participation, she felt like a student in first grade. It could be argued, in fact, that as language learners seek more contact in the wider community, their investments in their imagined communities may grow stronger, and the risk of non-participation in language courses may increase correspondingly. In addition, as Toohey (personal communication) notes, while language learners may be comfortable in being positioned as newcomers to the knowledge and skills of the grammar teacher, some may resist being positioned as newcomers to the practices of being an adult, such as renting an apartment, going to the doctor and taking a bus.

BEYOND THE IMAGINED COMMUNITY

Thus far I have argued that a language learner's non-participation in a second language class may result from a disjuncture between the learner's imagined community and the teacher's curriculum goals. This disjuncture is made more complex by the fact that a learner's expectations of the second language curriculum will likely change over time, partly as a result of the nature of the learner's interactions in the wider target language community. While non-participation is a highly complex practice, there are two points, drawn from my research, that may have pedagogical and research significance. The first point to note is that whether or not learner investments are recognized as an integral part of the second language curriculum, the methods that a teacher uses in the classroom will nevertheless engage the identities of learners in diverse and sometimes unsettling ways. If we do not acknowledge the imagined communities of the learners in our classrooms, we may exacerbate their non-participation. My research suggests that teachers might encourage learners to think of themselves as living in multiple communities, including the classroom community, the target language community and the imagined community. As teachers help learners interrogate their investments in their imagined community, with its unique possibilities and limitations, they may simultaneously address the risk of non-participation in the language classroom.

My second and concluding point concerns the implications of my findings for further research. The key to such research arises from the finding that learners have different investments in particular members of the target language community, and that learners may be most uncomfortable speaking to people in whom they have the greatest investment. Further, the people in whom learners have the greatest investment, my research suggests, may be the very people who represent or provide access to the imagined community of a given learner. I think it would be interesting for teachers, learners and researchers to ask to what extent such investments are productive for learner engagement in the wider target language community. To the extent that such investments are productive, they could be fostered and encouraged. However, if such investments compromise a learner's engagement with the wider target language community, in general, and second language class-rooms, in particular, they raise important questions for teachers, learners and researchers alike. Thus, while we may acknowledge a learner's imagined community, it may be problematic to celebrate this community uncondition-ally. This point is made convincingly by Simon (1992) who argues that mem-ories, images and desires should be the source for radical renewal, and that students should be encouraged to interrogate why they desire what they do, and whether such desires are consistent with a vision of future possibility. I hope that further research will shed light on the intriguing relationship between learners' non-participation and their imagined communities.

ACKNOWLEDGEMENT

Many thanks to Kelleen Toohey for her insightful comments on an earlier draft of this chapter.

Postscript: new directions for research on learner contributions

This postscript is a reflection on the particular research perspectives offered in the preceding chapters. It addresses three issues in turn:

- How might research on the social and affective contributions of the language learners relate to research that focuses upon psycholinguistic contributions?
- What further specific questions for research have been raised by the perspectives offered here?
- What broader challenges to the researcher are highlighted by a focus upon learner contributions?

My consideration of each of these will be necessarily brief. I will conclude with a tentative proposal regarding the basis on which both socially-oriented and psychologically-oriented approaches to second language acquisition (SLA) research may become mutually informing.

LEARNER CONTRIBUTIONS AND SLA THEORY AND RESEARCH

In introducing the chapters in this book, it was suggested that an adequate explanation of how people learn a second language has to account for four major variables: (1) what the learners contribute to the process, (2) the language data made available to the learners in the communicative environment in which the learning occurs, (3) how the learning is done through the interaction between learners and environment, and (4) the actual outcomes from the learning. Although taking the first of these variables as the explicit focus, several of the preceding chapters have explored the interrelationships between learners, language data and the situated learning process. A common purpose has been to inform, from different perspectives, an explanation of how these interrelationships may have an impact upon learning outcomes. The foregoing accounts of learner contributions to their own learning provide us with a comprehensive picture of the language learners as thinking, feeling and acting persons in a context of language use that is grounded in social relationships with other people. A key characteristic of the second language acquisition process, as compared with the acquisition of a first language, is that outcomes vary in significant ways. The closer study of how the contributions of the second language learners – engaged within both the limitations and opportunities of the available communicative environment – may account for differential learning outcomes is one of the crucial agendas for future SLA research. A further purpose of the present book has been to contribute to this agenda.

Two major contributions of the learners have not been directly addressed in this volume. We have not considered in detail the possible contribution of the learners' *first* language knowledge and abilities, including the prior sociolinguistic and pragmatic competencies that they bring to the learning of a new language (see especially Kasper and Kellerman, 1997; Rampton, 1995b). Nor have we explicitly addressed the crucial role of the learners' inherent language acquisition capacities and related psychological processes. A focus upon both these areas has exemplified important SLA research to the present time. Perhaps one of the remarkable achievements of the last thirty years of the twentieth century was the significant intensification of research in SLA, building on, and contributing to, a gradual sophistication of theory. However, it may be argued that, because both theory and research received a good deal of its initial impetus from *first* language acquisition studies, strongly influenced at the time by a Chomskyan paradigm, their primary psycholinguistic focus on the interaction between the learners' mental processes and language data accessed from the linguistic environment has tended to prevail over broader social perspectives on learner, language and context. With some justification, Long has recently claimed:

> Social and affective factors, the L2 *acquisition* literature suggests, are important, but relatively minor in their impact, in both naturalistic and classroom settings, and most current theories of and in SLA reflect that fact. . . . Simply asserting that this is not so . . . will not make it so. Nor will repeating the assertions, however often, as opposed to producing some evidence for them.
>
> (Long, 1997: 319, original emphasis)

It is the case, however, that those 'current theories' prevalent in the last thirty years that have promoted and accounted for language acquisition as primarily the interface between learners' mental processes and the grammatical system of the target language have pursued a research agenda that seeks to account for generalizable patterns of development across all learners. Intervening variables other than the cognitive and linguistic that may either enhance or seriously inhibit such development are likely to be positioned as a distraction from this agenda. It may be claimed that a different, complementary and equally valid research purpose is to uncover those variables that are very likely to account for *differences* in the achievements of second language learners. And among such variables will be a range of social and affective factors. Although many of the chapters in the present book have pursued this objective and proposed new directions in how such research may be undertaken, Long is right in asserting that we need more evidence that reveals the actual impact upon language acquisition of the kinds of learner conceptualizations, affects and actions that have been explored here.

That social and affective factors may appear 'relatively minor in their impact' may be, of course, a function of the relative lack of research upon them – or its lack of acceptability, perhaps – as compared with psycholinguistically grounded investigations. Despite Long's claim about 'naturalistic and classroom settings', currently influential SLA theory is derived from a relatively limited data base typified by texts of native speaker–non-native speaker, teacher–learner, or learner–learner talk. Furthermore, the activities from which such texts emerge are interpreted by some researchers and, thereby, naturalized in the literature as 'controlled' events taken to be affectively and interpersonally neutral for their participants. The data may be taken from settings other than the experimental, but prevalent interpretations of such data assume the emotional and social dimensions of the setting as constant or peripheral and, as a result, these are displaced as having little impact on how talk is conducted and what may be acquired from it. But even within this rather reductive view of the appropriate environmental conditions for acquisition, SLA research is still struggling to provide convincing evidence of genuine long-term acquisition in relation to such conditions. It therefore seems that the present state of SLA research in general suggests that we cannot afford to be exclusive in the paradigms upon which the research may be based.

In proposing certain new directions for research that may be complementary to psycholinguistic studies and that may offer a fuller explanation for differential achievement in the learning of language, it appears that the chapters in this book have raised as many new research questions as those that they have tried to address. In the section that follows, I will identify questions that seem to me particularly important in addition to those already proposed within the foregoing chapters.

SOME UNANSWERED QUESTIONS

What is the actual relationship between learner thinking and learner action?

There is little doubt that we need more research on learners' representations of reality, not least their views of the target language, how language is best learned, and of the benefits and limits of the classroom as a language learning environment. However, the purpose of such research should be to reveal how learners selectively work to facilitate their *learning* on the basis of such representations. In Chapter 3, Wenden illustrates this in tracing links between learner interpretations of task demands and their subsequent strategy selection. The question remains as to whether learners' interpretations of task demands may themselves be constrained by the specific repertoire of strategies to which the learners have access from prior experience. In other words, perhaps the strategies already familiar and available to me shape my definition of the task that confronts me. Therefore, how does interpretation of a task, itself based upon changing metacognitive knowledge, relate to the specific actions that are already within the control of the learners given that this relationship may be two-way?

Chamot's detailed account of the research on language learning strategies in Chapter 2 indicates the diverse and imaginative ways in which researchers have tried to gain access to learners' descriptions of their own behaviours that they see as helpful to them but which are unobservable to the researcher. While, as Chamot indicates, even very young learners can articulate the strategies they use, can we infer that learners who do not articulate certain strategic behaviour as part of their ways of working will not adopt such behaviour? This is an extension of the previous point in the sense that meta-awareness or consciousness may not only derive *from* the trying out of new ways of acting but also that it can sometimes function independently of action. Furthermore, some learners may not only be unable to articulate what they do, they may be unaware of what they do – whether it is strategically helpful or not. Degrees of consciousness and how these actually interrelate with learner action are, therefore, key issues within the investigation of strategies and also for research that claims that learners can 'notice the gap' between their own non-target-like production and how it may be reformulated by them in target form.

The puzzle confronting SLA research when uncovering the relationships between learner conceptualization and learner action is unlikely to be resolved by seeking uni-directional causal explanations. Does anxiety, for example, lead to poor performance or does poor performance lead to anxiety? Does willing participation in classroom discourse lead to greater proficiency or vice versa? Or does noticing the gap precede or follow acquisition? Such interrelations are more likely to be two-way and dynamic in their mutual influence while causal explanations have, in the past, served merely to mislead rather than enlighten us. And this has implications for pedagogic intervention, however well intentioned. Taking strategy training as an example, if some learners develop seemingly beneficial strategies without explicit training while others appear to require it, why might this be? Is the issue a matter of access to appropriate action, or having an appropriate definition of a task in hand, or is it both? And which may be a prerequisite for the other? It seems that to explore the actual interface between learner thinking and action we need to trace the development of *both* over time in order to discover mutual effects without assuming the primacy of either.

How should 'context' be defined?

A trend within recent debates on SLA research has been the condemnation of a generation of SLA research as invalid because it is seen to have relied upon evidence from experimental situations (see, for example, Firth and Wagner and replies to their paper in *The Modern Language Journal*, 81/3, 1997 and 82/1, 1998). The argument here is that an experimental situation

is a *particular* context that has a particular discourse and that both are different in certain ways from the more usual contexts in which people learn a
language, such as classrooms or communities of target language speakers.
This argument can be extended: different contexts are defined differently by
participants; what is meaningful and significant to them is likely to be context specific; and how they act in them – including how they interact and
what and how they learn through such interaction – is also likely to be
context specific. Therefore, the argument concludes, findings from one context, such as those from an experimental task undertaken in a university
observation laboratory, should not be generalized to all learning situations.
This argument has significant implications for language pedagogy in the
classroom. The issue here is the extent to which learning a language in a
classroom is so constrained by the conventions of classroom discourse that
learners may fail to develop both the language and the discursive practices
that would enable them to communicate in other contexts. Is the communicative competence that learners develop in a classroom generalizable across
other communicative events and situations? Clearly, different contexts providing opportunities for language learning, like different contexts of language use, are not discrete. However, it remains the case that, if only from
the evidence of recent debates about the social dimensions of language
acquisition, SLA research needs to develop a much more sophisticated
definition of context than we appear to have at present. 'Context' is attributed
with often quite distinct theoretical perspectives within research related to
language learning and the concept needs to be problematized if research is
to progress. Our capacity to find evidence of particular contextual variables
that do make a difference for language acquisition depends upon this.

One starting point may be to regard context as layered, metaphorically
speaking, like the skin of an onion. Some of the chapters in this volume have
considered four such layers that may have direct relevance to language learning. Focusing upon the specific context of a classroom, we might regard the
interaction between learners during a particular task as the heart of the
onion (Chapters 2 and 6), this interaction is located within activity (Chapter 7), both are located within discourse in terms of discursive and social
practices typical of classrooms (Chapter 6), and a classroom is but one community within and, for the learner, between other communities (Chapter 8).
Questions that remain to be answered by research can be applied to each of
these layers. For instance, Oxford's (Chapter 5) account of how learners
constructed their language teachers suggested a 'teaching–learning alliance'
that we may regard as part of the discursive practices of classrooms. However,
what is the nature of such an alliance and how is it jointly arrived at? Similarly, in what ways do learners exercise agency within activity in the classroom
context? What may enable or limit the exercise of agency in such a context?
If we applied a discoursal perspective on the classroom, what discursive practices do teachers and learners actually adopt and develop in their work
together? In what ways might such discursive practices provide us with a
window on to the co-construction of knowledge during joint activity?

At the outer layer of context there is the community or communities of which the learner is a member or seeks to become a member. How does the classroom as a 'learning community' relate to wider communities beyond it in terms of the impact of both upon a learner's transitions in membership and identity? If learning can be seen as the 'increasing participation in communities of practice' (Norton, Chapter 8), how do learners conceptualize the costs and benefits of investing themselves in the classroom community and, more widely, in the learning of the language of a new community? Issues of membership and identity perhaps most clearly remind us of the likely significance of motivation in language learning. Yet it is only very recently that some researchers have begun to explore the workings of motivation *within* specific contexts such as the classroom group (see especially Dörnyei, 1998, 2001).

Once we seek to discover relationships between contextual variables and language learning, two major challenges to research become apparent. First, recalling Oxford's account of learners' sometimes startling constructs of their teachers (Chapter 5), we might consider whether teachers are not only positioned by learners in certain ways through classroom interaction, but also by the immediate institutional and external curriculum constraints upon them. Similarly, Norton's account of learners as migrants within a new community (Chapter 8) suggests that the broader social-political context as perceived or 'imagined' by them is very likely to impact upon people's linguistic identity and, thereby, their whole approach to learning the language of the wider community. Even if we seek to investigate what may be described as the micro-context of classroom interaction, certain theoretical and research approaches to the discourse would imply that our account will be partial and seriously flawed unless the socio-political dimensions of interaction – such as power, authority, identity, access, and so on – are not also recognized and their influence explained (see, for example, Chouliaraki and Fairclough, 1999; Pennycook, 1994; Tollefson, 1995). In essence, even approaching the classroom as context may entail an investigative alertness to both the wider social-political influences upon it and how social and political positions and values of participants in the language classroom, not least the teacher's, will shape the learning that occurs there. The first major challenge to an adequate and researchable definition of context appears, therefore, to specify its dimensions – the extent of its reach – in ways that are both valid and informative for the language learning process.

The second, and related, challenge in how we may account for context concerns the pivotal role widely attributed to *meaning* in language learning process. What is meaningful and significant to learners will reverberate with cultural value. Culture clearly influences the conceptualizations of learners and, probably, their affective engagement in learning. Learners – and teachers – approach their tasks within the narrative of their cultural histories and, it may be claimed, construct together an interim culture of collective work in a language classroom. In essence, culture and context are indivisible. Their mutual entailment implies that the contextual layers of interaction, activity, discourse, community and the wider society in which the language learning may occur are all locations for the articulation, limitation and re-working of cultures and the meanings and significances that they entail. The fact that language itself is a crucial mediator of culture surely compounds the import-ance of the latter in the study of language learning. Nevertheless, for all the current talk about the need to be alert to cultural difference or our own potential cultural myopia as researchers, SLA research has hardly begun to try to relate a theory or operational definition of culture to the focus of its investigation. A possible reason for this may be that the prevailing cultural stance of much SLA research is largely modernist and 'western' in its psycho-logical, social and cultural values and presuppositions. Appeals to a reliance upon 'rationalism', the 'scientific' method, 'objectivity' and the like merely postpone serious discussion of concepts that are inherently cultural constructs and, thereby, open to different and, crucially, changing interpretation and instantiation. And 'culture', like 'context', is itself a multi-dimensional concept that is largely unproblematized in both the research and pedagogic literature. SLA theory and research to date seems to lack sufficient critical reflection within its own discipline, which is, perhaps, a symptom of its immaturity. It seems that the time is right for uncovering our underlying assumptions (see, for example, Pennycook, 1994; Rampton, 1987, 1995b). What, for instance, *are* the constructs of the learner, the environment of learning (including communicative data made available there), the learning process and its out-comes that currently characterize much SLA research? In what ways may these be enlightening or constraining in our understanding of language learning?

How we define and frame the layers of context and the meanings and significances that culture weaves into each layer therefore seem to be two current prerequisites for the future progress in how we conceptualize and investigate the learning of a new language. As a consequence, it is more likely that the ways in which, and the extent to which, social and affective variables actually do have an impact on the process will reveal themselves.

TOWARDS A SYNTHESIS

This book has offered perspectives on research that represent some initial steps in working towards a more integrated view of the language learners as thinking and feeling people acting with purpose that is generated by what they see as significant and meaningful for them *as learners* in particular social and cultural contexts. Perhaps indirectly, the chapters in this book collectively signal the need for research that seeks out evidence of the interdependency between psycholinguistic, affective, cultural and social variables in relation to language learning. However, in addition to unanswered questions concerning, in particular, how we may be defining context and meaning in language learning, this book highlights two difficulties that need to be addressed in such an enterprise. The first is the potential *complexity* of investigating learner contributions and how they relate to each other. The second problem, en-tailed in accounting for differences in the outcomes of language learning, is the likely discovery of variables that are *relative* as compared with variables and patterns of acquisition that may be generalizable across learners. In this concluding section, these two difficulties will be elaborated upon briefly as a means of identifying how we may begin to frame the interdependency of learner contributions in order to relate them to learning outcomes.

Complexity

In anticipating the chapters in this book in the introduction, a diagrammatic profile of learner contributions was offered as a summary. It is reproduced here (Figure 1) as a reminder, if one was needed, of the range of variables with which we are concerned in taking account of learner contributions and their possible interrelationships. Such a profile certainly presents a significant challenge to the construction of a theory of SLA that meets the possibly desirable criteria of simplicity or elegance! It is understandable that some researchers shy away from this challenge in favour of investigating what might be interpreted as universal, stable and predictable across language learners, although this appears to entail disregarding most of the learner contributions that this book has addressed. It has been argued here, however, that all of these learner attributes, conceptualizations, affects and actions are, at least potentially and to differing extents, engaged when learners' mental capacities and processes work upon linguistic data in a particular setting. It follows that the outcomes from such work are, at least potentially and to differing extents, constrained or facilitated by all of these contributions. One way of containing the seeming complexity of studying learner contributions will be to confirm overlaps and more local relationships between several of them. For example, although distinctive in their own ways, there are likely to be strong links between learner beliefs, attitudes and motivation. Similarly, in terms of learner action, the exercise of agency, strategic behaviour and participatory practices during learning are likely to be mutually related. Therefore, a contributory way of reducing the seeming complexity of tracing the impact of learner variables on learning is to explore how particular clusters of learner variables interrelate one with the other. It is also here that both context, appropriately defined (see above), and time are crucial to the facilitation of research. It is very likely that the learners will engage specific contributions in specific ways in relation to how they interpret particular aspects of context. In addition, most learner contributions are dynamic and mutable and imply the need to trace how they shift during learning over time. Research that is not longitudinal will not achieve this and is likely to miss moments of 'crisis' or important changes in learning that require of the learners reconceptualization, significant affective investment or adaptation in actions taken. Paradoxically, perhaps, the very dynamism of learner contributions renders them potentially more accessible to the researcher if the investigation is longitudinal. So, internal clusters of relationships among learner contributions, how they variously come into play under specific contextual conditions, and how they change – often in mutual ways – all reduce the seeming complexity of investigating

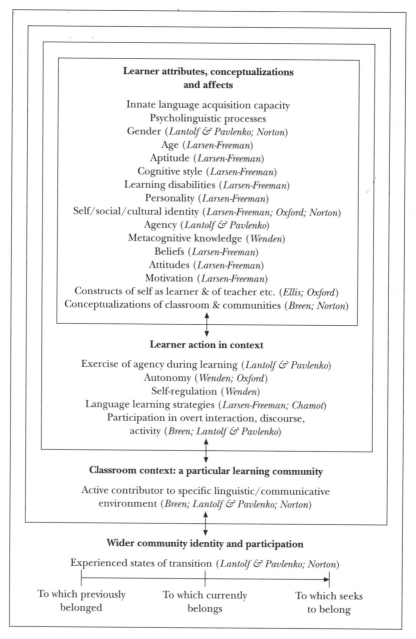

Figure 1   The profile of learner contributions to language learning

them. Complexity of our task may be further reduced if we can identify a kind of anchor or unifying means of integrating learner contributions in some way rather than divorcing them along dichotomous lines such as 'psychological' versus 'social' or 'innate' versus 'learned', and so on.

Relativism

One of the motives for a book that focuses upon learner contributions is to begin to explain the universal phenomenon of differences between learners in their outcomes from second language learning. We are necessarily engaged in the discovery of variables that account for relativity in relation to acquisition as compared with variables and patterns of acquisition that may be seen as seemingly much more generalizable across learners. The theoretical position and, therefore, the findings from the latter endeavour are sometimes claimed to be 'real' – rather than 'relative' – and, it is argued, entitled to greater trust. To assert that all or any theories of SLA – and the research related to them – are equally good or bad constructions of the 'reality' of SLA is clearly a matter of judgemental relativism that gravely hinders progress in our understanding. However, we could accept as complementary a theory that accounts for differences between learners in their attainment of proficiency alongside a theory that accounts for universals in SLA. This would not be a matter of mere judgemental relativism. Epistemic relativism, on the other hand, requires us to recognize that any theory and its related research *derive from the ways in which we discourse about reality* and that different discourses are positioned differently in our society and culture (Bhaskar, 1986; Collier, 1994). Different discourses are generated by, and reflect particular positions in, for instance, an academic community within a particular society. From this perspective on relativism, the comparative strengths or limitations of a theory can be open to constant evaluation in the course of ongoing research practice. We can therefore continually enquire of any theory how it may access reality as it gradually shapes the research and how the emergent evidence may, in turn, force a reconceptualization of the theory; whether or not it fits with experienced reality of language learning, whether or not it renders the reality of learning a language more transparent, and so on. Asserting a theoretical position as somehow 'given' is to position the discourse that generated it as beyond question or doubt. Epistemic relativism, therefore, can be seen as a positive check on theoretical and research stances that may be positioned by the discourse of a particular place and time as being sole arbiters of what counts as reality. As Ellis (Chapter 4), Breen (1996) and Firth and Wagner (1997) suggest, perhaps we are at an opportune moment to reassess how SLA research is itself constructing language learners and language learning in the ways in which we discourse about these things.

A TENTATIVE CONCLUSION

In reflecting briefly upon the particular contribution the present book provides to a richer understanding of the learner in the language learning process, this postscript has addressed the seeming irreconcilability of psycholinguistic and social and affective perspectives on the process by arguing for a complementary relationship in the future. It has also raised a number of questions for future SLA research or elaborated upon those identified as important by authors of some of the foregoing chapters. Further, it has suggested that future research and theory are confronted by certain challenges that have been highlighted by our particular focus upon learner contributions and that there are solutions to the complexity and relativism that might be attributed to the task.

A non-tentative conclusion is that we need to be wary of conceptual inclusivity in research. At this moment in time, we may have more evidence concerning certain things – rather than others – that do have an important influence on learning outcomes and which may encourage us to be more confident in a particular theoretical rationale rather than ones that, as yet, are not strongly confirmed by evidence. However, the goal of research, by definition, is to keep looking. A conceptual openness on the basis of a reflexive stance in relation to how we discourse about language learning may enable us to look into the dynamic of variables that it involves both more deeply and in different ways. One example of this may be that SLA research releases itself from its dependency on the paradigm of first language acquisition, recognizing the possibility that the key differences between learning a first language and an additional language may significantly outweigh their similarities.

I suggested earlier that there may be ways in which the seeming complexity of our task may be reduced, if we can identify a unifying means of integrating learner contributions and, thereby, integrating theoretical and research perspectives rather than retreating behind misleading dichotomies. As our profile of learner contributions (Figure 1) implies, there are relationships we need to explore between learner thinking and affect, learner action, and layers of context that might inform a more holistic account of the language learning process. However, the tentative conclusion is that the roots of such an account already exist in prevalent theories of SLA. Meaning is recognized as the pulse of language learning, and especially the ways in which learners comprehend, express and negotiate meanings when they interact with others. Therefore the learners' struggles to *make* meaning can be seen as *the* mediator in the language learning process. Earlier, I argued that what is likely to be meaningful and significant for learners is threaded with cultural value. I also proposed that what is invested with particular meanings and what becomes significant for the learners derive from their definition of the layers of context within which they position themselves as learners. In sum, meaning and significance seen as *actively constructed and reconstructed by learners* and these processes seen as grounded simultaneously *within* interaction, activity, discourse and the communities in which the learners participate, offer the potential for a more integrated exploration of language learning than we have been able to achieve so far. From this perspective, language learning is, in essence, cultural action towards meaning within context. And such action entails mental processes and affective engagement. It is hoped that the foregoing accounts of what learners bring to their learning may inform such a perspective.

References

Abraham, R.G. and Vann, R.J. 1987. Strategies of two language learners: A case study. In A. Wenden and J. Rubin (Eds), *Learner strategies in language learning*. Englewood Cliffs, NJ: Prentice-Hall.

Aida, Y. 1994. Examination of Horwitz, Horwitz, and Cope's construct of foreign language anxiety: The case of students of Japanese. *The Modern Language Journal* 78/2: 155–68.

Alexander, P.A. and Dochy, F. 1995. Conceptions of knowledge and beliefs: A comparison across varying cultural and educational communities. *American Educational Research Journal* 32/2: 413–42.

Allwright, D. 1984. Why don't learners learn what teachers teach? The interaction hypothesis. In D. Singleton and D. Little (Eds), *Language learning in formal and informal contexts*. Dublin: IRAL.

Allwright, D. 1989. Interaction in the language classroom: Social problems and pedagogic possibilities. *Language teaching in today's world: Vol. 3 of Proceedings of the 1989 Symposium of Language Teaching and Learning*. Paris: Les États Génréaux des Langues.

Allwright, D. 1996. Social and pedagogic pressures in the language classroom: The role of socialisation. In H. Coleman (Ed.), *Society and the language classroom*. Cambridge: Cambridge University Press.

Arries, J. 1999. Learning disabilities and foreign languages: A curriculum approach to the design of inclusive courses. *The Modern Language Journal* 83/1: 98–110.

Ashton-Warner, S. 1963. *Teacher*. New York: Simon and Schuster.

Aston, G. 1986. Trouble-shooting in interaction with learners: The more the merrier? *Applied Linguistics* 7/2: 128–43.

Atkinson, P.J. 1989. Humanistic approaches in the adult classroom: An affective reaction. *ELT Journal* 43/4: 268–73.

Auerbach, E. and McGrail, L. 1991. Rosa's challenge: Connecting classroom and community contexts. In S. Benesch (Ed.), *ESL in America: Myths and possibilities*. Portsmouth, NH: Heinemann.

Bailey, K.M. 1983. Competitiveness and anxiety in adult second language learning: Looking at and through the diary studies. In H.W. Seliger and M.H. Long (Eds), *Classroom-oriented research in second language acquisition*. Rowley, MA: Newbury House.

Bailey, K.M. and Nunan, D. (Eds) 1996. *Voices from the language classroom*. Cambridge: Cambridge University Press.

Bandura, A. 1982. Self-efficacy mechanism in human agency. *American Psychologist* 37: 122–47.

183

Barcelos, A.M. 1995. The culture of learning a foreign language (English) of language students. Unpublished Master's Thesis, UNICAMP, Sao Paulo, Brazil.

Barnett, M.A. 1988. Teaching reading strategies: How methodology affects language course articulation. *Foreign Language Annals* 21/2: 109–19.

Bartel, R. 1983. *Metaphors and symbols: Forays into language.* Urbana, IL: National Council of Teachers of English.

Bayley, R. and Preston, D.R. (Eds) 1996. *Second language acquisition and linguistic variation.* Amsterdam: John Benjamins.

Bedell, D.A. and Oxford, R.L. 1996. Cross-cultural comparisons of language learning strategies in the People's Republic of China and other countries. In R.L. Oxford (Ed.), *Language learning strategies around the world: Cross-cultural perspectives.* Honolulu, HI: Second Language Teaching and Curriculum Center, University of Hawaii Press, pp. 47–60.

Beebe, L. (Ed.) 1988. *Issues in second language acquisition: Multiple perspectives.* Boston, MA: Heinle and Heinle.

Beebe, L. and Takahashi, T. 1989. Sociolinguistic variation in face-threatening speech acts. In M. Eisenstein (Ed.), *The dynamic interlanguage: Empirical studies in second language variation.* New York: Plenum Press.

Beebe, S. and Butland, M. 1994. Emotional response and learning: Explaining affinity-seeking behaviors in the classroom. Paper presented at the Annual Meeting of the International Communication Association, Sydney, Australia.

Belmechri, F. and Hummel, K. 1998. Orientations and motivation in the acquisition of English as a second language among high school students in Quebec City. *Language Learning* 48: 219–44.

Benson, M.J. 1989. The academic listening task: A case study. *TESOL Quarterly* 23/3: 421–46.

Benson, P. 2000. *Teaching and researching autonomy.* London: Pearson Education.

Benson, P. and Lor, W. 1998. *Making sense of autonomous language learning.* English Centre, Monograph, No. 2. Hong Kong University, Hong Kong.

Bergman, J.L. 1992. SAIL – A way to success and independence for low-achieving readers. *Reading Teacher* 45/8: 598–602.

Berlin, I. 1976. *Vico and Herder: Two studies in the history of ideas.* London: Hogarth.

Bermudez, A.B. and Prater, D.L. 1990. Using brainstorming and clustering with LEP writers to develop elaboration skills. *TESOL Quarterly* 24: 523–8.

Berwick, R. 1990. *Task variation and repair in English as a foreign language.* Kobe, Japan: Kobe University of Commerce, Institute of Economic Research.

Bhaskar, R. 1986. *Scientific realism and human emancipation.* London: Verso.

Bialystok, E. 1997. The structure of age: In search of barriers to second-language acquisition. *Second Language Research* 13: 116–37.

Bialystok, E. and Hakuta, K. 1999. Confounded age: Linguistic and cognitive factors in age differences in second language acquisition. In D. Birdsong (Ed.), *Second language acquisition and the critical period hypothesis.* Mahwah, NJ: Lawrence Erlbaum Associates.

Bialystok, E. and Sharwood-Smith, M. 1985. Interlanguage is not a state of mind: An evaluation of the construct for second language acquisition. *Applied Linguistics* 6/2: 101–17.

Birdsong, D. 1992. Ultimate attainment in second language acquisition. *Language* 68: 706–55.

Birdsong, D. (Ed.) 1999. *Second language acquisition and the critical period hypothesis.* Mahwah, NJ: Lawrence Erlbaum Associates.

Blender, E. 1997. Group dynamics and study abroad groups: Practical applications of theory. Paper presented at the annual conference of the American Association of Teachers of Slavic and East European Languages, 1997.

Block, D. 1992. Metaphors we teach and learn by. *Prospect* 7/3: 42–55.

Block, D. 1994. A day in the life of a class: Teacher/learner perceptions of task purpose in conflict. *System* 22/4: 473–86.

Block, D. 1996. A window on the classroom: Classroom events viewed from different angles. In K. Bailey and D. Nunan (Eds), *Voices from the language classroom.* Cambridge: Cambridge University Press.

Block, D. 1997. Learning by listening to language learners. *System* 25: 347–60.

Block, D. 1999. Who framed SLA research? Problem framing and metaphoric accounts of the SLA research process. In L. Cameron and G. Low (Eds), *Researching and applying metaphor.* Cambridge: Cambridge University Press.

Blum-Kulka, S., House, J. and Kasper, G. (Eds) 1989. *Cross-cultural pragmatics: Requests and apologies.* Norwood, NJ: Ablex.

Bongaerts, T. 1999. Ultimate attainment in L2 pronunciation: The case of very advanced late L2 learners. In D. Birdsong (Ed.), *Second language acquisition and the critical period hypothesis.* Mahwah, NJ: Lawrence Erlbaum Associates.

Bongaerts, T., Planken, B. and Schils, E. 1995. Can late learners attain a native accent in a foreign language? A test of the critical period hypothesis. In D. Singleton and Z. Lengyel (Eds), *The age factor in second language acquisition.* Clevedon, UK: Multilingual Matters.

Bongaerts, T., van Summeren, C., Planken, B. and Schils, E. 1997. Age and ultimate attainment in the pronunciation of a foreign language. *Studies in Second Language Acquisition* 19: 447–65.

Bourdieu, P. 1977. The economics of linguistic exchanges. *Social Science Information* 16/6: 645–68.

Braidi, S.M. 1995. Reconsidering the role of interaction and input in second language acquisition. *Language Learning* 45: 141–75.

Bransford, J.D. 1979. *Human cognition.* Belmont, CA: Wadsworth Publishing Co.

Brecht, R. and Davidson, D. 1995. Predicators of foreign language gain during study abroad. In B. Freed (Ed.), *Second language acquisition in a study abroad context.* Amsterdam: John Benjamins.

Breen, M.P. 1985. The social context for language learning: A neglected situation? *Studies in Second Language Acquisition* 7: 135–58.

Breen, M.P. 1996. Constructions of the learner in SLA research. In J.E. Alatis, C.A. Straehle, M. Ronkin and B. Gellenberger (Eds), *Georgetown University Round Table on Languages and Linguistics 1996.* Washington, DC: Georgetown University Press.

Breen, M.P. 1998. Navigating the discourse: On what is learned in the language classroom. In W.A. Renandya and G.M. Jacobs (Eds), *Learners and language learning.* Anthology Series 39. Singapore: SEAMEO Regional Language Centre.

Breen, M.P. and Candlin, C. 1980. The essentials of a communicative curriculum for language teaching. *Applied Linguistics* 1/2: 89–112.

Bremer, K., Roberts, C., Vasseur, M.-T., Simonot, M. and Broeder, P. 1996. *Achieving understanding: Discourse in intercultural encounters.* London: Longman.

Briscoe, C. 1991. The dynamic interactions among beliefs, role metaphors and teaching practices: A case study of teacher change. *Science Education* 75: 185–99.

Brown, A.L., Campione, J.C. and Day, J.D. 1981. Learning to learn: On training students to learn from texts. *Educational Leadership* 10: 14–21.

Brown, A., Bransford, J.D., Ferrara, R. and Campione, J.C. 1983. Learning, remembering and understanding. In J.H. Flavell and E.M. Markman (Eds), *Carmichael's manual of child psychology: Volume 1*. New York: Wiley.

Brown, H.D. 1994. *Principles of language learning and teaching* (Third edition). Englewood Cliffs, NJ: Prentice-Hall.

Brown, R., Pressley, M., Van Meter, P. and Schuder, T. 1994. *A quasi-experimental validation of transactional strategies instruction with previously low-achieving grade-2 readers*. Amherst, NY: University at Buffalo, SUNY, Department of Educational Psychology.

Brown, T.S. and Perry, F.L., Jr. 1991. A comparison of three learning strategies for ESL vocabulary acquisition. *TESOL Quarterly* 25/4: 655–70.

Burke, K. 1966. *Language as symbolic action: Essays on life, literature, and method*. Berkeley, CA: University of California Press.

Burr, V. 1995. *An introduction to social constructionism*. London: Routledge.

Cameron, L. 1999. Operationalising 'metaphor' for applied linguistic research. In L. Cameron and G. Low (Eds), *Researching and applying metaphor*. Cambridge: Cambridge University Press.

Cameron, L. and Low, G. (Eds) 1999. *Researching and applying metaphor*. Cambridge: Cambridge University Press.

Canagarajah, A.S. 1993. Critical ethnography of a Sri Lankan classroom: Ambiguities in student opposition to reproduction through ESOL. *TESOL Quarterly* 27/4: 601–26.

Canale, M. and Swain, M. 1980. Theoretical bases of communicative approaches to second language teaching and testing. *Applied Linguistics* 1: 1–47.

Carpenter, T., Fennema, E., Peterson, P.L., Chiang, C. and Loef, M. 1989. Using knowledge of children's mathematics thinking in classroom teaching: An experimental study. *American Educational Research Journal* 26: 499–532.

Carrell, P.L. 1989. Metacognitive awareness and second language reading. *The Modern Language Journal* 73/2: 122–34.

Carrell, P.L., Pharis, B.G. and Liberto, J.C. 1989. Metacognitive strategy training for ESL reading. *TESOL Quarterly* 23/4: 647–78.

Carrell, P., Prince, M. and Astika, G. 1996. Personality types and language learning in an EFL context. *Language Learning* 46: 75–99.

Carrier, K. 1999. The social environment of second language listening: Does status play a role in comprehension? *The Modern Language Journal* 83/1: 65–79.

Chamot, A.U. 1987. The learning strategies of ESL students. In A. Wenden and J. Rubin (Eds), *Learner strategies in language learning*. Englewood Cliffs, NJ: Prentice-Hall.

Chamot, A.U. 1993. Student responses to learning strategy instruction in the foreign language classroom. *Foreign Language Annals* 26/3: 308–21.

Chamot, A.U. 1994. A model for learning strategy instruction in the foreign language classroom. In J.E. Alatis (Ed.), *Georgetown University Round Table on Languages and Linguistics 1994*. Washington, DC: Georgetown University Press.

Chamot, A.U. 1995a. Learning strategies in listening comprehension: Theory and research. In D. Mendelsohn and J. Rubin (Eds), *The theory and practice of listening comprehension for the second language learner*. San Diego, CA: Dominie Press.

Chamot, A.U. 1995b. Learning strategies of elementary foreign-language-immersion students. In J.E. Alatis (Ed.), *Georgetown University Round Table on Languages and Linguistics 1995*. Washington, DC: Georgetown University Press.

Chamot, A.U. 1999. Reading and writing processes: Learning strategies in immersion classrooms. In M.A. Kassen (Ed.), *Language learners of tomorrow: Process and Promise.* Lincolnwood, IL: National Textbook Company.

Chamot, A.U. and El-Dinary, P.B. 1999. Children's learning strategies in immersion classrooms. *The Modern Language Journal* 83/3: 319–41.

Chamot, A.U. and Küpper, L. 1989. Learning strategies in foreign language instruction. *Foreign Language Annals* 22: 13–24.

Chamot, A.U. and Küpper, L. 1990. *A study of learning strategy instruction in the foreign language classroom: Second year report.* McLean, VA: Interstate Research Associates. ERIC Clearinghouse on Languages and Linguistics.

Chamot, A.U. and O'Malley, J.M. 1994a. *The CALLA handbook: Implementing the cognitive academic language learning approach.* White Plains, NY: Addison Wesley Longman.

Chamot, A.U. and O'Malley, J.M. 1994b. Language learner and learning strategies. In N.C. Ellis (Ed.), *Implicit and explicit learning of languages.* San Diego, CA: Academic Press.

Chamot, A.U., Küpper, L. and Impink-Hernandez, M.V. 1988a. *A study of learning strategies in foreign language instruction: Findings of the longitudinal study.* McLean, VA: Interstate Research Associates. ERIC Clearinghouse on Languages and Linguistics.

Chamot, A.U., Küpper, L. and Impink-Hernandez, M.V. 1988b. *A study of learning strategies in foreign language instruction: The third year and final report.* McLean, VA: Interstate Research Associates. ERIC Clearinghouse on Languages and Linguistics.

Chamot, A.U., Dale, M., O'Malley, J.M. and Spanos, G.A. 1993. Learning and problem solving strategies of ESL students. *Bilingual Research Quarterly* 16/3 and 4, Summer/Fall: 1–38.

Chamot, A.U., Barnhardt, S., El-Dinary, P.B. and Robbins, J. 1996. Methods for teaching learning strategies in the foreign language classroom. In R.L. Oxford (Ed.), *Language learning strategies around the world: Cross-cultural perspectives.* Honolulu, HI: Second Language Teaching and Curriculum Center, University of Hawaii Press.

Chamot, A.U., Keatley, C., Barnhardt, S., El-Dinary, P.B., Nagano, K. and Newman, C. 1996. *Learning strategies in elementary language immersion programs.* Final report submitted to Center for International Education, US Department of Education. ERIC Clearinghouse on Languages and Linguistics.

Chamot, A.U., Keatley, C. and Mazur, A. 1999. Literacy development in adolescent English language learners: Project Accelerated Literacy (PAL). Paper presented at the 1999 Annual Meeting of the American Educational Research Association, Montreal, Canada.

Chamot, A.U., Barnhardt, S., El-Dinary, P.B. and Robbins, J. 1999. *The learning strategies handbook.* White Plains, NY: Addison Wesley Longman.

Chapelle, C. 1992. Disembedding 'disembedded figures in the landscape . . .': An appraisal of Griffiths and Sheen's 'reappraisal of L2 research on field dependence/independence'. *Applied Linguistics* 13: 375–84.

Chapelle, C. and Green, P. 1992. Field independence/dependence in second-language acquisition research. *Language Learning* 42: 47–83.

Chaudron, C. 1988. *Second language classrooms: Research on teaching and learning.* Cambridge: Cambridge University Press.

Cheng, Y.-S., Horwitz, E. and Schallert, D. 1999. Language anxiety: Differentiating writing and speaking components. *Language Learning* 49: 417–46.

Chinn, C.A. and Brewer, W.F. 1993. The role of anomalous data in knowledge acquisition: a theoretical framework and implications for science instruction. *Review of Educational Research* 63/1: 1–50.

Chomsky, N. 1959. Review of 'Verbal Behavior' by B.F. Skinner. *Language* 35: 26–58.

Chomsky, N. 1981. *Lectures on government and binding.* Dordrecht: Foris.

Chomsky, N. 1986. *Barriers.* Cambridge, MA: MIT Press.

Chouliaraki, L. and Fairclough, N. 1999. *Discourse in late modernity: Rethinking critical discourse analysis.* Edinburgh: Edinburgh University Press.

Clarke, P. 1982. On bandwagons, tyranny, and common sense. *TESOL Quarterly* 16/4: 437–48.

Claxton, G. 1984. *Live and learn: An introduction to the psychology of growth and change in everyday life.* London: Harper and Row.

Clément, R., Dörnyei, Z. and Noels, K. 1994. Motivation, self-confidence, and group cohesion in the foreign language classroom. *Language Learning* 44: 417–48.

Cohen, A.D. (Ed.) 1998. *Strategies in learning and using a second language.* London: Longman.

Cohen, A.D. and Aphek, E. 1981. Easifying second language learning. *Studies in Second Language Learning* 3: 221–36.

Cohen, A.D. and Cavalcanti, M.C. 1990. Feedback on composition: Teacher and student verbal reports. In B. Kroll (Ed.), *Second language writing: Research insights for the classroom.* Cambridge: Cambridge University Press.

Cohen, A.D. and Olshtain, E. 1993. The production of speech acts by EFL learners. *TESOL Quarterly* 27/1: 33–56.

Cohen, A.D., Weaver, S. and Li, T.-Y. 1998. The impact of strategies-based instruction on speaking a foreign language. In A.D. Cohen (Ed.), *Strategies in learning and using a second language.* London: Longman.

Cole, M. 1996. *Cultural psychology. A once and future discipline.* Cambridge, MA: Belknap Books.

Collier, A. 1994. *Cultural realism.* London: Verso.

Collins, C. 1991. Reading instruction that increases thinking abilities. *Journal of Reading* 34: 510–16.

Cook, V. 1993. *Linguistics and second language acquisition.* Basingstoke: Macmillan.

Cook, V. 1996. *Second language learning and language teaching.* London: Edward Arnold.

Corder, S.P. 1967. The significance of learners' errors. *International Review of Applied Linguistics* 5: 161–9.

Cortazzi, M. and Jin, L. 1996. Metaphors of teaching, learning, and language. Paper presented at the Symposium on Applying Metaphor, University of York, UK. In P. Riley (Ed.), *'Bats' and 'balls': Beliefs about talk and beliefs about language learning: Mélangues CRAPEL,* No. 23. Nancy, France: Université Nancy II.

Cortazzi, M. and Jin, L. 1999. Bridges to learning: Metaphors of teaching, learning and language. In L. Cameron and G. Low (Eds), *Research and applying metaphor.* Cambridge: Cambridge University Press.

Cotterall, S. 1995. Readiness for autonomy: Investigating learner beliefs. *System* 23: 195–205.

Cotterall, S. 1999. Variables affecting success in language learning: what do learners believe? In A. Wenden (Ed.), Special Issue on Metacognitive Knowledge and Beliefs in Language Learning. *System* 27/4: 493–514.

Coughlan, P. and Duff, P. 1994. Different activities: Analysis of an SLA task from an activity theory perspective. In J.P. Lantolf and G. Appel (Eds), *Vygotskian approaches to second language research.* Norwood, NJ: Ablex.

Crookes, G. and Schmidt, R. 1991. Language learning motivation: Reopening the research agenda. *Language Learning* 41: 469–512.

Cumming, A. and Gill, J. 1992. Motivation or accessibility? Factors permitting Indo-Canadian women to pursue ESL literacy instruction. In B. Burnaby and A. Cumming (Eds), *Socio-political aspects of ESL education in Canada*. Toronto: OISE Press.

Curran, C.A. 1972. *Counseling-learning: A whole-person model for education*. New York: Grune and Stratton.

Dadour, E.S. and Robbins, J. 1996. University-level studies using strategy instruction to improve speaking ability in Egypt and Japan. In R.L. Oxford (Ed.), *Language learning strategies around the world: Cross-cultural perspectives*. Honolulu, HI: Second Language Teaching and Curriculum Center, University of Hawaii Press.

Dahl, D. 1981. The role of experience in speech modifications for second language learners. *Minnesota Papers in Linguistics and Philosophy of Language* 7: 78–93.

Danziger, K. 1990. *Constructing the subject. Historical origins of psychological research*. Cambridge: Cambridge University Press.

Danziger, K. 1997. *Naming the mind. How psychology found its language*. London: Sage.

Davydov, V.V. 1999. The content and unsolved problems of activity theory. In Y. Engeström, R. Miettinen and R.-L. Punamäki (Eds), *Perspectives on activity theory*. Cambridge: Cambridge University Press.

Day, R. 1984. Student participation in the ESL classroom, or some imperfections in practice. *Language Learning* 34: 69–102.

Deignan, A. 1999. Corpus-based research in metaphor. In L. Cameron and G. Low (Eds), *Researching and applying metaphor*. Cambridge: Cambridge University Press.

Derry, S.J. 1990. Learning strategies for acquiring useful knowledge. In Jones, B.F. and Idol, L. (Eds), *Dimensions of thinking and cognitive instruction*. Hillsdale, NJ: Lawrence Erlbaum Associates.

Devine, J. 1993. The role of metacognition in second language reading and writing. In J.G. Carson and I. Leki (Eds), *Reading in the composition classroom: Second language perspectives*. Boston, MA: Heinle and Heinle.

Dewaele, J.-M. and Furnham, A. 1999. Extraversion: The unloved variable in applied linguistic research. *Language Learning* 49: 509–44.

Dewaele, J.-M. and Furnham, A. 2000. Personality and speech production: A pilot study of second language learners. *Personality and Individual Differences* 28/4: 355–65.

Dobinson, T. 1996. *The recall and retention of new vocabulary from second language classrooms*. Unpublished MA dissertation. Perth, Western Australia: Edith Cowan University.

Dole, J., Duffy, G., Roehler, L. and Pearson, P.D. 1991. Moving from the old to the new: Research in reading comprehension instruction. *Review of Educational Research* 61/2: 239–64.

Donato, R. 1994. Collective scaffolding in second language learning. In J.P. Lantolf and G. Appel (Eds), *Vygotskian approaches to second language research*. Norwood, NJ: Ablex.

Donato, R. and McCormick, D. 1994. A sociocultural perspective on language learning strategies: The role of mediation. *The Modern Language Journal* 78/4: 453–64.

Dörnyei, Z. 1994. Motivation and motivating in the foreign language classroom. *The Modern Language Journal* 78/3: 273–84.

Dörnyei, Z. 1995. On the teachability of communication strategies. *TESOL Quarterly* 29: 55–85.

Dörnyei, Z. 1998. Motivation in second and foreign language learning. *Language Teaching* 31: 117–35.

Dörnyei, Z. 2001. *Teaching and researching motivation*. London: Pearson Education.

Doughty, C. and Williams, J. (Eds) 1998. *Focus on form in classroom second language acquisition*. New York: Cambridge University Press.

Dubin, F. and Olshtain, E. 1986. *Course design*. Cambridge: Cambridge University Press.

Duff, P.A. 1996. Different languages, different practices: socialization of discourse competence in dual-language school classrooms in Hungary. In K.M. Bailey and D. Nunan (Eds), *Voices from the language classroom*. Cambridge: Cambridge University Press.

Duffy, G.G., Roehler, L.R., Sivan, E., Rackliffe, G., Book, C., Meloth, M.S., Vavrus, L.G., Wesselman, R., Putnam, J. and Bassiri, D. 1987. Effects of explaining the reasoning associated with using reading strategies. *Reading Research Quarterly* 22/3: 347–68.

Dulay, H. and Burt, M. 1977. Remarks on creativity in language learning. In M. Burt, H. Dulay and M. Finocchiaro (Eds), *Viewpoints on English as a second language*. New York: Regents Publishing Company.

Durkin, K. 1987. Minds and language: Social cognition, social interaction and the acquisition of language. *Mind and Language* 2/2: 105–40.

Ehrlich, S. 1997. Gender as a social practice. Implications for second language acquisition. *Studies in Second Language Acquisition* 19: 421–46.

Ehrman, M. 1993. Ego boundaries revisited: Toward a model of personality and learning. In J. Alatis (Ed.), *Georgetown University Round Table on Languages and Linguistics 1993*. Washington, DC: Georgetown University Press, pp. 331–62.

Ehrman, M. 1995. Personality, language-learning aptitude, and program structure. In J. Alatis, C. Straehle, B. Gallenberger and M. Ronkin (Eds), *Georgetown University Round Table on Languages and Linguistics 1995*. Washington, DC: Georgetown University Press, pp. 328–45.

Ehrman, M. 1996. *Understanding second language learning difficulties*. Thousand Oaks, CA: Sage.

Ehrman, M. and Dörnyei, Z. 1998. *Interpersonal dynamics in second language education: The visible and invisible classroom*. Thousand Oaks, CA: Sage.

Ehrman, M. and Oxford, R. 1995. Cognition plus: Correlates of language learning success. *The Modern Language Journal* 79/1: 67–89.

Eisner, E.W. 1991. *The enlightened eye: Qualitative inquiry and the enhancement of educational practice*. New York: Macmillan.

Elbaum, B.E., Berg, C.A. and Dodd, D.H. 1993. Previous learning experience, strategy beliefs, and task definition in self-regulated foreign language learning. *Contemporary Educational Psychology* 18: 318–36.

El-Dinary, P.B., Brown, R. and Van Meter, P. 1995. Strategy instruction for improving writing. In E. Wood, V.E. Woloshyn and T. Willoughby (Eds), *Cognitive strategy instruction for middle and high schools*. Cambridge, MA: Brookline Books.

Elliott, A.R. 1995. Foreign language phonology: field independence, attitude, and the success of formal instruction in Spanish pronunciation. *The Modern Language Journal* 79/4: 530–42.

Ellis, G. and Sinclair, B. 1989. *Learning to learn English: A course in learner training. Teacher's book*. Cambridge: Cambridge University Press.

Ellis, N.C. 1994. Vocabulary acquisition: The implicit ins and outs of explicit cognitive mediation. In N.C. Ellis (Ed.), *Implicit and explicit learning of languages*. San Diego, CA: Academic Press.

Ellis, N.C. 1996. Phonological memory, chunking, and points of order. *Studies in Second Language Acquisition* 18: 91–126.

Ellis, N.C. and Beaton, A. 1993. Psycholinguistic determinants of foreign language vocabulary learning. *Language Learning* 43: 559–617.

Ellis, R. 1984. *Classroom second language development.* Oxford: Pergamon.

Ellis, R. 1985. Teacher–pupil interaction in second language development. In S. Gass and C. Madden (Eds), *Input in second language acquisition.* Rowley, MA: Newbury House.

Ellis, R. 1986. *Understanding second language acquisition.* Oxford: Oxford University Press.

Ellis, R. 1994. *The study of second language acquisition.* Oxford: Oxford University Press.

Ellis, R. and Rathbone, M. 1987. *The acquisition of German in a classroom context.* Mimeograph. London: Ealing College of Higher Education.

Ely, C. 1986. An analysis of discomfort, risk-taking, sociability and motivation in the second language class. *Language Learning* 36: 1–25.

Engeström, Y. 1987. *Learning by understanding. An activity-theoretical approach to developmental research.* Helsinki: Orienta-Konsultit.

Engeström, Y. 1999. Activity theory and individual and social transformation. In Y. Engeström, R. Miettinen and R.-L. Punamäki (Eds), *Perspectives on activity theory.* Cambridge: Cambridge University Press.

Engeström, Y. and Middleton, D. (Eds), 1996. *Cognition and communication at work.* Cambridge: Cambridge University Press.

Englert, C.S., Raphael, T.E., Anderson, L.M., Anthony, H.M. and Stevens, D.D. 1991. Making strategies and self-talk visible: Writing instruction in regular and special education classrooms. *American Educational Research Journal* 28: 337–72.

Enkvist, I. 1992. *Conceptions of learning and study goals: First semester students of Spanish at a Swedish university.* Studies of Higher Education and Research 3. Stockholm: The Council for Studies of Higher Education, Sweden.

Eubank, L. and Gregg, K. 1999. Critical periods and (second language acquisition): Divide et impera. In D. Birdsong (Ed.), *Second language acquisition and the critical period hypothesis.* Mahwah, NJ: Lawrence Erlbaum Associates.

Eysenck, M.W. 1986. *A handbook of cognitive psychology.* London: Lawrence Erlbaum Associates.

Færch, C. and Kasper, G. (Eds) 1983. *Strategies in interlanguage communication.* London: Longman.

Fairclough, N. 1989. *Language and power.* London: Longman.

Fairclough, N. 1992. *Discourse and social change.* Cambridge: Polity Press.

Faltis, C. 1997. Case study methods in researching language and education. *Encyclopedia of Language and Education,* Volume 8: 145–52.

Firth, A. and Wagner, J. 1997. On discourse, communication, and (some) fundamental concepts in SLA research. *The Modern Language Journal* 81/3: 285–300.

Flavell, J. 1979. Metacognition and cognitive monitoring: a new area of cognitive developmental inquiry. *American Psychologist* 34: 906–11.

Flavell, J. 1981. Monitoring social cognitive enterprises: something else that may develop in the area of social cognition. In J.H. Flavell and L. Ross (Eds), *Social cognitive development: Frontiers and possible futures.* New York: Cambridge University Press.

Flavell, J.H. 1987. Speculation about the nature and development of metacognition. In F.E. Weinert and R.H. Kluwe (Eds), *Metacognition, motivation and understanding.* Hillsdale, NJ: Lawrence Erlbaum Associates.

Flege, J. 1995. Second language speech learning. Theory, findings, and problems. In W. Strange (Ed.), *Speech perception and linguistic experience.* Timonium, MD: York Press.

Flege, J. 1999. Age of learning and second language speech. In D. Birdsong (Ed.), *Second language acquisition and the critical period hypothesis.* Mahwah, NJ: Lawrence Erlbaum Associates.

Flege, J., Munro, M. and MacKay, I. 1995. Factors affecting strength of perceived foreign accent in a second language. *Journal of the Accoustical Society of America* 97: 3125–34.

Flowerdew, J., Li, D. and Miller, L. 1998. Attitudes towards English and Cantonese among Hong Kong Chinese university lecturers. *TESOL Quarterly* 32: 201–31.

Foster, P. 1998. A classroom perspective on the negotiation of meaning. *Applied Linguistics* 19/1: 1–23.

Fotos, S. 1994. Motivation in second language learning: A critical review. *Senshu University Annual Bulletin of the Humanities* 24: 29–54.

Frawley, W.J. 1997. *Vygotsky and cognitive science.* Cambridge, MA: Harvard University Press.

Freire, P. 1970. *Pedagogy of the oppressed.* New York: Seabury.

Gadd, N. 1998. Toward less humanistic teaching. *ELT Journal* 52/3: 223–35.

Gagné, E.D., Yekovich, C.W. and Yekovich, F.R. 1993. *The cognitive psychology of school learning* (Second edition). New York: HarperCollins.

Ganschow, L. and Sparks, R. 1993. 'Foreign' language learning disabilities: Issues, research and teaching implications. In S.A. Vogel and P.B. Adelman (Eds), *Success for college students with learning disabilities.* New York: Springer-Verlag.

Ganschow, L. and Sparks, R. 1995. Effects of direct instruction in Spanish phonology on the native-language skills and foreign-language aptitude of at-risk foreign-language learners. *Journal of Learning Disabilities* 28: 107–20.

Ganschow, L. and Sparks, R. 1996. Anxiety about foreign language learning among high school women. *The Modern Language Journal* 80/2: 199–212.

Ganschow, L., Javorsky, J., Sparks, R., Skinner, S., Anderson, R. and Patton, J. 1994. Differences in language performance among high-, average-, and low-anxious college foreign language learners. *The Modern Language Journal* 78/1: 41–55.

Gardner, H. 1983. *Frames of mind: The theory of multiple intelligences.* New York: Basic Books.

Gardner, R. 1980. On the validity of affective variables in second language acquisition: Conceptual, contextual, and statistical considerations. *Language Learning* 30: 255–70.

Gardner, R. 1985. *Social psychology and second language learning: The role of attitude and motivation.* London: Edward Arnold.

Gardner, R.C. and Lambert, W.E. 1972. *Attitudes and motivation in second language learning.* Rowley, Mass: Newbury House.

Gardner, R. and MacIntyre, P. 1991. An instrumental motivation in language study. *Studies in Second Language Acquisition* 13: 57–72.

Gardner, R. and MacIntyre, P. 1993. On the measurement of affective variables in second language learning. *Language Learning* 43: 157–94.

Gardner, R. and Tremblay, P. 1994a. On motivation, research agendas, and theoretical frameworks. *The Modern Language Journal* 78/3: 359–68.

Gardner, R. and Tremblay, P. 1994b. On motivation: measurement and conceptual considerations. *The Modern Language Journal* 78/4: 524–7.

Gardner, R., Tremblay, P. and Masgoret, A. 1997. Towards a full model of second language learning: An empirical investigation. *The Modern Language Journal* 81/3: 344–62.

Gaskins, I.W. and Elliot, T.T. 1991. *Implementing cognitive strategy instruction across the school: The benchmark manual for teachers.* Cambridge, MA: Brookline Books.

Gass, S.M. 1998. Apples and oranges: Or, why apples are not oranges and don't need to be. A response to Firth and Wagner. *The Modern Language Journal* 82/1: 83–90.

Gass, S.M. and Varonis, E.M. 1985. Task variation and nonnative/nonnative negotiation of meaning. In S.M. Gass and C.G. Madden (Eds), *Input in second language acquisition.* Rowley, MA: Newbury House.

Genesee, F. 1976. The role of intelligence in second language learning. *Language Learning* 26/2: 267–80.

Gergen, K.J. 1985. The social constructionist movement in modern psychology. *American Psychologist* 40: 266–75.

Giles, H. (Ed.) 1977. *Language, ethnicity and intergroup relations.* New York: Academic Press.

Gillette, B. 1994. The role of learner goals in L2 success. In J.P. Lantolf and G. Appel (Eds), *Vygotskian approaches to second language research.* Norwood, NJ: Ablex.

Giltrow, J. and Colhoun, E. 1992. The culture of power: ESL traditions, Mayan resistance. In B. Burnaby and A. Cumming (Eds), *Socio-political aspects of ESL in Canada.* Toronto: OISE Press.

Glaser, B. and Strauss, A.M. 1967. *Discovery of grounded theory.* Chicago, IL: Aldine.

Glucksberg, S., Keysar, B. and McGlone, M. 1992. Metaphor understanding and accessing conceptual schema; Reply to Gibbs. *Psychological Review* 99: 578–81.

Goldstein, T. 1996. *Two languages at work: Bilingual life on the production floor.* Mouton de Gruyter: New York.

Green, J.M. and Oxford, R. 1995. A closer look at learning strategies, L2 proficiency, and gender. *TESOL Quarterly* 29/2: 261–97.

Gregg, K. 1989. Second language acquisition theory: The case for a generative perspective. In S. Gass and J. Schachter (Eds), *Linguistic perspectives on second language acquisition.* Cambridge: Cambridge University Press.

Gregg, K. 1993. Taking explanation seriously: or, let a couple of flowers bloom. *Applied Linguistics* 14: 276–94.

Griffiths, R. 1991. Pausological research in an L2 context: a rationale and review of selected studies. *Applied Linguistics* 12: 276–94.

Griffiths, R. and Sheen, R. 1992. Disembedded figures in the landscape: A reappraisal of L2 research on field dependence/independence. *Applied Linguistics* 13: 133–48.

Grotjahn, R. 1991. The research programme subjective theories: A new approach in second language research. *Studies in Second Language Acquisition* 13: 187–214.

Gurney, B.F. 1995. Tugboats and tennis games: Preservice conceptions of teaching and learning revealed through metaphors. *Journal of Research in Science Teaching* 32/6: 569–83.

Hamayan, E. and Tucker, R. 1980. Language input in the bilingual classroom and its relations to second language achievement. *TESOL Quarterly* 14: 453–68.

Hargreaves, A. (Ed.) 1996. *Rethinking educational change with heart and mind.* Alexandria, VA: Association for Supervision and Curriculum Development.

Harley, B. and Hart, D. 1997. Language aptitude and second language proficiency in classroom learners of different starting ages. *Studies in Second Language Acquisition* 19: 379–400.

Harré, R. 1983. *Personal being: A theory for individual psychology.* Oxford: Basil Blackwell.

Harris, K.R. and Graham, S. 1992. *Helping young writers master the craft: Strategy instruction and self-regulation in the writing process.* Cambridge, MA: Brookline Books.

Hartmann, E. 1991. *Boundaries in the mind: A new psychology of personality.* New York: Basic Books.

Hatch, E. 1978. Discourse analysis and second language acquisition. In E. Hatch (Ed.), *Second language acquisition.* Rowley, MA: Newbury House.

Henzel, V. 1979. Foreigner talk in the classroom. *International Review of Applied Linguistics* 17: 159–65.

Hermann, G. 1980. Attitudes and success in children's learning of English as a second language: The motivational versus the resultative hypothesis. *English Language Teaching Journal* 34: 247–54.

Herron, C. 1982. Foreign language learning: Approaches as metaphor. *The Modern Language Journal* 66/2: 235–42.

Higgs, T. and Clifford, R. 1982. The push towards communication. In T. Higgs (Ed.), *Curriculum, competence, and the foreign language teacher.* Skokie, IL: National Textbook Company.

Ho, B. 1996. Developing strategic knowledge about technical report-writing through reflective activities. Paper presented at the International Conference, The Development of Learning Independence in Language Learning, King Mongut Institute of Technology, Bangkok, Thailand.

Hoffman, E. 1989. *Lost in translation. A life in a new language.* New York: Penguin.

Hoffman, R. and Kemper, S. 1987. What could reaction-time studies be telling us about metaphor comprehension? *Metaphor and Symbolic Activity* 2: 149–86.

Hofstede, G. 1986. Cultural differences in teaching and learning. *International Journal of Intercultural Education* 10: 301–20.

Hofstede, G. 1991. *Cultures and organizations: Software of the mind.* London: McGraw-Hill.

Holec, H. 1981. *Autonomy and foreign language learning.* Oxford: Pergamon Press.

Holec, H. 1987. The learner as manager: managing learning or managing to learn. In A. Wenden and J. Rubin (Eds), *Learner strategies in language learning.* London: Prentice-Hall.

Horowitz, E.K. 1987. Surveying student beliefs about language learning. In A. Wenden and J. Rutin (Eds), *Learner strategies in language learning.* London: Prentice-Hall.

Horowitz, E.K. 1988. The beliefs about language learning of beginning university foreign language students. *The Modern Language Journal* 72/3: 283–94.

Horowitz, E.K. 1999. Cultural and situational influences on learner beliefs about language learning. In A. Wenden (Ed.), Special Issue on Matacognitive Knowledge and Beliefs in Language Learning. *System* 27/4: 557–76.

Hosenfeld, C. 1976. Learning about learning: Discovering our students' strategies. *Foreign Language Annals* 9: 117–29.

Hosenfeld, C. 1999. Some beliefs of language learners are emergent phenomena. Paper presented at the 12th World Congress of Applied Linguistics, Tokyo, Japan.

Hosenfeld, C., Arnold, V., Kirchofer, J., Laciura, J. and Wilson, L. 1981. Second language reading: A curricular sequence for teaching reading strategies. *Foreign Language Annals* 14/5: 415–22.

Huang, S.C., Lloyd, P. and Mikulecky, L. 1998. Assessing ESL learners' perceptions of self-efficacy in reading and writing. Paper presented at the American Association for Applied Linguistics Annual Conference, Miami, Florida.

Huberman, M. (Ed.) 1989. Research on teachers' professional lives. Special issue of *International Journal of Educational Research* 13/4.

Huberman, M. 1993. *The lives of teachers.* New York: Teachers College Press.

Huda, N. 1998. Relationship between speaking proficiency, reflectivity-impulsivity, and L2 learning strategies. In W. Renandya and G. Jacobs (Eds), *Learners and language learning*. Singapore: SEAMEO Regional Language Centre.

Hurford, J. and Kirby, S. 1999. Co-evolution of language size and the critical period. In D. Birdsong (Ed.), *Second language acquisition and the critical period hypothesis*. Mahwah, NJ: Lawrence Erlbaum Associates.

Ibrahim, A. 1999. Becoming Black: Rap and hip-hop, race, gender, identity and the politics of ESL learning. *TESOL Quarterly* 33: 349–69.

Idol, L. and Jones, B.F. 1991. *Educational values and cognitive instruction: Implications for reform*. Hillsdale, NJ: Lawrence Erlbaum Associates.

Ioup, G., Boustagui, E., El Tigi, M. and Moselle, M. 1994. Re-examining the critical period hypothesis: A case study of successful adult SLA in a naturalistic environment. *Studies in Second Language Acquisition* 16: 73–98.

Jehng, J.-C., Johnson, S.D. and Anderson, R.C. 1993. Schooling and students' epistemological beliefs about learning. *Contemporary Educational Psychology* 18: 23–35.

Jiménez, R.T. and Gámez, R. 1998. Literature-based cognitive strategy instruction for middle school Latino students. In R.M. Gersten and R.T. Jiménez (Eds), *Promoting learning for culturally and linguistically diverse students*. Belmont, CA: Wadsworth.

Johnson, J.A., Dupuis, Y.L., Musial, D., Hall, G.E. and Gollnick, D.N. 1996. *Introduction to the fundamentals of American education* (Tenth edition). Needham Heights, MA: Allyn and Bacon.

Jones, B.F. and Idol, L. 1990. Introduction. In B.F. Jones and L. Idol (Eds), *Dimensions of thinking and cognitive instruction*. Hillsdale, NJ: Lawrence Erlbaum Associates.

Kasanga, L.A. 1996. Peer interaction and L2 learning. *Canadian Modern Language Review* 52/4: 611–39.

Kasper, G. (Ed.) 1996a. The development of pragmatic competence. Special issue of *Studies in Second Language Acquisition* 18/2.

Kasper, G. 1996b. Introduction: Interlanguage pragmatics in SLA. *Studies in Second Language Acquisition* 18/2: 145–8.

Kasper, G. 1997. 'A' stands for acquisition. A response to Firth and Wagner. *The Modern Language Journal* 81/3: 307–12.

Kasper, G. and Kellerman, E. (Eds) 1997. *Communication strategies: Psycholinguistic and sociolinguistic perspectives*. London: Longman.

Katz, A. 1996. Teaching style: A way to understand instruction in language classrooms. In K.M. Bailey and D. Nunan (Eds), *Voices from the language classroom*. Cambridge: Cambridge University Press.

Keatley, C., Chamot, A.U., Barnhardt, S. and El-Dinary, P.B. 1999. Learning strategy use by children in language immersion classrooms. Paper submitted to *Language Learning*.

Kelchtermans, G. 1996. Teacher vulnerability: Understanding its moral and political roots. *Cambridge Journal of Education* 26/3: 307–23.

Kellerman, E. 1995. Age before beauty: Johnson and Newport revisited. In L. Eubank, L. Selinker and M. Sharwood Smith (Eds), *The current state of interlanguage: Studies in Honor of William E. Rutherford*. Amsterdam: John Benjamins.

Kellerman, E. and Sharwood Smith, M. (Eds) 1986. *Cross-linguistic influence in second language acquisition*. Oxford: Pergamon.

Kelly, G. 1955. *The psychology of personal constructs* (Vols 1 and 2). New York: Norton.

Kern, R.G. 1995. Students' and teachers' beliefs about language learning. *Foreign Language Annals* 28: 71–92.

Kimura, M. 1999. A cross-sectional study of Japanese college students' English proficiency and their strategies for foreign language learning: Differences between general students and returnees. Paper presented at AILA 1999, Tokyo, Japan.

Klein, W. 1995. Language acquisition at different ages. In D. Magnusson (Ed.), *The lifespan development of individuals: Behavioral, neurobiological, and psychosocial perspectives. A synthesis.* New York: Cambridge University Press.

Kliefgen, J. 1985. Skilled variation in a kindergarten teacher's use of foreigner talk. In S. Gass and C. Madden (Eds), *Input in second language acquisition.* Rowley MA: Newbury House.

Kline, R. 1993. *The social practice of literacy in a program of study abroad.* Unpublished PhD dissertation, Pennsylvania State University, Philadelphia, PA.

Knox, A.B. 1977. *Adult development and learning.* San Francisco, CA: Jossey-Bass.

Koch, S. and Deetz, S. 1981. Metaphor analysis of social reality in organizations. *Journal of Applied Communication Research* 9: 1–15.

Kramsch, C. 1993. *Context and culture in language teaching.* Oxford: Oxford University Press.

Kramsch, C. 1995. The applied linguist and the foreign language teacher: Can they talk to each other? *Australian Review of Applied Linguistics* 18: 1–16.

Krapels, A.R. 1990. An overview of second language writing process approach. In B. Kroll (Ed.), *Second language writing.* Cambridge: Cambridge University Press.

Krashen, S. 1981. *Second language acquisition and second language learning.* Oxford: Pergamon.

Krashen, S. 1985. *The input hypothesis: Issues and implications.* London: Longman.

Krashen, S. 1994. The input hypothesis and its rivals. In N.C. Ellis (Ed.), *Implicit and explicit learning of languages.* San Diego, CA: Academic Press.

Krashen, S. 1998. Comprehensible output? *System* 26: 175–82.

Krashen, S. and Terrell, T. 1983. *The natural approach: Language acquisition in the classroom.* Oxford: Pergamon.

Krashen, S., Long, M. and Scarcella, R. 1979. Age, rate, and eventual attainment in second language acquisition. *TESOL Quarterly* 13: 573–82.

Kuhlmeier, H., van den Bergh, H. and Melse, L. 1996. Attitudes and achievements in the first year of German language instruction in Dutch secondary education. *The Modern Language Journal* 80/4: 494–508.

Kumaravadivelu, B. 1991. Language-learning tasks: Teacher intention and learner interpretation. *ELT Journal* 45/2: 98–107.

Kumaravadivelu, B. 1994. The postmethod condition: (E)merging strategies for second/foreign language teaching. *TESOL Quarterly* 28/1: 27–48.

Lakoff, G. 1986. A figure of thought. *Metaphor and Symbolic Activity* 1: 215–25.

Lakoff, G. 1987. *Women, fire and dangerous things.* Chicago, IL: University of Chicago Press.

Lakoff, G. and Johnson, M. 1980. *Metaphors we live by.* Chicago, IL: University of Chicago Press.

Lakoff, G. and Turner, M. 1989. *More than cool reason: A field guide to poetic metaphor.* Chicago, IL: University of Chicago Press.

Lambert, W. and Taylor, D. 1996. Language in the lives of ethnic minorities: Cuban American families in Miami. *Applied Linguistics* 17: 477–500.

Lantolf, J. 1996. SLA theory building: 'Letting all the flowers bloom!' *Language Learning* 46: 713–49.

Lantolf, J. and Appel, G. 1994. *Vygotskian approaches to second language research.* Norwood, NJ: Ablex.

Lantolf, J.P. and Genung, P.B. 2000. An activity theoretic perspective on foreign language learning in the classroom setting: A case study. In S. Pekarek (Ed.), Special issue of *Acquisition et Interaction en Lengue Etrangère*. April 2000.

LaPierre, D. 1994. Language output in a cooperative learning setting: Determining its effects on second language learning. Unpublished MA thesis, University of Toronto (OISE), Toronto.

Lapkin, S., Hart, D. and Swain, M. 1991. Early and middle French immersion programs: French language outcomes. *Canadian Modern Language Review* 48/1: 11–40.

Larsen-Freeman, D. 1983. The importance of input in second language acquisition. In R. Andersen (Ed.), *Pidginization and creolization as language acquisition*. Rowley, MA: Newbury House. pp. 87–93.

Larsen-Freeman, D. 1991. Second language acquisition research: Staking out the territory. *TESOL Quarterly* 25: 315–50.

Larsen-Freeman, D. 1997. Chaos/complexity science in second language acquisition. *Applied Linguistics* 18: 141–65.

Larsen-Freeman, D. 1998. On the scope of second language acquisition research: 'The learner variety' and beyond. *Language Learning* 48: 551–6.

Larsen-Freeman, D. and Long, M. 1991. *An introduction to second language acquisition research*. London: Longman.

Lave, J. 1988. *Cognition in practice*. Cambridge: Cambridge University Press.

Lave, J. and Wenger, E. 1991. *Situated learning. Legitimate peripheral participation*. Cambridge: Cambridge University Press.

Leary, D. 1990. Psyche's muse: The role of metaphor in the history of psychology. In D. Leary (Ed.), *Metaphors in the history of psychology*. New York: Cambridge University Press.

Leki, I. 1995. Coping strategies of ESL students in writing tasks across the curriculum. *TESOL Quarterly* 29/2: 235–60.

Leont'ev, A.N. 1978. *Activity, consciousness, and personality*. Englewood Cliffs, NJ: Prentice-Hall.

Leont'ev, A.N. 1981. *Psychology and the language learning process*. Oxford: Pergamon Press.

Lewin, K., Lippitt, R. and White, R. 1939. Patterns of aggressive behavior in experimentally created 'social climate'. *Journal of Psychology* 10: 271–99.

Liddicoat, A. 1997. Interaction, social structure, and second language use: A response to Firth and Wagner. *The Modern Language Journal* 81/3: 313–17.

Lightbown, P.M. 1980. The acquisition and use of questions by French L2 learners of English. In S. Felix (Ed.), *Second language development: Trends and issues*. Tubingen: Gunter Narr.

Lightbown, P.M. 1991. What have we here? Some observations on the effect of instruction on L2 learning. In R. Phillipson et al. (Eds), *Foreign/second language pedagogy research*. Clevedon, UK: Multilingual Matters.

Lightbown, P.M. and Halter, R.H. 1993. *Comprehension-based ESL program in New Brunswick: Grade 8*. Ottawa: Department of the Secretary of State for Education.

Lightbown, P. and Spada, N. 1993. *How languages are learned*. Oxford: Oxford University Press.

Lin, A. 1997. Bilingual education in Hong Kong. *Encyclopedia of Language and Education*. Volume 5: 281–90.

Lindstromberg, S. 1991. Metaphor and ESP: A ghost in the machine. *English for Specific Purposes* 10: 207–25.

Lippi-Green, R. 1997. *English with an accent: Language, ideology and discrimination in the United States*. London: Routledge.

LoCastro, V. 1994. Learning strategies and learning environments. *TESOL Quarterly* 28: 409–14.

Long, M.H. 1981. Input, interaction and second language acquisition. In H. Winitz (Ed.), *Native language and foreign language acquisition.* New York: Annals of the New York Academy of Sciences, 379.

Long, M.H. 1989. Task, group, and task-group interactions. *University of Hawaii Working Papers in ESL* 8: 251–86.

Long, M.H. 1990. Maturational constraints on language development. *Studies in Second Language Acquisition* 12: 251–86.

Long, M.H. 1991. Focus on form: A design feature in language teaching methodology. In K. deBot, R. Ginsberg and C. Kramsch (Eds), *Foreign language research in cross-cultural perspective.* Amsterdam: John Benjamins.

Long, M.H. 1993a. Assessment strategies for SLA theories. *Applied Linguistics* 14: 225–49.

Long, M.H. 1993b. Second language acquisition as a function of age. Research findings and methodological issues. In K. Hyltenstam and A. Viberg (Eds), *Progression and regression in language: Sociocultural, neuropsychological and linguistic perspectives.* New York: Cambridge University Press.

Long, M.H. 1996. The role of the linguistic environment in second language acquisition. In W. Ritchie and T. Bhatia (Eds), *Handbook of second language acquisition.* New York: Academic Press.

Long, M.H. 1997. Construct validity in SLA research: A response to Firth and Wagner. *The Modern Language Journal* 81/3: 318–23.

Lukmani, Y. 1972. Motivation to learn and language proficiency. *Language Learning* 22: 261–73.

Luria, A.R. 1973. *The working brain: An introduction to neuropsychology.* New York: Basic Books.

Luria, A.R. 1979. *The making of mind.* Cambridge, MA: Harvard University Press.

Lyster, R. 1998. Recasts, repetition, and ambiguity in L2 classroom discourse. *Studies in Second Language Acquisition* 20/1: 51–81.

Lyster, R. and Ranta, E. 1997. Corrective feedback and learner uptake: Negotiation of form in communicative classrooms. *Studies in Second Language Acquisition* 19: 37–61.

MacIntyre, P. 1995. How does anxiety affect second language learning? A reply to Sparks and Ganschow. *The Modern Language Journal* 79/1: 90–9.

MacIntyre, P. and Charos, C. 1996. Personality, attitudes, and affect as predictors of second language communication. *Journal of Language and Social Psychology* 15: 3–26.

MacIntyre, P. and Gardner, R. 1991a. Methods and results in the study of anxiety and language learning: A review of the literature. *Language Learning* 41: 85–117.

MacIntyre, P. and Gardner, R. 1991b. Language anxiety: Its relationship to other anxieties and to processing in native and second languages. *Language Learning* 41: 513–34.

MacIntyre, P. and Gardner, R. 1994. The subtle effects of language anxiety on cognitive processing in the second language. *Language Learning* 44: 283–305.

MacIntyre, P., Noels, K. and Clément, R. 1997. Biases in self-ratings of second language proficiency: The role of language anxiety. *Language Learning* 47: 265–87.

MacIntyre, P., Clément, R., Dörnyei, Z. and Noels, K. 1998. Conceptualizing a willingness to communicate in a L2: Situational model of L2 confidence and affiliation. *The Modern Language Journal* 82/4: 545–62.

Mackey, A. 1996. Can interaction step up the pace? An empirical study of conversational interaction and interlanguage development. Paper given at the 1996 Annual American Association for Applied Linguistics Conference, Chicago, IL.

Magnan, S. (Ed.) 1990. *Shifting the instructional focus to the language learner.* Middlebury, VT: Northeast Conference on the Teaching of Foreign Languages.

Maley, A. 1984. 'I got religion' – Evangelism in language teaching. In S.J. Savignon and M.S. Berns (Eds), *Initiatives in communicative language teaching: A book of readings.* Reading, MA: Addison-Wesley.

Mantle-Bromley, C. 1995. Positive attitudes and realistic beliefs: Links to proficiency. *The Modern Language Journal* 79/3: 372–86.

McCombs, B. and Whistler, J.S. 1997. *The learner-centered classroom and school.* San Francisco, CA: Jossey-Bass.

McDonough, S. 1995. *Strategy and skill in learning a foreign language.* London: Edward Arnold.

McGroarty, M. 1998. Constructive and constructivist challenges for applied linguistics. *Language Learning* 48: 591–622.

McKay, S. and Wong, S. 1996. Multiple discourse, multiple identities: Investment and agency in second-language learning among Chinese adolescent immigrant students. *Harvard Educational Review* 66: 577–608.

McLaughlin, B. 1987. *Theories of second language learning.* London: Edward Arnold.

McNamara, T.F. 1997. 'Interaction' in second language performance assessment: Whose performance? *Applied Linguistics* 18/4: 446–66.

Mendelsohn, D. 1994. *Learning to listen: A strategy-based approach for the second-language learner.* San Diego, CA: Dominie Press.

Miles, M.B. and Huberman, M. 1984. *Qualitative data analysis: A sourcebook of new methods.* Beverly Hills, CA: Sage.

Miller, J. 1999. Becoming audible: social identity and second language use. *Journal of Intercultural Studies* 20: 149–65.

Mori, Y. 1999a. Epistemological beliefs and language learning beliefs: What do language learners believe about their learning? *Language Learning* 49: 377–415.

Mori, Y. 1999b. Beliefs about language learning and their relationship to the ability to integrate information from word parts and context in interpreting novel Kanji words. *The Modern Language Journal* 83/4: 534–47.

Moyer, A. 1999. Ultimate attainment in L2 phonology. *Studies in Second Language Acquisition* 21: 81–108.

Munby, H. 1986. Metaphor in the thinking of teachers: An exploratory study. *Curriculum Studies* 18/2: 197–206.

Muñiz-Swicegood, M. 1994. The effects of metacognitive reading strategy training on the reading performance and student reading analysis strategies of third grade bilingual students. *Bilingual Research Journal* 18/1 and 18/2: 83–97.

Musumeci, D. 1996. Teacher–learner negotiation in content-based instruction: Communication to cross purposes? *Applied Linguistics* 17/3: 286–325.

Naiman, N., Fröhlich, M., Stern, H.H. and Todesco, A. 1978. *The good language learner.* Toronto: Ontario Institute for Studies in Education.

Naiman, N., Fröhlich, M., Stern, H.H. and Todesco, A. 1996. *The good language learner.* Clevedon, UK: Multilingual Matters. (Original work published 1978.)

Nam, C. and Oxford, R.L. 1998. Portrait of a future teacher: Case study of learning styles, strategies, and learning disability. *System* 26/1: 52–72.

Nation, I.S. 1982. Beginning to learn foreign vocabulary: A review of research. *RELC Journal* 13/1: 14–33.

Neisser, U. 1976. *Cognition and reality*. San Francisco, CA: W.H. Freeman and Co.

Nelson, C. 1999. Sexual identities in ESL: Queer theory and classroom inquiry. *TESOL Quarterly* 33: 371–91.

Nelson, G.L. and Brown, K. n.d. Hofstede's four-dimensional model of cultural differences: Pedagogical applications. Unpublished manuscript, Georgia State University, Atlanta, GA.

Newton, J. and Kennedy, G. 1996. Effects of communication tasks on grammatical relations marked by second language learners. *System* 24/3: 309–22.

Nobuyoshi, J. and Ellis, R. 1993. Focused communication tasks and second language acquisition. *ELT Journal* 47/3: 203–10.

Noels, K. and Clément, R. 1996. Communication across cultures: Social determinants and acculturative consequences. *Canadian Journal of Behavioural Science* 28: 214–28.

Noels, K., Pon, A. and Clément, R. 1996. Language, identity, and adjustment: The role of linguistic self-confidence in the acculturation process. *Journal of Language and Social Psychology* 15: 246–64.

Noels, K., Clément, R. and Pelletier, L. 1999. Perceptions of teachers' communicative style and students' intrinsic and extrinsic motivation. *The Modern Language Journal* 83/1: 23–34.

Norton, B. 1997. Language, identity, and the ownership of English. *TESOL Quarterly* 31: 409–29.

Norton, B. 2000. *Identity and language learning: Gender, ethnicity and educational change*. London: Longman.

Norton Peirce, B. 1995. Social identity, investment, and language learning. *TESOL Quarterly* 29/1: 9–31.

Norton Peirce, B., Harper, H. and Burnaby, B. 1993. Workplace ESL at Levi Strauss: 'Dropouts' speak out. *TESL Canada Journal* 10/2: 9–30.

Nunan, D. 1988. *The learner-centered curriculum*. Cambridge: Cambridge University Press.

Nunan, D. 1992. The teacher as decision-maker. In J. Flowerdew, M. Brock and S. Hsia (Eds), *Perspectives on second language teacher education*. Hong Kong: City Polytechnic of Hong Kong.

Nunan, D. 1996. Learner strategy training in the classroom: An action research study. *TESOL Journal* 6/1: 35–41.

Nunan, D. 1999. *Second language teaching and learning*. Boston, MA: Heinle and Heinle.

Nyikos, M. and Oxford, R.L. 1993. A factor analytic study of language learning strategy use: Interpretations from information-processing theory and social psychology. *The Modern Language Journal* 77/1: 11–22.

Nystrom, N. 1983. Teacher–student interaction in bilingual classrooms: four approaches to error feedback. In H. Seliger and M. Long (Eds), *Classroom oriented research in second language acquisition*. Rowley, MA: Newbury House.

Ohta, A.S. 1999. Broadening the notion of 'uptake': What private speech reveals about the role of corrective feedback in L2 development. Paper given at the 1999 Annual American Association for Applied Linguistics Conference, Stamford, CT.

Oller, J. and Perkins, K. 1978. Intelligence and language proficiency as sources of variance in self-reported affective variables. *Language Learning* 28: 85–97.

O'Malley, J.M. and Chamot, A.U. 1990. *Learning strategies in second language acquisition*. Cambridge: Cambridge University Press.

O'Malley, J.M. and Chamot, A.U. 1998. Accelerating academic achievement of English language learners: A synthesis of five evaluations of the CALLA model. Submitted to *Bilingual Research Journal*.

O'Malley, J.M., Chamot, A.U., Stewner-Manzanares, G., Küpper, L. and Russo, R.P. 1985a. Learning strategies used by beginning and intermediate ESL students. *Language Learning* 35: 21–46.

O'Malley, J.M., Chamot, A.U., Stewner-Manzanares, G., Russo, R.P. and Küpper, L. 1985b. Learning strategy applications with students of English as a second language. *TESOL Quarterly* 19: 285–96.

O'Malley, J.M., Chamot, A.U. and Walker, C. 1987. Some applications of cognitive theory to second language acquisition. *Studies in Second Language Acquisition* 9: 287–306.

O'Malley, J.M., Chamot, A.U. and Küpper, L. 1989. Listening comprehension strategies in second language acquisition. *Applied Linguistics* 10/4: 418–37.

Oser, F.K., Dick, A. and Patry, J.-L. 1992. *Effective and responsible teaching.* San Francisco, CA: Jossey-Bass.

Oxford, R.L. 1986. *Development and psychometric testing of the Strategy Inventory for Language Learning.* Alexandria, VA: US Army Research Institute for the Behavioral and Social Sciences.

Oxford, R.L. 1990. *Language learning strategies: What every teacher should know.* Rowley, MA: Newbury House.

Oxford, R.L. 1993. Research on second language learning strategies. *Annual Review of Applied Linguistics* 13: 175–87.

Oxford, R.L. 1996a. Employing a questionnaire to assess the use of language learning strategies. *Applied Language Learning* 7: 25–45.

Oxford, R.L. 1996b. When emotion meets (meta)cognition in language learning histories. In A. Moeller (Ed.), *The teaching of culture and language in the second language classroom: Focus on the learner.* Special issue of *International Journal of Educational Research,* 23/7: 581–94.

Oxford, R.L. 1996c. *Language learning strategies around the world: Cross-cultural perspectives.* Honolulu, HI: Second Language Teaching and Curriculum Center, University of Hawaii Press.

Oxford, R.L. 1999. Strategy Inventory for Language Learning: Theoretical context, research, and concerns. Paper presented at AILA 1999, Tokyo, Japan.

Oxford, R.L. 2000. ESL/EFL learning strategies: Synthesis of research. In R. Carter and D. Nunan (Eds), *English language teaching handbook.* Cambridge: Cambridge University Press.

Oxford, R.L. and Burry-Stock, J.A. 1995. Assessing the use of language learning strategies worldwide with the ESL/EFL version of the *Strategy Inventory for Language Learning. System* 23/2: 153–75.

Oxford, R.L. and Ehrman, M. 1993. Second language research on individual differences. In W. Grabe (Ed.), *Annual Review of Applied Linguistics* XIII: 188–205.

Oxford, R.L. and Lavine, R.Z. 1991. Teacher–student 'style wars' in the language classroom: Research insights and suggestions. *Journal of American Departments of Foreign Languages* 23/2: 38–45.

Oxford, R.L. and Leaver, B.L. 1996. A synthesis of strategy instruction for language learners. In R.L. Oxford (Ed.), *Language learning strategies around the world: Cross-cultural perspectives.* Honolulu, HI: University of Hawaii Press.

Oxford, R.L. and Nam, C. 1997. Learning styles and strategies of a 'partially bilingual' student diagnosed as learning disabled: A case study. In J. Reid (Ed.), *Understanding learning styles in the second language classroom.* Englewood Cliffs, NJ: Prentice-Hall.

Oxford, R.L. and Shearin, J. 1994. Language learning motivation: Expanding the theoretical framework. *The Modern Language Journal* 78/1: 12–28.

Oxford, R.L., Ehrman, M.E. and Lavine, R.Z. 1991. Style wars: Teacher–student style conflicts in the language classroom. In S.S. Magnan (Ed.), *Challenges for the 1990s for college language programs*. Boston, MA: Heinle and Heinle/Thomson International.

Oxford, R.L., Tomlinson, S.C., Barcelos, A., Harrington, C., Lavine, R., Saleh, A. and Longhini, A. 1998. Clashing metaphors about classroom teachers: Toward a systematic typology for the language teaching field. *System* 26/1: 3–51.

Padron, Y.N. and Waxman, H.C. 1988. The effects of ESL students' perceptions of their cognitive strategies on reading achievement. *TESOL Quarterly* 22: 146–50.

Palincsar, A.S. and Brown, A.L. 1986. Interactive teaching to promote independent learning from text. *The Reading Teacher* 39/2: 771–7.

Palincsar, A.S. and Klenk, L. 1992. Examining and influencing contexts for intentional literacy learning. In C. Collins and J.N. Mangieri (Eds), *Teaching thinking: An agenda for the twenty-first century*. Hillsdale, NJ: Lawrence Erlbaum Associates.

Paris, S.G. and Byrnes J.Y.P. 1989. The constructivist approach to self-regulation of learning in the classroom. In B.J. Zimmerman and D.H. Schunk (Eds), *Self-regulated learning and academic achievement*. New York: Springer-Verlag.

Park, G. 1994. Beliefs and learning strategies: What can we do to help our students be more effective self-directed learners? Unpublished manuscript, University of Texas at Austin, Austin, TX.

Patkowski, M. 1994. The critical age hypothesis and interlanguage phonology. In M. Yavas (Ed.), *First and second language phonology*. San Diego, CA: Singular Publishing Group. pp. 205–21.

Pavlenko, A. 1998. Second language learning by adults: Testimonies of bilingual writers. *Issues in Applied Linguistics* 9: 3–19.

Pavlenko, A. (forthcoming). Bilingualism, gender, and ideology. *The International Journal of Bilingualism*.

Pavlenko, A. and Lantolf, J.P. 2000. Second language learning as participation and the (re)construction of selves. In J.P. Lantolf (Ed.), *Sociocultural theory and second language learning*. Oxford: Oxford University Press.

Pennycook, A. 1989. The concept of method, interested knowledge, and the politics of language teaching. *TESOL Quarterly* 23/4: 589–618.

Pennycook, A. 1994. *The cultural politics of English as an international language*. London: Longman.

Perdue, C. (Ed.) 1993. *Adult language acquisition: Cross-linguistic perspectives* (Vols I and II). Cambridge: Cambridge University Press.

Perkins, D.N. and Salomon, G. 1989. Are cognitive skills context-bound? *Educational Researcher* 1: 16–25.

Pica, T. 1992. The textual outcomes of native speaker/non-native speaker negotiation: What do they reveal about second language learning? In C. Kramsch and S. McConnell-Ginet (Eds), *Text in context: Crossdisciplinary perspectives on language study*. Lexington, MA: D.C. Heath.

Pica, T. 1994. Research on negotiation: What does it reveal about second-language learning, conditions, processes, and outcomes? *Language Learning* 44/3: 493–527.

Pica, T., Holliday, L., Lewis, N. and Morgenthaler, L. 1989. Comprehensible output as an outcome of linguistic demands on the learner. *Studies in Second Language Acquisition* 11/1: 63–90.

Platt, E. and Brooks, F.B. 1994. The 'acquisition-rich environment' revisited. *The Modern Language Journal* 78/4: 497–511.

Plough, I. and Gass, S. 1993. Interlocutor and task familiarity: effects on interactional structure. In G. Crookes and S. Gass (Eds), *Tasks and language learning: Integrating theory and practice.* Clevedon, UK: Multilingual Matters.

Polanyi, L. 1995. Language learning and living abroad: Stories from the field. In B. Freed (Ed.), *Second language acquisition in a study abroad context.* Amsterdam: John Benjamins.

Politzer, R., Ramirez, A. and Lewis, S. 1981. Teaching standard English in the third grade: classroom functions of language. *Language Learning* 31: 171–93.

Potter, J. 1996. *Representing reality: discourse, rhetoric and social construction.* London: Sage.

Pressley, M., Levin, J.R. and Delaney, H.D. 1982. The mnemonic keyword method. *Review of Educational Research* 52: 61–91.

Pressley, M., Borkowski, J.G. and Schneider, W. 1987. Cognitive strategies: good strategy users coordinate metacognition and knowledge. In R. Vasta and G. Whitehurst (Eds), *Annals of child development: Volume 5.* Greenwich, CT: JAI Press.

Pressley, M., Johnson, C., Symons, S., McGoldrick, J. and Kurita, J. 1989. Strategies that improve memory and comprehension of what is read. *Elementary School Journal* 90: 3–32.

Pressley, M., Woloshyn, V. and Associates. 1995. *Cognitive strategy instruction that really improves children's academic performance* (Second edition). Cambridge, MA: Brookline Books.

Pulvermuller, F. and Schumann, J. 1994. Neurobiological mechanisms of language acquisition. *Language Learning* 44: 681–734.

Rampton, B. 1987. Stylistic variability and not speaking 'normal' English: Some post-Labovian approaches and their implications for the study of interlanguage. In R. Ellis (Ed.), *Second language acquisition in context.* Englewood Cliffs, NJ: Prentice-Hall.

Rampton, B. 1995a. *Crossing: Language and ethnicity among adolescents.* London: Longman.

Rampton, B. 1995b. Politics and change in research in applied linguistics. *Applied Linguistics* 16: 233–56.

Rampton, B. 1999. Dichotomies, difference and ritual in second language learning and teaching. *Applied Linguistics* 20: 316–40.

Reddy, M. 1993. The conduit metaphor: A case of frame conflict in our language about language. In A. Ortony (Ed.), *Metaphor and thought* (Second edition). Cambridge: Cambridge University Press.

Richard-Amato, P.A. 1988. *Making it happen: Interaction in the second language classroom – From theory to practice.* London: Longman.

Richards, J. and Gravatt, B. 1998. University of Auckland Students' beliefs about foreign languages. *Institute of Language Teaching & Learning Occasional Papers II.* Auckland: Institute of Language Teaching and Learning.

Richards, J. and Rodgers, T. 1986. *Approaches and methods in language teaching.* Cambridge: Cambridge University Press.

Richards, M. 1997. Learner strategies and teacher responses in language learning. Paper presented at the ISATT '97 Meeting, Kiel, Germany.

Ritchie, W.C. and Bhatia, T.K. 1996. *Handbook of second language acquisition.* San Diego, CA: Academic Press.

Rivers, W. and Temperley, M. 1978. *A practical guide to the teaching of English as a second or foreign language.* Cambridge: Cambridge University Press.

Robbins, J. 1996. Between 'hello' and 'see you later': Development of strategies for interpersonal communication in English by Japanese EFL students. Published PhD dissertation, University Microfilms, International. UMI number: 9634593. Ann Arbor, MI: University of Michigan.

Robinson, P. 1995. Aptitude, awareness, and the fundamental similarity of implicit and explicit second language learning. In R. Schmidt (Ed.), *Attention and awareness in foreign language learning* (Technical Report No. 9). Honolulu, HI: University of Hawaii Press.

Robinson, P. 1997. Individual differences and the fundamental similarity of implicit and explicit adult second language learning. *Language Learning* 47: 45–99.

Rockhill, K. and Tomic, P. 1995. Situating ESL between speech and silence. In J. Gaskell and J. Willinsky (Eds), *Gender in/forms curriculum: From enrichment to transformation*. Toronto: OISE Press/Teachers College Press.

Ross, S. and Rost, M. 1991. Learner use of strategies in interaction: Typology and teachability. *Language Learning* 41/2: 235–73.

Rubin, J. 1975. What the 'good language learner' can teach us. *TESOL Quarterly* 9: 41–51.

Rubin, J. 1981. The study of cognitive processes in second language learning. *Applied Linguistics* 11/2: 117–31.

Rubin, J. and Thompson, I. 1994. *How to be a more successful language learner* (Second edition). Boston, MA: Heinle and Heinle.

Rubin, J., Quinn, J. and Enos, J. 1988. *Improving foreign language listening comprehension*. Report to US Department of Education, International Research and Studies Program.

Saito, Y., Horwitz, E. and Garza, T. 1998. Foreign language reading anxiety. *The Modern Language Journal* 83/2: 202–18.

Sakui, K. and Gaies, S. 1999. Investigating Japanese learners' beliefs about language learning. In A. Wenden (Ed.), *System*. Special Issue on Learner Beliefs. 27/4: 473–92.

Salager-Mayer, F. 1990. Metaphors in medical English prose: A comparative study with French and Spanish. *English for Specific Purposes* 9: 145–59.

Samimy, K.K. and Tabuse, M. 1992. Affective variables and a less commonly taught language: A study in beginning Japanese classes. *Language Learning* 42: 377–98.

Sasaki, M. 1993a. Relationships among second language proficiency, foreign language aptitude, and intelligence: A structural equation modeling approach. *Language Learning* 43: 313–44.

Sasaki, M. 1993b. Relationships among second language proficiency, foreign language aptitude, and intelligence: A protocol analysis. *Language Learning* 43: 469–505.

Sasaki, M. 1996. *Second language proficiency, foreign language aptitude, and intelligence: Quantitative and qualitative analyses*. New York: Peter Lang.

Scarcella, R. and Oxford, R. 1992. *The tapestry of language learning: The individual in the communicative classroom*. Boston, MA: Heinle and Heinle.

Schieffelin, B.B., Woolard, K.A. and Kroskrity, P.V. 1998. *Language ideologies. Practice and theory*. Oxford: Oxford University Press.

Schmidt, R. 1994. Deconstructing consciousness in search of useful definitions for applied linguistics. In J. Hulstijn and R. Schmidt (Eds), *Consciousness in second language learning. AILA Review 11*. Brussels: AILA.

Schmidt, R. 1997. Comment on SLART-L listserve, 27 August.

Schmidt, R. and Frota, S. 1986. Developing basic conversational ability in a second language: A case study of an adult learner of Portuguese. In R.R. Day (Ed.),

Talking to learn: Conversation in second language acquisition. Rowley, MA: Newbury House.

Schmidt, R., Boraie, D. and Kassabgy, O. 1996. Foreign language motivation: Internal structure and external connections. In R.L. Oxford (Ed.), *Language learning motivation: Pathways to the new century.* Honolulu, HI: University of Hawaii Press.

Schommer, M. 1990. Effects of beliefs about the nature of knowledge on comprehension. *Journal of Educational Psychology* 82: 498–504.

Schulman, L.S. 1992. Toward a pedagogy of cases. In J.H. Schulman (Ed.), *Case methods in teacher education.* New York: Teachers College Press.

Schumaker, J.B. and Deshler, D.D. 1992. Validation of learning strategy interventions for students with learning disabilities: Results of a programmatic research effort. In B.Y.L. Wong (Ed.), *Contemporary intervention research in learning disabilities: An international perspective.* New York: Springer-Verlag.

Schumann, J.H. 1998. The neurobiology of affect. *Language Learning* 48: Supplement 1.

Seedhouse, P. 1999. Task-based interaction. *ELT Journal* 53/3: 149–56.

Seliger, H. 1977. Does practice make perfect? A study of interaction patterns and L2 competence. *Language Learning* 27: 263–78.

Selinker, L. 1992. *Rediscovering interlanguage.* London: Longman.

Senior, R. 1999. The good language class: Teachers' perceptions. Unpublished PhD thesis, Perth, Western Australia: Edith Cowan University.

Shaw, J. 1998. *The effect of experiential language learning on epistemological beliefs: A case study of language learners in an MBA program.* Unpublished manuscript, Asian Institute of Technology, Bangkok, Thailand.

Sheen, R. 1992. A rebuttal to Chapelle's response to Griffiths and Sheen. *Applied Linguistics* 14: 98–100.

Shotter, J. 1993a. *Cultural politics of everyday life: Social constructionism, rhetoric, and knowing of the third kind.* Milton Keynes: Open University Press.

Shotter, J. 1993b. *Conversational realities: Constructing life through language.* London: Sage.

Siegal, M. 1996. The role of learner subjectivity in second language sociolinguistic competency: Western women learning Japanese. *Applied Linguistics* 17: 356–82.

Silver, E.A. and Marshall, S.P. 1990. Mathematical and scientific problem solving: Findings, issues, and instructional implications. In B.F. Jones and L. Idol (Eds), *Dimensions of thinking and cognitive instruction.* Hillsdale, NJ: Lawrence Erlbaum Associates.

Silverman, D. 1993. *Interpreting qualitative data: Methods for analysing talk, text, and interaction.* London: Sage.

Simon, R. 1992. *Teaching against the grain: Texts for a pedagogy of possibility.* New York: Bergin and Garvey.

Skehan, P. 1989. *Individual differences in second-language learning.* London: Edward Arnold.

Skehan, P. 1991. Individual differences in second language learning. *Studies in Second Language Acquisition* 13: 275–98.

Skehan, P. 1996. A framework for the implementation of task-based instruction. *Applied Linguistics* 17/1: 38–61.

Skehan, P. 1998. *A cognitive approach to language learning.* Oxford: Oxford University Press.

Slavoff, G. and Johnson, J. 1995. The effects of age on the rate of learning a second language. *Studies in Second Language Acquisition* 17: 1–16.

Slimani, A. 1989. The role of topicalisation in classroom language learning. *System* 17: 223–34.

Slimani, A. 1992. Evaluation of classroom interaction. In J. Alderson and A. Beretta (Eds), *Evaluating second language acquisition.* Cambridge: Cambridge University Press.

Snow, C. and Hoefnagel-Hohle, M. 1982. School age second language learners' access to simplified linguistic input. *Language Learning* 32: 411–30.

Snyder, B. and Pressley, M. 1990. Introduction to cognitive strategy instruction. In M. Pressley, V. Woloshyn and Associates, *Cognitive strategy instruction that really improves children's academic performance.* Cambridge, MA: Brookline Books.

Spada, N. and Lightbown, P.M. 1993. Instruction and the development of questions in L2 classrooms. *Studies in Second Language Acquisition* 15: 209–31.

Sparks, R. and Javorsky, J. 1999. A response to Arries: 'Learning disabilities and foreign languages: A curriculum approach to the design of inclusive courses'. *The Modern Language Journal* 83/4: 569–75.

Sparks, R., Artzer, M., Javorsky, J., Patton, J., Ganschow, L., Miller, K. and Hordubay, D. 1998. Students classified as learning disabled (LD) and non learning disabled students: Two comparison studies of native language skill, foreign language aptitude, and foreign language proficiency. *Foreign Language Annals* 31: 535–51.

Spolsky, B. 1989. *Conditions for second language learning.* New York: Oxford University Press.

Steen, G. 1994. *Understanding metaphor in literature.* London: Longman.

Stempel, G.H. III. 1989. Content analysis. In G.H. Stempel III and B. Westley (Eds), *Research methods in mass communication* (Second edition). Englewood Cliffs, NJ: Prentice-Hall.

Stern, H.H. 1975. What can we learn from the good language learner? *Canadian Modern Language Review* 31: 304–18.

Stevick, E. 1976. *Memory, meaning and method: Some psychological perspectives on language learning.* Rowley, MA: Newbury House.

Stevick, E. 1980. *Teaching languages: A way and ways.* Rowley, MA: Newbury House.

Stevick, E. 1990. *Humanism in language teaching.* Oxford: Oxford University Press.

Strauss, A.M. 1987. *Qualitative analysis for social scientists.* Cambridge: Cambridge University Press.

Strong, M. 1983. Social styles and second language acquisition of Spanish-speaking kindergarteners. *TESOL Quarterly* 17: 241–58.

Strong, M. 1984. Integrative motivation: Cause and result of successful language acquisition. *Language Learning* 34: 1–14.

Swain, M. 1985. Communicative competence: some roles of comprehensible input and comprehensible output in its development. In S. Gass and C. Madden (Eds), *Input in second language acquisition.* Rowley, MA: Newbury House.

Swain, M. 1991. French immersion and its offshoots: Getting two for one. In B.F. Freed (Ed.), *Foreign language acquisition research and the classroom.* Lexington, MA: D.C. Heath.

Swain, M. 1995. Three functions of output in second language learning. In G. Cook and B. Seidlhofer (Eds), *For H.G. Widdowson: Principles and practice in the study of language.* Oxford: Oxford University Press.

Swain, M. and Lapkin, S. 1994. Problems in output and the cognitive processes they generate: A step towards second language learning. Manuscript of the Modern Language Centre, University of Toronto (OISE), Toronto.

Swales, J. 1990. *Genre analysis.* Cambridge: Cambridge University Press.

Takeuchi, O. 1999. Language learning strategies used by Japanese college students of English: A synthesis of four empirical studies. Paper presented at AILA 1999, Tokyo, Japan.

Taylor, C. 1985. *Human agency and language. Philosophical papers 1.* Cambridge: Cambridge University Press.

Taylor, W. 1984. Metaphors of educational discourse. In W. Taylor (Ed.), *Metaphors in education.* London: Heinemann.

Thesen, L. 1997. Voices, discourse, and transition: In search of new categories in EAP. *TESOL Quarterly* 31/3: 487–512.

Thompson, I. and Rubin, J. 1996. Can strategy instruction improve listening comprehension? *Foreign Language Annals* 29/3: 331–42.

Thompson, J.B. 1991. Editor's introduction. In J.B. Thompson (Ed.), *Pierre Bourdieu. Language and symbolic power.* Cambridge, MA: Harvard University Press.

Thornbury, S. 1991. Metaphors we work by: EFL and its metaphors. *ELT Journal* 45/3: 193–200.

Tittle, M. 1998. Assessing foreign language students' epistemological beliefs about language learning. Research in progress. Department of Educational Psychology, University of Urbana-Champaign.

Tollefson, J.W. 1991. *Planning language, planning inequality.* London: Longman.

Tollefson, J.W. (Ed.) 1995. *Power and equality in language education.* New York: Cambridge University Press.

Toohey, K. 1998. 'Breaking them up and taking them away': ESL students in Grade 1. *TESOL Quarterly* 32: 61–84.

Toohey, K. 2000. *Learning English in schools: Identity, social relations, and classroom practice.* Clevedon, UK: Multilingual Matters.

Tremblay, P. and Gardner, R. 1995. Expanding the motivational construct in language learning. *The Modern Language Journal* 79/4: 505–20.

Tudor, I. 1996. *Learner-centeredness as language education.* Cambridge: Cambridge University Press.

Tumposky, N.R. 1991. Students' beliefs about language learning. *Carlton Papers in Applied Language Study* 8: 50–65.

Underhill, A. 1989. Process in humanistic education. *ELT Journal* 43/4: 250–60.

van Lier, L. 1988. *The classroom and the language learner.* London: Longman.

van Lier, L. 1996. *Interaction in the language curriculum.* London: Longman.

Vandergrift, L. 1997a. The comprehension strategies of second language (French) listeners: A descriptive study. *Foreign Language Annals* 30/3: 387–409.

Vandergrift, L. 1997b. The Cinderella of communication strategies: Reception strategies in interactive listening. *The Modern Language Journal* 81/4: 494–505.

Vann, R.J. and Abraham, R.G. 1990. Strategies of unsuccessful language learners. *TESOL Quarterly* 24/2: 177–98.

Varela, E.E. 1997. Speaking solo: Using learning strategy instruction to improve English language learners' oral presentation skills in content-based ESL. Unpublished doctoral dissertation. Washington, DC: Georgetown University.

Victori, M. 1995. ESL writing knowledge and strategies: An integrative study. Unpublished doctoral dissertation. Department of English Philology, Autonomous University of Barcelona, Spain.

Victori, M. 1999. An analysis of writing knowledge in EFL composing: A case study of two effective and two less effective writers. In A. Wenden (Ed.), Special Issue on Metacognitive Knowledge and Beliefs in Language Learning. *System* 27/4: 537–56.

Vygotsky, L. 1956. *Izbrannie psichologicheskie issledovania (Selected psychological research).* Moscow: Izdatel'stvo Akademii Pedagogicheskikh Nauk.

Vygotsky, L. 1978. *Mind in society: The development of higher psychological processes.* Ed. and Trans. by M. Cole, V. John-Steiner and E. Souberman. Cambridge: Cambridge University Press.

Vygotsky, L. 1986. *Thought and language* (New edition). Ed. by A. Kozulin. Cambridge, MA: MIT Press.

Vygotsky, L. 1987. *The collected works of L.S. Vygotsky: Vol. 1. Problems of general psychology.* Trans. N. Minick. New York: Plenum.

Vygotsky, L. 1997. *The collected works of L.S. Vygotsky: Vol. 3. Problems of the theory and history of psychology.* Trans. R. van der Veer. Ed. by R.W. Rieber and J. Wollock. New York: Plenum.

Wallace, B. and Oxford, R.L. 1992. Disparity in learning styles and teaching styles in the ESL classroom: Does this mean war? *AMTESOL Journal* 1/1: 45–68.

Weaver, S.J. and Cohen, A.D. 1997. *Strategies-based instruction: A teacher-training manual.* Minneapolis, MN: Center for Advanced Research on Language Acquisition, University of Minnesota.

Weber-Fox, C. and Neville, H. 1999. Functional neural subsystems are differentially affected by delays in second language immersion: ERP and behavioral evidence in bilinguals. In D. Birdsong (Ed.), *Second language acquisition and the critical period hypothesis.* Mahwah, NJ: Lawrence Erlbaum Associates.

Weiner, B. 1986. *An attributional theory of motivation and emotion.* New York: Springer-Verlag.

Weinstein, C.E. and Mayer, R.E. 1986. The teaching of learning strategies. In M.R. Wittrock (Ed.), *Handbook of research on teaching* (Third edition). New York: Macmillan.

Wen, Q. and Johnson, R. 1997. L2 learner variables and English achievement: A study of tertiary-level English majors in China. *Applied Linguistics* 18: 27–48.

Wenden, A.L. 1982. The processes of self-directed learning: A case study of adult language learners. Unpublished doctoral dissertation, Teachers College, Columbia University, New York.

Wenden, A.L. 1986. What do second language learners know about their language learning? A second look at retrospective accounts. *Applied Linguistics* 7/2: 186–205.

Wenden, A.L. 1987. How to be a successful language learner: Insights and prescriptions from L2 learners. In A. Wenden and J. Rubin (Eds), *Learner strategies in language learning.* London: Prentice-Hall.

Wenden, A.L. 1991a. *Learner strategies for learner autonomy.* London: Prentice-Hall.

Wenden, A.L. 1991b. Metacognitive strategies in L2 writing: A case for task knowledge. In J.E. Alatis (Ed.), *Georgetown Roundtable on Languages and Linguistics 1991.* Washington, DC: Georgetown University Press.

Wenden, A.L. 1995. Learner training in context: A knowledge-based approach. In L. Dickinson and A. Wenden (Eds), *System.* Special Issue on Learner Autonomy. 23/2: 183–94.

Wenden, A.L. 1997. The nature and function of monitoring. Paper presented at the Conference of the American Association of Applied Linguistics, Miami, Florida.

Wenden, A.L. 1998a. Metacognitive knowledge and language learning. *Applied Linguistics* 19/4: 515–37.

Wenden, A.L. 1998b. *Learner training in foreign/second language learning: A curricular perspective for the 21st century.* Eric Document Reproduction Service No. ED 416 673.

Wenger, E. 1998. *Communities of practice: Learning, meaning, and identity.* Cambridge: Cambridge University Press.

Wertsch, J.V. 1985. *Vygotsky and the social formation of mind.* Cambridge, MA: Harvard University Press.

Wertsch, J.V. 1998. *Mind as action.* New York: Oxford University Press.

Wesche, M.B. 1994. Input, interaction and acquisition: The linguistic environment of the language learner. In B. Richards and C. Gallaway (Eds), *Input and interaction in language acquisition.* Cambridge: Cambridge University Press.

Wesche, M.B., Edwards, H. and Wells, W. 1982. Foreign language aptitude and intelligence. *Applied Psycholinguistics* 3: 127–40.

White, C. 1999. Expectations and emergent beliefs of self-instructed language learners. In A. Wenden (Ed.), Special Issue on Metacognitive Knowledge and Beliefs in Language Learning. *System* 27/4: 443–58.

White, L. 1989. *Universal grammar and second language acquisition.* Amsterdam: John Benjamins.

White, L. and Genesee, F. 1996. How native is near-native? The issue of ultimate attainment in adult second language acquisition. *Second Language Research* 12: 233–65.

Widdowson, H. 1978. *Teaching language as communication.* Oxford: Oxford University Press.

Widdowson, H. 1979. *Explorations in applied linguistics.* Oxford: Oxford University Press.

Williams, M. and Burden, R. 1997. *Psychology for language teachers.* Cambridge: Cambridge University Press.

Williams, M. and Burden, R. 1999. Students' developing conceptions of themselves as language learners. *The Modern Language Journal* 83/2: 193–201.

Willing, K. 1988. *Learning styles in adult migrant education.* Adelaide: National Curriculum Resource Center Research Series.

Willing, K. 1991. Learning-how-to-learn: A review of current learning strategies publications. *Prospect* 6/2: 51–7.

Witherell, C. and Noddings, N. (Eds) 1991. *Stories lives tell: Narrative and dialogue in education.* New York: Teachers College Press.

Wode, H. 1994. Nature, nurture, and age in language acquisition. The case of speech perception. *Studies in Second Language Acquisition* 16: 325–45.

Wolfson, N. 1989. *Perspectives: Sociolinguistics and TESOL.* Rowley, MA: Newbury House.

Wolfson. N. and Judd, E. (Eds) 1983. *Sociolinguistics and second language acquisition.* Rowley, MA: Newbury House.

Wong-Filmore, L. 1982. Instructional language as linguistic input: second language learning in classrooms. In L. Wilkinson (Ed.), *Communicating in the classroom.* New York: Academic Press.

Wood, E., Woloshyn, V.E. and Willoughby, T. 1995. *Cognitive strategy instruction for middle and high schools.* Cambridge, MA: Brookline Books.

Wool, G. 1989. Relational aspects of learning. In K. Field, B.J. Cohler and G. Wool (Eds), *Learning and education: Psychoanalytic perspectives.* Madison, CT: International Universities Press.

Woolfolk, A.E., Rosoff, B. and Hoy, W.K. 1990. Teachers' sense of efficacy and their beliefs about managing students. *Teaching and Teacher Education* 6/2: 137–48.

Wright, A. 1987. *Roles of language teachers.* Oxford: Oxford University Press.

Yang, N.D. 1999. The relationship between EFL learners' beliefs and learning strategy use. In A. Wenden (Ed.), Special Issue on Metacognitive Knowledge and Beliefs in Language Learning. *System* 27/4: 515–36.

Yaroshevsky, M.G. and Gurgenidze, G.S. 1997. Epilogue. In L. Vygotsky, *The collected works of L.S. Vygotsky. Vol. 3. Problems of the theory and history of psychology.* Trans. R. van der Veer. Ed. by R.W. Rieber and J. Wollock. New York: Plenum.

Yeni-Komshian, G., Flege, J. and Liu, H. 1997. Pronunciation proficiency in L1 and L2 among Korean-English bilinguals: The effect of age of arrival in the US. *Journal of the Acoustical Society of America* 1102(A): 3138.

Zamel, V. 1983. The composing processes of advanced ESL students: Six case studies. *TESOL Quarterly* 17: 165–87.

Zinchenko, V.P. 1995. Cultural-historical psychology and the psychological theory of activity: Retrospect and prospect. In J.V. Wertsch, P. del Río and A. Alvarez (Eds), *Sociocultural studies of mind.* Cambridge: Cambridge University Press.

Zinchenko, V.P. 1996. Developing activity theory: The zone of proximal development and beyond. In B. Nardi (Ed.), *Context and consciousness: Activity theory and human-computer interaction.* Cambridge, MA: MIT Press.

Zobl, H. 1995. Converging evidence for the 'acquisition-learning' distinction. *Applied Linguistics* 16: 35–56.

Author Index

Subject Index